4111855300

D1429401

The Power of the Financial Press

2850

For Eileen and Benjamin Parsons,
Mary, John and Ben

The Power of the Financial Press

Journalism and economic opinion in Britain and America

Wayne Parsons

Edward Elgar

Published by
Edward Elgar Publishing Limited
Gower House
Croft Road
Aldershot
Hants GU11 3HR
England

British Library Cataloguing in Publication Data

Parsons, D. W.
The power of the financial press: journalism and economic opinion in
Britain and America
1. Capitalism. Theories. Formulation. Role of press
I. Title.
330.12′2

ISBN 185278 039 8

Printed in Great Britain by
Billing & Sons Ltd, Worcester

*Though the familiar use of things about us
take off our wonder, yet it cures not our ignorance*
John Locke
An Essay Concerning Human Understanding

Contents

Preface

Writing this book has been an exciting challenge for someone interested in the history of ideas and the relationship between economic ideas, policy and opinion. Inevitably, the book has evolved in the writing. The original plan was to make a more limited study of developments in the financial media and information business over the last decade or so. However, as is the way of research, it became more and more evident that a far wider historical and intellectual remit had to be taken in order to make more sense out of the contemporary scene. To begin with, for example, there was the question of the way in which, almost by definition, the business press and the whole structure of financial information and news largely sustains the *cultural* context within which capitalism and the market economy has evolved. Again, by definition, the very existence of a financial press is the consummate manifestation of what a capitalist society is all about. The financial pages are thus the clearest expression of the way in which the *language* of capitalism – its discourse and rhetoric – are disseminated and legitimated. So, in the course of examining the development of financial information the author became fascinated by the fact that, in propagating economic, financial and business news, the press is also in the market for selling economic *ideas* and values as well as purely economic information (if there is such a thing). Furthermore, as my examination of this relationship between ideas and information progressed, I became more and more interested in the ebb and flow of ideas across the Atlantic.

During so many chapters of our history there has been an interplay between British and American economic opinion and ideas. This continuing transatlantic intellectual exchange thus became a major focus of the study. My observations of British and American intellectual history also meant that I became increasingly aware that viewing economics from the standpoint of its diffusion was an excellent perspective from which one could examine the demand and supply for economists and economic ideas. With these problems in mind, I soon determined that the book would mainly concentrate on the role that *élite* as opposed to *mass* communication has played in setting the political agenda and in defining the terms of debate and the dominant discourse of the day. The significance of the power of the financial press so to influence the prevailing political climate is not then an issue which I sought to tackle, since to a large extent such explanations are implicit in so much of the sociological analyses offered by students of the mass media. In a capitalist society communications are capitalist.

Whatever its merits, this study would not have been completed without the help and support of many. I am particularly grateful to the British Academy and the Leverhulme Trust for their absolutely invaluable financial assistance; Lady Zuzanna Shonfield, Samuel Brittan of the *Financial Times*, Sir Gordon Newton, former editor of the *Financial Times*, Sir Alastair Burnet, former editor of *The Economist*, Leonard Silk of the *New York Times* and Robert Bartley of the *Wall Street Journal* for their hospitality and words of wisdom; and all those friends and colleagues who have bourne with great fortitude my researches and rantings for far too long. At Queen Mary College I have benefited from discussions with colleagues in the department of economics but special thanks must be given to Professor The Lord Peston, Professor Bernard Corry and Professor David Currie for commenting on some of my arguments. Within my own department, the encouragement of Professor Trevor Smith, Professor William Fishman, Dr Elizabeth Vallance and Dr Andrew Massey has oftentimes boosted my flagging morale. It must be said, of course, that I take full responsibility for the final product.

The librarians at Queen Mary College, the University College of Wales, Aberystwyth, the British Library, the National Library of Wales and the Colindale newspaper library have been especially helpful.

My greatest thanks must, as always, go to my wife Mary and children John and Ben for keeping me sane and happy.

Introduction

We live, so we are told, in an 'information age'. It is, however, true to say that man has always lived in an age of information. But today, even more so than in the past, the development of our economic and social systems are being powerfully influenced by our modes of communication. This book is about one particular aspect of this continuing revolution in information and knowledge: the way in which economic ideas and information have been propagated. Almost by definition the price system and the market economy are dependent upon the existence of an information network. As markets develop beyond a specific geographical location, and as the nature of the information being exchanged becomes more complex so the mode of information exchange and economic communications necessarily becomes more sophisticated. As Wiles has observed:

> In origin the [perfect market is] merely the coming together on a vacant plot of primitive higglers, who want to reduce the risk inherent in decentralized pricing, it has come to own an expensive downtown building with paid officials, professional brokers who have bought themselves a seat and subjected themselves to the rules, and modern communications terminals... From here it fulfils a most important social function: it centralizes information, digests it, and issues a 'planning criterion' to anyone who can afford the *Financial Times* or a teleprinter.[1]

Historically, therefore, the development of printed information was a vital stage in the construction of a communications structure and information network which could facilitate a decentralized price system. The fact that, in May 1987, it was announced that China would begin publishing a *Financial Times* is, for example, an important indicator of the desire to shift towards a more market-based society. The growth of economic communications was and is a precondition of capitalist development and the spread of capitalism as a concept or ideology.[2] And yet, it is only

1

comparatively recently that, as Stigler expressed it in 1961, information has come out of its 'slum dwelling in the town of economics'.[3] Markets and prices are themselves, of course, information systems, yet manifestly the mode and technology of market information and commercial intelligence has had a tremendous impact on how capitalism and the price system are actually disseminated. From the earliest days of commercial society in Britain and America the existence of printed economic information, opinions and gossip have been at the very basis of our economic systems and values. The aim of this book is to examine the evolution of this relationship between the market economy and the market for information and ideas by focusing on one vitally important cog in the market mechanism: the newspaper.

Newspapers have, almost from their inception, been about selling markets: providing information for the businessman, and opportunities for the business community to advertise its products, services and prices. Newspapers in many senses, therefore, could be said to lie at the very core of the capitalist process and the 'free market' idea and consequently have a key role to play in the way in which what Peter Berger describes as 'economic culture'[4] is communicated and its myths and discourse sustained and propagated. Newspapers thereby assist in the integration and mediation of economic values, ideas and language. Paul Samuelson, for example, recounts that this 'persuasive social propaganda' awoke in the young economist an early awareness of the prevailing economic culture:

> As a boy entrepreneur I used to sample my wares and read in the *Saturday Evening Post* ... the success stories of American businessmen. Although they appeared in the non-fiction columns, they read like fiction. (Only after 1929 did I learn that they actually were part fiction.)[5]

Given that newspapers are so imbedded in capitalism and the structures of power, it is inevitable that they also constitute a significant medium through which economic ideas and opinions are legitimated. They not only sell (to make a profit) the information which keeps the wheels of the economy turning but in so doing they also purvey and reinforce the values and ideas, language and culture, which underpin the existence of the market economy. As Milton Friedman has noted:

The transmission of information through prices is enormously facilitated by organised markets and by specialised communication facilities. It is a fascinating exercise to look through the price quotations published in, say, the *Wall Street Journal*, not to mention the numerous more specialised trade publications. These prices mirror almost instantly what is happening all over the world . . . The *Wall Street Journal* does not provide this information out of altruism or because it recognises how important it is for the operation of the economy. Rather, it is led to provide this information by the very price system whose functioning it facilitates.[6]

The development of the press and the price system are, therefore, inextricably linked both with one another and with the political system since economic and financial commentaries and news provide a context or agenda within which political and social events impact upon and communicate themselves to the business community. The press serves as a crucial mediator between the price system and the political system, and enables politicians, business men and men of ideas to set the parameters of ruling opinion. The business pages are also, as a consequence, places where the interplay between economic thought and opinion[7] is most in evidence.

Over the period covered by this book newspapers and magazines have been a major point of entry for economic theory and language into more general currency and (mis)usage.[8] The financial press – the term we shall use to describe economic and business reporting as well as strictly financial coverage – is then a unique interpreter, less of 'mass opinion' than of the views and values of a more limited and narrower élite which composes the readership of the financial pages. Given the bias of *media studies* towards *mass* communication it is not surprising that, despite its importance, the study of élite communications networks have been badly neglected.[9] This book, on the other hand, is predicated on the rather obvious fact that there is (and has always been) a differential pattern of access to economic information: the information rich and the information poor have always been with us. Inevitably, the role played by that section of the press geared to a small band of affluent and powerful readers has changed a good deal over the past few hundred years. In the beginning, for example, newsheets like *Lloyd's List* simply carried details of price movements and foreign reports that might have affected trade. By the early nineteenth century newspapers also provided a platform for the dissemination of economic theories and discourse. As technology has developed and economic theory has become more technical, so the place of the press in the economic world has altered. In the nineteenth century newspapers were great synthesizers of economic sentiment and opinion as well as prime sources of useful information. By the 1980s however, as Rita Cruise O'Brien and G. K. Helleiner point out:

> For those 'in the trade', published sources, even 'hot from the press', are typically too obsolete to be useful for daily decision-making. The linking of computerised data banks and telecommunications facilities have altered the business information environment dramatically . . . [10]

With the advent of new methods of electronic communication and academic specialization, so the pre-eminence of the press as the most 'important single medium for the communication of ideas' [11] – as well as information – has declined. Nevertheless, in spite of the coming of new modes of communications and computer technology the financial press continues to stand, in Palmer's words, at a 'crucial intersection between the world of finance and the world of government'. [12] In this book we take a look at how that intersection has functioned; both in terms of the traffic in information and the flow of economic ideas.

In tackling these two themes the chapters which follow take a largely chronological approach. We begin at the beginning, by discussing the dissemination of economic information and intelligence in the eighteenth century and examine the role of the press and journals of opinion in propagating economic discourse. The first chapter focuses on the way in which printers and newspaper publishers were quick to respond to the informational needs of the business and financial community. Newsletters in Britain and in the American colonies grew out of the identification of the demand for good commercial coverage – both news and advertising. The press evolved largely to fulfil the desires of the profit motive and the self-interest of the commercial classes. During the early decades of the nineteenth century the British press came to provide, for the first time, a channel both for market information and new ideas about how that market actually worked. The consummate product of that new economic journalism was the London *Economist* founded in 1843. Perhaps one of the main characteristics of what its famous editor, Walter Bagehot, termed the 'economic age', was that it witnessed the victory of *laissez-faire* political economy as a widely shared form of public discourse and political rhetoric. In so doing it became the victim of its own success. As Donald McCloskey notes, economics soon left its 'reputation in the hands of politicians and journalists'.[13] From the early nineteenth century the role of economic discourse in social life, as well as in business and politics became something which has largely been shaped by the (amateur) disseminators and users of economic ideas and concepts rather than by their (professional) originators. Through publications like the *Edinburgh Review* and *Economist*, economic ideas became, as it were, a common language of public debate: its terms and concepts entered, as Bagehot thought, into the life of the nation. This was, however, not to last. The enthusiasm which the political economists had shown for engaging in issues of public concern via journalistic theorizing was not to be displayed by those who followed in their footsteps. As financial journalism expanded in the latter part of the nineteenth century – thanks to the repeal of stamp duty and the investment booms of the 1880s – the economics profession contracted into a more academic and non-controversial mode of inquiry. The subject was shaped less by outside events (news) than by problems generated from inside the profession.[14] The old political economy *qua* public discourse died with Bagehot and the arrival of Marshall *et al*. And thus it could be said that the so called 'marginalist revolution' also in a sense intellectually marginalized political economy by its expulsion of the amateur. 'Economics' lost much of its literary and journalistic character that was such an essential part of the vitality and relevance of political economy in the early part of the century when arguments about free trade and the value of money and the poor law created a demand for economic theories and terminology. It is significant that, as Chapter 2 shows, it was not until the 1920s and 1930s that economic theory and ideas once again interplayed more fully with public opinion. Like the classical political economists of the nineteenth century, Keynes was to employ the press to great effect to publicize his views and influence the agenda of the day. The 'Keynesian revolution' in economic theory was to bring in its wake a revolution in economic journalism which was as significant as that which had taken place during the 'Ricardian revolution' of the early nineteenth century. In the 1920s and 1930s Keynes was to make many converts in the press, including Walter Lippman and some of the leading British economic journalists of the day. The impact of Keynesianism on the evolution of British economic journalism was, as Chapter 3 discusses, to be manifested in the postwar period in the emergence of a group of journalists who had in many ways, as Fred Hirsch once observed, a greater influence over the climate of postwar British policymaking and upon the dissemination of Keynesian ideas than did the academic community itself.[15]

Meanwhile, as they say in the very best kind of detective story, in America the course of financial journalism was somewhat different to that in Britain, even though there was an exchange of men and ideas across the Atlantic. As was the case in Britain, the financial press was greatly expanded in the closing decades of the nineteenth century. By this time the American press served as something of a model for British editors like Harry Marks of the *Financial News*. But in intellectual terms the US press tended to look to London as the place where ideas happened – as in the post-Second World War era London looked to the US. The kind of analysis to be found in the *Economist* or the *Financial Times* was thin on the ground in Wall Street. Like the old merchants of the eighteenth century, what the American investor wanted was facts and gossip that could make him a profit, not lessons in economic theory from journalistic professors. Nevertheless, a 'Bagehot' did emerge in the form of one Alexander Dana Noyes, who wrote a 'Market Place' column in the *New York Times*. Noyes was one of the few journalists who came out of the Wall Street crash with his reputation enhanced, and the generally low status of financial reporting was to continue into the postwar period. Unlike the situation in Britain, however, the American press was not to develop much by way of a tradition of economic journalism – although there were exceptions in the case of the work of Leonard Silk and Eileen Shanahan on the *New York Times*. Chapter 4 compares the way in which 'economic journalism' developed in Britain and America and focuses on the fact that leading academics, like Galbraith, Samuelson and Friedman, emerged as celebrities and were in demand as commentators and gurus. This in itself was, we suggest, as much symptomatic of editorial differences between British and American papers, as of differences in the public and popular status enjoyed by the social sciences in the two countries.

The 1960s and early 1970s was a time when the standing of the American economics profession was at its height. With the onset of the world economic recession in the mid-1970s the prestige of the largely Keynesian academic community was to fall as inflation and unemployment rose. The financial press in both Britain and America played a leading role in challenging the prevailing economic wisdom by giving over space to the discussion of 'supply-side' and 'monetarist' ideas. An example of this was, as Chapter 5 illustrates, the successful selling of supply-side economic in the *Wall Street Journal* and the way in which Milton Friedman skilfully publicized his ideas. As Chapter 6 shows, a similar picture of the press playing a leading role in the counter-Keynesian revolution was also to be found in Britain. If, as Hirsch argues, journalists had a significant role in the propagation of (a certain variety) of Keynesian ideas in the 1960s, it was appropriate that in the 1970s Friedman's 'monetarism' was taken up and spread more readily by journalists – notably Samuel Brittan in the *Financial Times* and Peter Jay in *The Times* than was the case in the academic world. Like the 'supply-side revolution' in the US, therefore, the rise of 'monetarism' in Britain during the 1970s had much more to do with its impact on influential sectors of press and political opinion than with its ability to make converts in economics departments in British universities through the weight of its scientific arguments. In so charting the role of the press in the formation of economic opinion in the nineteenth and twentieth centuries the book does not wish to exaggerate the power of the media to effect a revolution in economic thought, but rather to emphasize that at times it does have, as Peter Jackson argues, an importance in 'forming the ideas of others, especially politicians and their personal advisors'.[16] The power of the financial press may thus be characterized in terms of its capacity to establish a community of economic discourse as opposed to an ability to change the attitudes and opinions of its readers.

In retrospect, the mid-1970s appear as almost a golden age of economic controversy. The conflict which the financial press on both sides of the Atlantic reflected was that of a struggle for the victory of ideas: it was a fight which the 'anti-Keynesians' won and a loss from which the 'Keynesians', and indeed the economics profession, has yet to recover. As in the 1880s, the 1980s have witnessed a growth in the financial press and information services which has been fuelled, in part, by the deregulation of the financial markets and increasing share ownership and privatization as well as by advances in information technology. Now, as in the 1920s, speculation is a game all the family can play for the 'price of an evening paper' – as Jesse Livermore commented at the time.[17] Thanks to the long bull market which came to a dramatic end in 1987, tipsters have been in greater demand than teachers and scholarly journalists. The financial press and the flourishing 'investment' newsletter industry have come into their own – as in other periods of economic uncertainty and stockmarket booms. Economic theories and academic gurus have been just one more casualty of the information revolution and economic crisis. Knowing what is going on at the moment – economic news – and what is going up or down tomorrow – investment advice – is clearly of more market value than a smart theory which tells you what it all means. It was a point which was nicely made by Patrick Sergeant when celebrating one hundred years of Fleet Street in 1982. Macro economics, he suggested, was safe territory for a financial journalist such as himself since 'nobody else knows anything about it', but 'you must be careful about the price of fish and chips'.[18] News, after all, makes markets and money for punters and so nowadays you are more likely to read a piece by an economist from a firm of stockbrokers on the latest set of figures or predictions than a professor from a university offering some explanation or solutions. As the final chapter discusses, therefore, we may have learnt in the 1980s to live with uncertainty and crisis, big government and big deficits, and big bangs, by having resolved to abandon big old theories and trust in new micro information technologies. In conclusion, we argue that the changes which have occurred in financial journalism over recent years, and indeed, over the last hundred years, have really mirrored and echoed the more profound intellectual changes which have taken place in the wider economic agenda itself and in the relationship between information and knowledge. The increased emphasis on the coverage of the 'micro' and 'market' context by financial newspapers, the booming sales of money and investment magazines and the new information technologies may have heralded an informationally rich society confronting the prospect of being knowledge-poor. Such are the paradoxes of an information revolution.

NOTES

1. P. J. D. Wiles, *Economic Institutions Compared* (Blackwell, Oxford, 1977) p. 273.
2. See Rita Cruise O'Brien (ed.), *Information, Economics and Power: the north–south dimension*, (Hodder and Stoughton, London, 1983).
3. G. J. Stigler, 'The economics of information', *Journal of Political Economy*, vol. 69, No. 3, (1961) p. 171.
4. Peter L. Berger, *The Capitalist Revolution: fifty propositions about prosperity, equality and liberty* (Wildwood House, Aldershot, 1987), see pp. 7–8.
5. Paul Samuelson, 'Personal Freedoms and Economic Freedoms in the Mixed Economy', in *The Collected Scientific Papers of Paul A Samuelson*, vol. 3 (MIT Press Cambridge Mass., 1972) p. 609.
6. Milton and Rose Friedman, *Free to Choose* (Penguin, Harmondsworth, 1980) pp. 34–5.
7. Hutchison makes the important distinction between thought and opinion in these terms:

   'economic thought' is used comprehensively to include economic opinion along with economic 'theory', 'analysis', and 'ideas'. 'Economic opinion' will be, to an important extent, that of non-economists, among politicians, the public, and civil servants, who may be somewhat influenced by 'theories' and 'analysis' and 'ideas', but who will mainly be swayed by the 'ideas' of economists, and will select from and distort these and influence them with their own political purposes.

   T. W. Hutchison, *On Revolutions and Progress in Economic Knowledge* (Cambridge University Press, Cambridge, 1978).
8. See, for example, in a related context two studies which examine the way in which economic theory has influenced the literary scene: Kurt Heinzelmann, *The Economics of the Imagination* (University of Massachusetts Press, Amhurst 1980); and Marc Shell, *The Economy of Literature* (Johns Hopkins University Press, Baltimore 1978).
9. Thus, studies of the press have tended to treat economics in terms of economics *of* the press industry, rather than its actual economic content and coverage or with ownership or its impact on mass opinion. For an exception to this see Ithiel de Sola Pool *et al.*, *The Prestige Press: a comprehensive study of political symbols* (MIT Press, Cambridge, Mass., 1970).
10. O'Brien (ed.), op. cit., p. 15.
11. A. J. Lee, *The Origins of the Popular Press, 1855–1914* (Croom Helm, London, 1976) p. 18.
12. John Palmer, 'The harlot's prerogative', in R. Boston (ed.) *The Press We Deserve* (Routledge and Kegan Paul, London, 1970) pp. 98–9.
13. Donald McCloskey, *The Rhetoric of Economics* (Wheatsheaf Books, Brighton, 1986).
14. See, J. J. Spengler, 'Exogenous and Endogenous Influences in the Formation of Post-1870 Economic Thought', in R. V. Eagly (ed.), *Events, Ideology and Economic Theory: determinants of progress in the development of economic analysis*, (Wayne State University Press, Detroit, 1968).
15. Fred Hirsch, *The Social Limits to Growth* (Routledge and Kegan Paul, London, 1977) p. 127. Hirsch had been the Financial Editor of *The Economist*. He had earlier examined the economics of the press and economics in the

press in a book written jointly with David Gordon, *Newspaper Money: Fleet Street and the search for the affluent reader* (Hutchinson, London, 1975).

16. Peter Jackson (ed.), *Implementing Government Policy Initiatives: the Thatcher Administration, 1979–1983* (Royal Institute of Public Administration, London, 1985) p. 28.

17. Cited in Gordon Thomas and Max Morgan-Witts, *The Day the Bubble Burst: a social history of the Wall Street Crash* (Hamish Hamilton, London, 1979) p. 181.

18. Patrick Sergeant, 'Tip for Tap in the City', in *100 Years of Fleet Street* (Press Club, London, 1982) p. 66.

1. Information and the economic age

As long as there have been markets, there has been a market for information. The growth of commerce, trade and finance has, from the earliest times, been dependent upon the development of an information network and a commercial grapevine. Economic 'revolutions' and change are therefore processes which are intimately linked to 'revolutions' in the field of economic communications. As commercial enterprises and industry have grown in complexity, scale and location, so too has the demand for information to facilitate that expansion. Indeed, the whole notion of 'economic' change really presupposes the idea of changes in modes of communication and knowledge.

The demand for information is as old as civilization itself. Joseph, for instance, did very nicely for himself by giving the Pharaoh advance warning of an agricultural depression! The demand for economic news and commercial communications of a less divine origin grew rapidly from the seventeenth century in response to the expansion of trade and commerce which was taking place in Europe at the time. At first, the flow of information went, as it had always done, through strictly private hands. The great commercial families of Fugger, Medici, Thurn and Taxis all had their own sources of intelligence which they used to their own economic advantage. It was the financier and banker Joseph Fugger of Augsburg who was, perhaps, the first to realize that there was money to be made from selling information as a commodity to clients and friends. By the middle of the seventeenth century the market for economic news and news that could affect markets had grown considerably. Although political censorship of the news was rife, governments freely allowed the development of services which met the needs of commercial and speculative interests. Indeed, the freedom of economic information has been one area of press liberty which, as Storey notes, has been

11

'kept intact' at all times.[1] It is significant, for example, that the development of commercial and financial newspapers in Europe in the sixteenth century, starting with the publication of price currents in Antwerp and Venice (1540–80), actually *predated* the arrival of the political press. All the major centres of commerce and trade, including London, Amsterdam and Hamburg, had a thriving business press by the early seventeenth century in the form of price currents, bills of entry and rates of exchanges and marine lists. Indeed, as McCusker notes, the surprise is that it took so long for businessmen to make use of the printing press to disseminate regular and reliable market information.[2] The earliest business press in London may be dated from the publication of bills of entry in the 1580s and price currents in the 1620s and 1630s. Thus well before 1700, as McCusker has shown, business newspapers had become 'an essential part of English commerce and finance'.[3]

The development of printing technologies were quickly identified as having great potential for extending the efficiency of markets beyond their immediate locality at an early stage of European economic growth. Printing meant that news of products, commodities and services could be advertised more widely than ever before. And, as trade and the population increased, so did the need for some system of regular communication between buyers and sellers. In the case of England, for instance, by the seventeenth century one-fifth of the population lived in the Thames Valley area, and as Nevett points out:

> The pattern of life in London had become so complex, and the numbers of people so large, that there was often no effective way of bringing information to the notice of those to whom it might be relevant . . . The corantos and newsletters provided political and commercial information which the capital needed . . . The advertisements they carried were therefore able to put buyers and sellers and investors in touch on an unprecedented scale.[4]

Communications were still poor; the mails were slow and not reliable and news from abroad was very patchy. After the passing of the Licensing Act of 1685 the *London Gazette* provided some news for the business community, but under strict government censorship. There was at this stage, then, no single publication to which merchants could refer for details of the course of exchanges, prices or shipping traffic. Bills of entry were lists of exports and imports of commodities at various ports; price currents contained details of the market prices of commodities; marine lists, the most famous of which was *Lloyd's List*, published information on shipping; and exchange currents provided information on foreign bills of exchange and stock market prices. Some of the earliest instances of the business press were the *Collection of the Improvement of Husbandry and Trade* (1692) which gave an account of commercial and financial news, and from time to time gave 'tips',[5] the *Course of Exchange* and *Lloyd's List* (1734). In these conditions, where information on the state of markets and trade was so thin on the ground, 'personal intercourse' was, as Wright and Fayle point out, 'everything':

> The merchant who wanted to know what was the prices of indigoes at India House; what ships were sailing for Jamaica ... what firms had gone under in a commercial crisis ... had to obtain his news by the exchange of information with his fellows. From an hour's talk in mixed company he could learn more than from the Gazettes of a week.[6]

None the less, it was the published information that still provided the staple diet which fed the talk. The Reverend Robert Kirk arriving in London – by then the largest town in Europe – noted that:

> The City is a vast great wilderness, few in it know a fourth part of its streets, far less can they get intelligence of a hundreth part of the special affairs and remarkable passages in it, unless by the printed papers, which come not to every man's notice.[7]

London was a town for making money, and journalism and coffee thrived on the passion for profit. Thus it was that coffee houses emerged to provide a means by which personal exchange of information, gossip and rumour could take place more easily and where a variety of newspapers were available to the clientele. When the Licensing Act expired in 1695, newsheets and coffee houses increased to meet the thirst for up-to-date intelligence and hot coffee. In 1696 Edward Lloyd, the proprietor of a coffee house, brought out one of the earliest such publications: *Lloyd's News*. Even so, the paper still carried little commercial news, apart from shipping intelligence: it gave no coverage of the course of the exchange or the price of stocks. *Lloyds News* was discontinued in 1697. Lloyd's coffee house, as other houses, however, continued to be the news centres of the time. Coffee houses both provided somewhere where personal information could be exchanged and also where newspapers could be read.[8] By the early eighteenth century 'coffee men' were becoming concerned that the quality of commercial information being provided by 'newswriters' was not up to the standard which was demanded by businessmen. Lloyd's coffee house again stepped in to meet this new demand for accurate information with the publication, in 1734, of *Lloyds List*, which is still in print today. The paper was specifically aimed at providing business men with reliable information on shipping news, but the details of the London exchanges and the prices of commodities were also included. The editor of the newspaper, Richard Baker, developed a close relationship with the post office which provided special service for Lloyd's correspondence. It was a service which reflected the importance which the government attached to the role of the business press in the growth of British trade and naval power. The reputation for accuracy commended *Lloyd's List* to both the governments of Britain and France, as well as the business community in general. Another major publication started around the same time (1697) was the *Course of Exchange*, a twice-weekly paper published by John Castaing, which, like *Lloyd's List*, continues to be published today (as *The Stock Exchange Daily Official List*). Castaing's paper provided, for the first time, reliable information for the investor during a period of rapid growth in the stock market and government securities.[9] Together, Baker and Castaing laid the foundations of accurate business reporting and set a high standard for the emerging financial news industry both in Britain and America where a business press was also growing up to provide information about all manner of events which might affect trade. As Middleton notes, the commercial tone and content of the American press had become established long before the revolution. After the war of independence it was, he argues, in the interest of publishers to serve the 'special commercial and political interests of business-men'.[10]

It was in the first half of the eighteenth century that the new business press came into its own as an effective mode of communication amongst the commercial classes eager to make a profit from the growth of joint stock companies during the spectacular boom of 1719–20. The importance of the role of newspapers in conveying speculative information and fostering involvement in trade and new commercial ventures should not be underestimated. Advertisements and news stimulated economic activity, and the speculative mentality by catering to the appetite for profits. It was not long before there was one of the most notorious instances of speculative mania – the South Seas Bubble of 1720. The existence of a newspaper press meant that speculative excitement spread, as Carswell observes, 'all over the British Isles, and to all classes save the humblest. Dublin, Edinburgh, Bristol and Norwich became as expectant as London, Berne, Basle, Paris and Amsterdam'.[11] Quotations of the South Sea stock began appearing in local papers up and down the land and in the early months of that year investment advertisements were occupying significant proportions of page space in daily papers like the *Daily Post*, *Daily Courant*, *Post Man*, *Post Boy* as well as in the *Weekly Journal* and the *Saturday Post*. In the *Daily Post*, for example, on 9 June 1720 some 23 pages out of 32 were given over to business and speculative advertising! Much of the journalism which accompanied this advertising was (like that which emanated from the pen of Daniel Defoe, promoting the stock of the Royal African Company) for sale.[12] And, by the time Defoe wrote his essays on the evils of the stock market, stocks and shares had become a common mode of gambling and making a quick profit. Little wonder, then, that newspapers had become such a British habit that one Swiss visitor noted in 1727: 'All Englishmen are great newsmongers. Workmen habitually begin the day by going to coffee rooms in order to read the daily news.'[13] Advertisement promoted trade, provided a means by which employers and potential employees could get in contact with one another, listed the current prices of commodities and shares and in general greatly facilitated the movement of capital and the pace of economic life. The impact of 'greater domestic intelligence' was not missed by Samuel Johnson who observed in the *Idler* for January 1759 that:

> Every man now knows a ready method of informing the public of all that he desires to buy and sell, whether his wares be material or intellectual; whether he makes clothes, or teaches the mathematics; whether he be a tutor that wants a pupil or a pupil that wants a tutor.[14]

Newspapers in the eighteenth century were, therefore, as Minchinton argues, an important way in which the machinery for 'articulating economic demand was improved'.[15] They spread information, whilst at the same time helping to propagate the new values of a vibrant commercial society. Newspapers served, as Brewer maintains:

> not only as a business seismograph, informing merchants, middlemen and traders of tremors that could lead to a financial earthquake, but also taught precisely those virtues and values which were necessary for survival in an economically expansive though debt ridden society.[16]

One of the most interesting aspects of this growing demand for economic news was the amount of space which even provincial local newspapers devoted to foreign news. Of course, from one point of view, it was less controversial than reporting domestic politics, but such news was also catering to the business community which was becoming, by the eighteenth century, increasingly aware of the wider world context within which they traded. Again, as John Brewer has noted:

> As long as the prospect, outbreak and course of war affected interest rates, the availability of credit, and the degree of confidence in the economy, there was good reason for the local trader to keep himself politically informed. Commercialization – especially the growth of credit – encouraged political involvement and gave political events an economic portentousness they had previously lacked. The newspaper catered to a curiosity that had already grasped that politics, commerce and credit were all part and parcel of the same problem.[17]

By the end of the eighteenth century a new kind of journalism had developed to satisfy the commercial curiosity in Britain and also in the American colonies. As the pace of economic life quickened, competition inevitably became more intense and the first American daily newspapers – *Pennsylvania Evening Post and Daily Advertiser* (1783), *Pennsylvania Packet and Daily Advertiser* (1784), the *New York Morning Post* (1785) and the *New York Daily Advertiser* (1785) – were, for the most part, aimed, like their British counterparts, at the merchant classes eager for news of trade, commerce, shipping and commodities and desirous of getting news of their products to consumers. Mercantile newspapers thus emerged as an important channel of commercial information which subsequently played a not unimportant role in the panic of 1792. As Sobel notes in his history of American financial crises, by this time although: 'None had what we would recognise today as a financial page, or even a column devoted to such news prices appeared regularly, along with accounts of speculation'.[18] Early local newspapers well appreciated the increasing importance attached to accuracy when it came to reporting the statistics which informed the commercial communities. Newspapers, even before the middle of the eighteenth century, were publishing data on prices, stocks and shares, shipping news and, most importantly in an age of credit, bankruptcies. By the second half of the century, as Cranfield comments, 'remarks on trade.' had become an accepted part of every newspaper'.[19] Provincial and London papers carried lists of bankruptcies, prices of commodities and stocks, and shipping news. They also, of course, carried a considerable amount of advertising, but very little by the way of what could be termed economic commentary or opinion. However, the 'penny sheet wars' over the Methuen Treaty of 1713 between the *Mercator* and the *British Merchant* were early signs that commercial interests would not be slow in coming to realize the potential of newsprint as disseminators of business *opinion* as well as commercial news and financial data. Henry Martin's articles in the *British Merchant* were an important, if not somewhat neglected, forerunner of the free-trade theories of Adam Smith.[20] It was during this period that the commercial classes, through pamphlets and newspapers became habituated to what Robbins termed 'intelligent discussion of financial affairs'[21] in their daily and weekly press. It was a habit that, perhaps, bore its greatest fruit in the letters of Ricardo to the *Morning Chronicle* on the subject of sterling exchanges at the time of the Napoleonic Wars. Newspapers slowly developed, therefore, from being purely a medium of economic information to being a forum of economic debate. An instance of this was the controversy over wool exports in the 1780s. As Richard Wilson concludes in his study of this episode of British commercial history:

> In its coverage of the controversy about the export of wool in the 1780s, the press, both in London and the provinces discussed issues in unprecedented detail. Hitherto there had been little comment about businessmen and economic affairs unless they had been closely linked with war or ministerial policy . . . Both sides in the controversy for the first time realised that the newspapers were essential for circulating information and informing opinion. The traditional use of markets,

meetings and correspondence was no longer sufficient ... many (printers) were beginning to see the potential of economic issues and discussions about the interests of the business community beyond the space devoted to stolen horses, runaway apprentices and lists of prices and bankrupts ... [22]

There has been a tendency – as Jeremy Black shows – to overemphasize the 'modernizing' impact of the press on society and political opinion in the eighteenth century.[23] However, there can be little doubt that such debates as those on wool exports and the general importance of the business press to the business community was vital to the exchange of commercial values and information, if not of actual economic ideas, values and rhetoric. Whereas the evidence for the role of the press in shaping (mass) public opinion is, as Black has demonstrated, somewhat conjectural, we can be more certain about its impact on the formation of economic attitudes, and discourse and commercial sentiment. The emergence of political economy in the latter part of the eighteenth century should not be divorced from the fact that, through newspapers, economic values had so well been expressed and disseminated in the preceeding decades.

By the late eighteenth century newspapers had evolved as a means of articulating consumer demand, whilst at the same time they had developed as a medium for communicating and aggregating commercial opinion and sentiment and, at times, spreading panic. It was no coincidence that, in both London and New York, the newspaper industry grew up in such close proximity to the financial districts: newspapers were the only thing actually made or produced in the City or Wall Street! And it is significant that this revolution in newspaper production and distribution coincided with the start of a revolution in economic ideas led by Adam Smith. As Feather has shown, the press had become, by the time of the publication of *The Wealth of Nations* in 1776, a 'national medium of information, opinion and advertising', which was vital to the book trade. The distribution of books was dominated by newspaper proprietors and newspaper advertisements facilitated the creation of an unprecedented demand for books and ideas. It was consequently through the newspaper and its distribution network that the 'philosophic paragraphs of Adam Smith penetrated the consciousness of provincial England.'[24] As is well known, the political economists were prolific journalists. Mill,

Torrens and McCulloch put forward their ideas at length in a journalistic form and economic controversy raged in the review press. The cut and thrust of theoretically informed debate was also to be found in many daily newspapers like the *Morning Chronicle* and Torrens's papers, the *Globe and Traveller* and the *Champion*. As O'Brien notes in the case of McCulloch, the *Scotsman* and the *Edinburgh Review*, as well as other occasional journalism, provided him with an outlet to expand his views, an income and influence over those in authority.[25] And, if judged by the controversy they stirred up, his articles must have had considerable impact. As a journalist, and the first real economist to write regularly in a newspaper, McCulloch was, so O'Brien concludes:

> of considerable importance in supplying economic material at an intellectually respectable level and in forcing on his readers problems which were, to say the least of it, outside the run of everyday experience. It is true to say that the readers did not like this ... but what newspaper readers even today would take kindly to lengthy theoretical discussions of the incidence of various forms of taxation occupying the entire front page of their newspaper?[26]

The letter pages were also extremely busy and provided a vital channel for the communication of new ideas. Most important, of course, were those of Ricardo to the *Morning Chronicle* in 1809.[27] The editor of the *Chronicle*, John Black, was himself a noted exponent of the political economy school of journalism which many felt to be more appropriate to the reviews than daily newspapers. He was a friend of McCulloch and James Mill and other political economists and was consequently, as Gilbert comments:

> strategically placed to influence and be influenced by, men of strong and advanced views – and one well positioned to carry those views to the wider public.[28]

The letter pages of the provincial press also provided a major platform for the political economists to sound off their views and garner the support of this wider public opinion. Examples of these are, for instance, Thomas Attwood in the *Birmingham Gazette* and *Birmingham Journal* and in *The Times, Globe* and *Morning Post* between 1816 and 1843, and Torrens's correspondence to the *Bolton Chronicle* in 1830.

It was, however, through the *Edinburgh Review* (1803–32) that the economic doctrines of Scottish political economy became more widely disseminated than through any other medium. The political economists, like Francis Horner in the *Edinburgh Review* between 1802 and 1806, were, as Fetter has argued, responsible for spreading an attitude that 'economic problems were important, and that they should be discussed in the light of an analysis of the facts'.[29] The periodical press was essentially an 'opinion forming' medium, which as Shattock and Wolff note, 'reached . . . an extraordinary audience which was in turn critical, articulate, influential, and, at least for most of the reign, homogeneous to a degree scarcely recognisable in its late twentieth century counterpart'.[30] The literary journals also reached a much larger audience than any book or pamphlet. One estimate is that (in 1814) the *Edinburgh Review* reached an audience of some 50 000 within a month of publication! Furthermore, as Fetter suggests, it is reasonable to assume that Ricardo's initial interest in economics was stimulated by Horner's pen.[31] And the influence of the *Edinburgh Review* and the other reviews was not confined to Britain since all but *Blackwoods* appeared frequently in American editions.[32] Thus, in Fetter's words: 'the pages of the *Edinburgh* provided for the gentry a shortened version of the economic classics, of the brochures of controversy and of the parliamentary reports'.[33] With the later emergence of the *Westminster, Quarterly* and *Blackwoods*, a similar service was provided by the middle-class reformers. In criticizing the political economists these other reviews further facilitated the popularization of the opinions and theories of the economists. Repetition is a great reinforcer of prevailing sentiment.[34]

The reviews' emphasis on political economy was as much a revolution in economic journalism and the communication of economic language as the ideas themselves. Significantly, what the *Edinburgh Review* mainly achieved was not the dissemination of the actual theories of Smith and Ricardo *et al.*, so much as its rhetoric and terminology. The distinction is an important one, for as Fontana's comprehensive examination of the impact of the *Edinburgh Review* points out, in the end the *Review* promoted doctrines which were 'very loosely (if at all) [in] the Smithian tradition':

> On balance, the impact of the reviewers upon the political language of their time was more of superficial brilliance and eclat than one of

genuine and durable substance ... the *Review* itself proved extra-
ordinarily successful in transmitting to the British political class and to
the educated public at large the central ideals of 'philosophical
Whiggism': the identification of modern European civilisation with the
progress of commercial society, the belief in the necessity of economic
expansion, the non-partisan commitment to civil liberty, and the
aspiration towards a professional and scientific style of politics.[35]

Indeed, perhaps the most interesting aspect of the economic
controversy in Ricardian England was the fact that the influence of
the political economists was such that, despite the manner in which
in private they disagreed amongst themselves, a unified set of ideas
was communicated to the public. What was propagated via the
journalism of the time was far from being the whole story. As far
as the general public was concerned, however, there was little
distinction between Ricardo, Malthus, Say or McCulloch. The
economic opinion which their ideas generated consequently led to
what Checkland once termed a 'specious clarity – that all political
economy was the same thing':

> The conditions in which the debate took place had a profound effect on
> its outcome. It was conducted, as it were in camera. Though a good
> deal of the writings of the parties had a fair circulation, there was no
> general appreciation that the pamphlets and books were the weapons
> in a battle of ideas moving into a critical stage. The public was for the
> most part ignorant of or indifferent to the synthesis to which these
> writings led.[36]

As is often the case in the history of ideas, the political economists
fell victim to their own powers of propagation and to the very
speed at which some of their theories became established as a body
of opinion. McCulloch, the great communicator of Ricardian
economics in the nineteenth century, was not the villain of the
piece. It was simply that the ideas of the economists all too well
fitted what J. S. Mill expressed as the conditions of successful
influence: 'Ideas, unless outward circumstances conspire with
them, have in general no very rapid or immediate efficacy on
human affairs.'[37] The existence of newspapers and magazines
which served to spread the ideas so quickly inevitably meant that
the separation of popular received opinion and the economic
theories themselves took place before those theories could be
developed into a more complete synthesis.

The *Edinburgh Review*, together with those publications which were antagonistic to political economy, transmitted a way of discussing economic and social issues in a scientific way, rather than a specific body of doctrines and theories: they introduced a new focus and language to public affairs. A notable instance of this was in the case of the series of articles published in the *Morning Chronicle* between 1849 and 1851 on the conditions of labour and the poor. Despite their obvious limitations, the reports constituted one of the most detailed social and economic surveys of the country and brought a new factual coherence to the issue of the 'condition of England.'[38] (The articles were later published in the US in the *Philadelphia Inquirer*.) The chief legacy of the political economists in terms of journalism was that of shaping the discourse of economic opinion rather than the diffusion of their economic theories. The power of periodical literature so to popularize economic ideas amongst the middle and upper classes no doubt owed a good deal to what Louis James refers to as the intimacy of this literary form which informed, educated and entertained specific social groups in a sustained and committed manner.[39] And, as Steinfels observes in the context of American neo-conservatism in the 1970s and 1980s: 'The geography of the intellectual's world is a geography of journals'[40] The success of the Victorian periodicals in influencing the political spirit of the times is ever thus a model for all who wish to change public opinion.

The great debates on *laissez-faire* political economy, free trade, the poor law, sterling and the machinery question which raged in the literary journals and in the letter pages of daily newspapers, reflected the growth in wealth and commerce of the late eighteenth and early nineteenth centuries. The tremendous expansion of banking in London and New York, and the emergence of entrepreneurs on the look out for good bets on the stock market (in one year alone, 1825, the dealings on the London Stock exchange doubled) led to the development of a new kind of 'City' and 'Wall Street' journalism that was very distinct from the work of McCulloch *et al*. Up until the 1820s financial reporting was, for the most part, confined to tables of market information. In 1785 *The Times* had pledged that it would give due attention to 'the interests of the trade, which are so greatly promoted by advertisements' and facilitate 'commercial intercourse between different parts of the community'. In common with other papers, however, in interpreting its role as a channel of commercial communication it did not go beyond listing prices and advertising. A report of the goings-on in the City first emerged in the Sunday papers, the *Observer*, the *Englishman*, and in an evening paper, the *Courier* in 1818. W. I. Clement, the editor of the *Observer*, was so taken by the City coverage that when he took over the *Morning Chronicle* in 1821 he made the City a daily news item. This was soon copied by other papers, like the *Morning Herald* and *The Times*. However, as Morgan and Thomas note in their history of the stock exchange, it was not until the 'boom' of 1825 that City journalism finally became an established feature of *The Times* and other London and major provincial papers.[41] The most important development at this time was the introduction of a 'money' column in *The Times* (Money, Market and City Intelligence). Thomas Massa Alsanger, financial editor of *The Times* appointed in 1817, soon established himself as the leading financial journalist of his day, and may rightly be seen as the real father of financial journalism as McCulloch was of the profession of economic journalist. Alsanger was bravely independent in his views. Despite, for example, the extensive advertising coverage given in *The Times* (as in other papers) to the railway boom, Alsanger gave many a warning that the bubble would inevitably burst. The editor backed him against the complaints of the advertisers and thereby increased the paper's reputation when the boom eventually came to an end. Alsanger was also an acknowledged authority on money and was regularly consulted by the Bank of England. The Bank itself, desirous of influencing the debate then ranging on the banking and financial system, began to publish a weekly *Circular to Bankers* so as to keep the 'facts' before the public. The circular frequently drew upon Alsanger's expertise.

The Times came to fill an important gap in the market for financial news: unbiased and critical reporting. The dominance of *The Times* as the organ of governing opinion was, of course, reinforced by the restrictive influence of taxes on newspapers which made them a relatively expensive commodity for ordinary people. Nevertheless, the predominance of *The Times* in business opinion as in political opinion was to survive even after the abolition of advertising duty in 1853 and paper excise duty in 1861. With such a captive market it could afford to take a critical and independent line on the City and the way it worked. In 1840, for example, *The Times* was sued by Alan Bogle over its story alleging forgery. Although the paper actually lost the action it received the grateful thanks of the City for the way in which it had exposed dubious practices. The City duly arranged for the erection of a memorial tablet to commemorate the role of *The Times* in the affair and endowed scholarships in the newspaper's name at the City of London School and Christ's Hospital. The paper also took the view that, rather than print the reports of company meetings composed by the companies themselves it would only publish a report written by one of its own journalists. Such integrity was, however, a rare commodity in nineteenth-century financial journalism. In America business journalism also began to enter a new phase in the 1820s. There were commercial advertisers and also journals, like the *Courier* and *Enquirer* that began to give over more space to financial news and comment. The editors of these papers were, as Weisberger argues:

> often spokesmen for a viewpoint profoundly important in the growing nation. They trumpeted the glories of nationalism and industrialism, and involved the pride of Americans with economic expansion.[42]

Perhaps the greatest exponent of this brand of journalism was one Hezekiah Niles, whose (Baltimore) *Weekly Register* (1811–48) was an influential model for American business journalism. In New York, Gordon Bennett's *Herald* and Henry J. Raymonds's *Times* were also setting new standards in business journalism. It was Bennett who more than any other figure revolutionized American financial journalism.[43] A Scots émigré, Bennett earned his living in the early days as a lecturer in political economy and by writing for newspapers. By 1826 he had become a full time journalist and in 1835 started – as a one man show – the *Herald*. From the beginning he was determined to publish a paper with more than partisan opinions and his coverage of Wall Street provided for the first time a specialized financial news service which was subsequently imitated by other publications. He exposed financial rogues – something which did not endear him to the stock-broking community – and pioneered money market reports, detailed stock exchange news and new technology – something which did. In very different ways Gordon Bennett's approach to Wall Street left as indelible a mark on the style and approach of American financial journalism as Walter Bagehot was to leave on the British scene.

If Alsanger and Gordon Bennett had come to fill one kind of gap in daily financial journalism by the 1840s – authoritative, informed and (somewhat more) independent reporting than had been available up until that point in time – then the London *Economist* filled another, more intellectual hiatus in terms of providing ideas and facts with the benefit of weekly hindsight. The object of the London *Times* and the New York *Herald* was, as all other papers, to make money through advertising revenue; the aim of the *Economist*, however, was to advance the cause of an idea – free trade and political reform. The advertising of *The Times* and of other newspapers propagated the culture and values of a commercial society: the articles of the *Economist* had no small role to play in spreading the theories and ideas which, as Bagehot noted, were 'paradoxes everywhere else in the world' but which came to 'settle down into the common sense of the nation'.[44] For, as Bagehot himself argued, a good deal of the credit for the way in which *laissez- faire* political economy spread in Britain was due to the *Economist*:

> through the pages of this journal certain doctrines, whether true or false, have been diffused, far more widely than they ever were in England before, – far more widely than from their abstract nature we could expect them to be diffused . . .[45]

The *Economist* was the great aggregator of commercial information and *laissez-faire* ideas. The paper organized and articulated the opinions of a readership well able to make use of the information it provided for profit or political argument. At the same time it was also, as Gordon Scott has shown, important in the formation and development of the doctrine of free trade and *laissez-faire* political economy:

> if we wish to find the origin of the mid-nineteenth century theory of *laissez-faire*, we can find it nowhere better than in the *Economist*.[46]

The paper was successful in diffusing ideas largely because it brought together the two strands of economic journalism which had emerged up to that point: the reporting of facts and the discussion of opinions. It was a great advocate of free trade and political economy and also of better information for the business-man. Although the paper was founded by James Wilson as an organ of the Anti-Corn Law League it avoided, right from the start, being too doctrinaire by placing an emphasis on 'facts' and taking the kind of quantitative approach to economic news to be found in other papers to an altogether more sophisticated level. The *Economist* aimed to be more than simply a propaganda organ for the League, but aspired to be an educator of the middle classes on the lines of the periodical press. For this, and other reasons, Cobden himself was very doubtful about the venture as the movement already had a propaganda organ – the *League*.[47] In February 1844 the *Economist* announced that it would endeavour to provide 'the most accurate statement of prices of government funds, foreign securities and stocks and of the various descriptions of joint stock companies in Great Britain and Ireland, with the most recent information respecting the same'. In this emphasis on reporting the facts of economic life the *Economist* was to lead the way in the development of economic information which was to be widely imitated. As the history of the paper records:

> From the very beginning *The Economist* has adopted the policy of collecting and publishing as many statistics as possible on all aspects of economic life, not only in this country but also . . . abroad. Thus *The Economist* of September 2nd 1843 already contains an extensive survey of the commodity markets, with statistics of imports, exports and prices and a short list of bond prices. The number and variety of records grew steadily as new data became available on prices, production, trade, transport, finance, the Stock Exchanges, unemployment and so on.[48]

Wilson therefore created a whole new kind of economic journalism geared to the needs of the business community; one that strove to maintain a high standard of factual reporting as well as campaigning for certain ideas. It was a journalism which provided a meeting ground between practical business, abstract theories and political argument. Wilson, thought Bagehot, had a rare talent to communicate:

> Nor is this faculty of exposition by any means a triffling [sic] power. On many subjects it is a common saying 'that he only discovers who proves', but in practical politics we may almost say that he only discovers who convinces. It is no use to have practical truths received by extraordinary men, unless they are also accepted by ordinary men.[49]

As Bagehot realized, the 'economic age', as he termed it, was an age for 'ordinary men' – the new and growing middle classes. The *Economist* was, to use Bagehot's expression, a great 'belief producer' for this class. And the importance of Wilson and Bagehot lay less in their actual reputation as economic *theorists* so much as their invention of a style or method of economic commentary which was pragmatically intellectual. Their influence was in terms of establishing for the Victorian business community a coherent context of ideas, information and news whilst at the same time giving an effective voice to the business mentality. Since, as Bagehot explained:

> Men of business can no more put into words much of what guides their life than they could tell another person how to speak their language . . . [50]

Bagehot's economic journalism provided businessmen with a set of ideas they could understand, and gave a highly articulate voice to the emerging commercial and financial classes. For some 18 years, at a time when British economic power was at its height, Bagehot gave business a language and legitimacy which it had hitherto lacked; his weekly comments put capitalism into words and thereby provided for a new forum of communication between business and the wider world. In a sense, it could be said that Bagehot's genius as an economist was that he imbued the economic attitudes of mid-nineteenth-century middle-class England with the same sort of coherency and intellectual respectability that his *English Constitution* provided for the political order. He was, as Keynes well expressed it: 'a psychologist – a psychological analyser, not of the great or the genius, but of those of a middle position, and primarily of business men, financiers, and politicians'.[51] He was, above all, as Robert Giffen once observed, a great 'describer of the modern business world' and was deferred to as an 'economic authority', which he was not. He wrote with the business community in mind. Hence, he aimed

> at an excessive simplicity in part formed by his habit of writing for the City . . . He had always some typical City man in his mind's eye – a man not skilled in literature or the turnings of phrases, with a limited vocabulary and knowledge of theory but keen as to the facts and reading for the sake of information and guidance respecting what

vitally concerned him. To please this ideal City man Bagehot would use harsh and crude or redundant expressions, sometimes ungrammatical . . . anything to drive his meaning home.[52]

There can be little doubt that Bagehot was the greatest interpreter of commercial sentiment and economic ideas of his day. Like Horner and McCulloch, Bagehot brought economic ideas and method into the domain of business and political affairs. At the same time, he also gave expression to the attitudes and psychology of the City and commercial world. Standing as he did at the centre point in the flow of economic ideas and business opinion he was thus a singularly important mediator of the economic agenda. His *Lombard Street: a description of the money market* (1873) represents the consummate product of his facility for capturing and interpreting the theory and practice of commerce. For this reason, as for his many other gifts, he was much respected by both politicians and businessmen: Gladstone called him his 'spare Chancellor', the City saw him as their tame intellectual. (He is credited with giving Sir Stafford Northcote the idea of the treasury bill in 1877 as a new way of raising government finance.) He was also close to what was going on at the academic level: in 1876/7, for example, he is recorded as having examined Political Economy at London University. What fascinated him above all was the relationship between the two dimensions of economic life which as a journalist he saw as his job to analyse: the abstract world of the theorist and the practical world of the business man. At its best, and at its most influential, political economy was, so Bagehot thought, the result of a fusion of business experience and a scientific disposition. The greatest advances in economics had, he maintained, come about through an interaction between these two worlds. As he argues with regard to Smith and Ricardo:

Adam Smith [took] up the subject in a solid straightforward way, such as he knew would suit the Glasgow merchants. He impressed practical men by his learning, at the same time he won them by his lucidity and assured them by his confidence.

. . .

The trade in which Ricardo spent his life, and in which he was so successful, is of all trades the most abstract. Perhaps some people may smile when they hear that his money was made on the stock exchange. But there is no place where the calculations are so fine, or where they are employed on data so impalpable. . .[53]

As a *journalist* Bagehot was preoccupied less with economics than, as Keynes argues, the 'psychology of economic writing' and with how the business mind worked. Thus he viewed economic commentary and news as a place wherein ideas and practice could interact as they had done in the age of Smith and Ricardo. For Bagehot the press in England was not only a powerful political force which could make and unseat governments (which he thought not to be the case in America since, as he says in the *English Constitution*, the term of Presidential office is fixed and consequently Americans only 'glance' at the papers and do not enter upon a discussion) but also a medium through which events and ideas, facts and theories, could come together to shape the climate of economic opinion at those crucial moments when opinion was wavering. In shaping a common ground it had a major intellectual role to play in the life of the nation. This common ground was necessary because, as he put it, 'theorists do not see ... business and the men of business will not reason out ... theories'.[54] There was, he believed, an inherent gap between the actuality of commerce and the ideas of economists which, in the absence of practical theorists and abstract business men, it was the task of journalists such as himself and Wilson to fill. Bagehot thus bequeathed the idea of there being a major role for economic journalism in the activity of formulating a political economy which can serve as a focus for political debate and commercial discussion.

The success of the *Economist* stimulated the growth of other weekly publications which aimed at a high level of economic analysis and statistical information. The most important being the *Statist* founded by Sir Robert Giffen (he of the Giffen good) and Thomas Lloyd in 1878. Lloyd, a gentleman of Irish stock, was very interested in the question of monetary policy and theory and had published a number of books, including *The Theory of Distribution and Consumption*. Sir Robert Giffen had been a journalist and a civil servant in the Board of Trade. Their aim in setting up the *Statist* was to publish a 'weekly journal for economists and men of business' with an emphasis on a 'scientific' and statistical approach, which would seek to avoid 'party politics'. In this goal of producing a paper providing an analytical understanding of the economic issues of the day the *Statist* was undoubtedly successful. Sadly, due to its close rivalry with the *Economist* it does not survive today: the last number came out in April 1967. In its early years the *Statist*, along with the *Economist*, made an enormous contribution to formulating a statistical context for economic debate. At a time when government figures on the economy were sparse, the two papers were a vital informational resource.

This shift towards a more statistically informed journalism, as advanced by Giffen and Lloyd and later on by Sir George Paish, an expert on the American railway industry and father of Frank Paish, marked a wider change in the relationship between economics and society. By this time Bagehot could discern that political economy was 'dead in the public mind';[55] no longer did ideas excite public opinion, but had rather become the accepted axioms of political debate. At the same time the gap between the worlds of business and policy-making and the more abstract activities of economic theorists had grown ever wider with the onset of what became known as the 'marginalist revolution'. Yet, in one sense, the two had never been so close, as the involvement of academically orientated journalists-cum-civil servants like Giffen and Paish in the *Statist* bear witness, and as the importance of information provided by the financial press to academic economists, like Marshall and Jevons, also attests. What Bagehot had in mind, however, was really the demise of the kind of fundamental economic controversy – over the poor law, trade and currency – which had taken place in the early days of the *Economist*'s history. Bagehot's own explanation of this decline in the demand for economic ideas was simple: in times of crisis men need ideas, when times are untroubled they do not:

> Business being bad there was great interest in the 'science of business', which ought to explain why it was thus bad, and might be able to show how it was to be made good. While the economic condition of countries is bad men care for Political Economy, which may tell us how it may be improved; when that condition is improved, Political Economy ceases to have the same popular interest, for it can no longer prescribe anything which helps people's lives.[56]

The 'ideas cycle' followed the business cycle.

The bias towards statistics, investment and tipping in the financial media, in the latter part of the century, as opposed to that of political economy in the preceeding years was, from this point of view, a sign of the fact that, at the height of Victorian economic prosperity (1862–79), the age of economic controversy was over.

Readers wanted facts, not ideas, technique and not teachers. As King notes, for example, with respect to money market reporting:

> The period from 1890 to 1914 was not a spectacular one in money market history – not, at least, by contrast with the crowded incidents, the blunderings, the crises, and the burning controversies of earlier years. The market, too was growing up; it needed sober instruction upon technical problems rather than noisy chiding on first principles.[57]

The financial press, rather unimaginatively, as King comments, gave the market exactly what it needed. In turn, the focus on analysing institutions, markets and companies complemented and reinforced the theoretical preoccupations of the economics profession. The *Economist* made an especially important contribution to the development of statistical tools by which economic change could be monitored by publishing figures on wholesale prices, overseas trade, capital issues, profits, shipping rates, insurance and business activity. In addition to this there were regular supplements, starting with the *Commercial History Supplement* (1864), and the *Monthly Trade Supplement* (1845), *Banking Supplement* (1861), *Budget Supplement* (1863) and the *Investors' Monthly Manual* (1864). Such statistics were particularly important prior to the development of more extensive materials published by the government. The techniques developed by Newmarch and Jevons in measuring price movements, for example, owed much to the 'Records and Statistics' published in the paper, and the availability of detailed accounts and reports of the stock exchange and the money markets undoubtedly meant that the perception of the 'economy' was greatly affected by the data available to business men and politicians. In reality, what this amounted to was a narrowing of the range of economic problems deemed as analytical/theoretical issues as well as what counted as economic news. Economic news, not that such a term was used, was effectively news which impacted upon the state of the market and City opinion. The economic condition of the people, for example, was not something which, as Lucy Brown shows in her study of the Victorian press, greatly preoccupied the attention of financial journalists and newspaper editors. In 1878, for instance, there was, she notes 'no general discussion of the economic trend . . . [and] no attempt . . . [to] present a coordinated account of the recession as a general phenomenon'.[58] Papers which were catering to the needs of the investing classes were then inherently biased against taking a wider perspective on the 'economy'. Economic news as such was simply news that was of importance to financial and business interests: the word 'unemployment' did not enter The Oxford English Dictionary until 1888. The hardship and poverty of the East End of London, a district which was but a stones' throw from the financial centre of an Empire, was of a very marginal interest and consequently had little political impact. The financial press at this time clearly served to insulate the political and, in a broader sense, the intellectual agenda from the economic events which were actually taking place. As Brown comments: 'This kind of reporting may have been satisfactory to the London business-man, but politically it was misleading.'[59]

The narrowness of economic perspective was not, however, the sole prerogative of the financial press. It was an interesting paradox that, thanks to Reuters and the opening of the Atlantic cable in 1866 (the 'Big Ditch'), as the information network which fed the London and New York stock exchanges and supplied financial journalists with raw news was becoming ever more international – with transatlantic communication time being cut from days to minutes – the professional economics community was in the process of becoming ever more national and specialized in charac-ter. By the latter part of the nineteenth century economists were tending towards inhabiting an increasingly insular world far re-moved from the influence of outsiders and amateurs. Economics as O'Brien and Presly point out, was becoming more professional-ized and 'closing . . . its discourse to outsiders – something which Marshall (and to some extent Edgeworth) tried to resist but which rolled relentlessly forward'.[60] At the same time, financial journal-ists themselves were becoming more specialized. The amateur was, in economics as in other branches of knowledge, becoming a rare breed. Perhaps the last flowering of the amateur economist in nineteenth century England was Miss Harriet Martineau (1802–76), both in her famous *Illustrations of Political Economy* which turned her into a great celebrity,[61] and in later life through her prolific leader writing in the *Daily News*. In America the distinc-tion of being the last non-professional of any note went to a printer-turned-journalist Henry George (1839–97) – a name later to be invoked by supply-side economists in the 1970s. George began his career on the *San Francisco Evening Post and The*

Standard, and soon developed an interest in political economy: he was at one stage even considered for the chair of political economy at the University of California. As far as George was concerned, however, the subject was not one which needed 'special knowledge' or equipment: anyone could do it. For George political economy was about thinking for yourself. Such a notion hardly made him a suitable candidate for an academic post and thus it was that he went on to pursue a career as an economic publicist which culminated with the publication of *Progress and Poverty* in 1879 – next to the works of Veblen, one of the most widely read American economics texts until the era of Samuelson, Friedman and Galbraith. George also pursued – through his Single Tax Party – a political career and almost succeeded in becoming Mayor of New York. The professional economic community had nothing but contempt for his simplistic theory that rent was the cause of poverty and that the solution was a single tax on land, but because his ideas were so well known they had actually to take him to task. Many of their criticisms, however, just went over his head, and as he himself admitted, George did not really understand the 'Anglo-German jargon' which had come to dominate economic discourse by the 1880s.[62] Yet if he was the last of the non-academics to (just) get into the histories of economic thought, he was also the first of another type: the economist as a political celebrity. After Henry George, economic journalists, a species that had done so much to develop and disseminate economic ideas and excite public interest in the early decades of the nineteenth century, became virtually extinct; something about which Marshall, writing in 1897 – the year of Henry George's death – was delighted: the old generation of general practitioners was at last giving way to the new scientific specialists.[63] The age of Miss Martineau and Henry George was over – leastways, for the time being. As we shall see in Chapters 5 and 6, however, their successors made a comeback in the 1970s when the academic specialists were no longer considered to have all the answers.

This professionalization of economics which was welcomed by Marshall and resented by the likes of Henry George was marked by the founding of the Royal Economics Society (1890) with, ironically, a former journalist as its first president, Robert Giffen; the setting up of the London School of Economics (1895), and the Cambridge Economics Tripos (1903), and more generally by the fact that after 1870 external events – news – were less of an influence on the development of economic theory than, as Stigler observed, the 'internal values and pressures of the discipline'. After 1870 the 'production incentives'[64] of economics were those of the profession, whereas before – particularly during the high tide of political economy – the incentives were largely generated by the kind of context or news agenda set by the press and periodicals, and there was a much closer relationship between the internal agenda of economists and the external agenda of political debate. It was natural, therefore, that newspapers and journals of opinion should have become the media through which economists expressed their ideas. In the first half of the century the press and literary magazines were really the only means of conducting a theoretical discussion. In the closing decades of the century, the internal pressures on economics led to a withdrawal from open public debate in favour of more specialized professional and closed discourse. (The *Quarterly Journal of Economics* was founded in 1886, and the *Economic Journal* in 1890.) It was a time for synthesizing and improving rather than disseminating and winning converts. It was also a time when, as Kadish comments, 'the reputation of the study of political economy reached an unprecedented nadir . . . the economists' work was held in unusually low esteem by various sections of the general public'.[65] The marginalist revolution could, therefore, be said to have also marginalized economics. As economics became almost exclusively the subject of university dons it was inevitable that its discourse would become less universally understood and perceived as less useful. This found its most obvious manifestation through the evolution of a research community which had little use for newspapers and communicating to the wider non-professional public or, indeed, the process of what Bagehot described as 'discovering by convincing'. It was also reflected in the rise and rise of something which the *Economist* and the *Statist* had done much to foster: economic statistics. The growth of the statistical approach, both in academic economics and in financial reporting had, as Hutchison notes, 'pervasive and imponderable effect[s] on social self-consciousness and sophistication'.[66] The energies which Mill, McCulloch *et al.* applied to journalism their successors were to invest, with an almost missionary zeal, into extra-mural teaching. Whereas the early political economists welcomed the chance to apply their ideas to contemporary issues the marginalists avoided it like a veritable plague. Economists, thought Marshall, should not wash their theories in public as disagreement exposed their science to the 'contempt of ordinary men'. This is not to say that Marshall was entirely averse to newspaper controversy, but it did mean a break with what he called an 'almost absolute rule against controversial correspondence'. Though he, like other economists, occasionally wrote to *The Times*, it was to clarify a technical point or offer some professional elucidation rather than to provoke an argument or advance his opinions as Keynes was later to do. As far as Keynes was concerned, this was a major failing of Marshall. The controversial nature of economics meant that, for Keynes as for the political economists, thinking aloud was an essential part of the process of theoretical progress. As Keynes argues in his essay on Marshall:

> in view of the transitory character of economic facts, and the bareness of economic principles in isolation, does not the progress and daily usefulness of economic science require that pioneers should eschew the Treatise ... economics all the world over might have progressed much faster, and Marshall's authority and influence would have been far greater, if his temperament had been a little different.[67]

Unquestionably, however, it was this expansion of what Keynes termed 'transitory' economic facts which was the major influence on the growth of the economic media. The demand for accurate and fast financial information was something which Reuter and other news agencies had spotted in the late 1840s. Though quickly accepted by the City, the new telegraph systems were not generally employed by the press until 1859. This improvement in the speed of communications came on top of the repeal of stamp duty on newspapers in 1855 and led the way to an explosion of financial newspapers to cater for the demand for information and tips. In the first instance, the extension of 'penny journalism' led, as the *Financier* (1870) noted in its first edition, to a 'diminution of the amount of space and attention devoted to financial and commercial affairs'. To meet the demand for daily information a mass of publications came on the market from the 1860s onwards. Most had only a brief existence. Wilson and Bagehot had written for the political and business classes at a time when, in Gordon Scott's words, that class had to be 'fully armed during the following week for any chance encounter with a protectionist enemy'.[68] They wrote for an audience in the market for ideas or debating points as much as they were in business for financial gain: Wilson and Bagehot were teachers and not tipsters. Their readership had been weaned on the *Edinburgh Review*. The financial press which grew in the 1880s was geared to a very different market altogether – a readership more interested in speculation than ideas or economic analysis. (Rather like the way in which the *Sporting Life*, also around this time, catered for the growing demand for starting prices from the gambling fraternity. The availability of this information for punters meant that more people took to bookmaking – as they took to the stock market – as a way of making money.)[69] During the 1880s the market for the financial press widened with the growth in the investing public. As middle-class Britain and America became wealthier, participation in the stock market became a less exclusive activity than it had been in the past. Publications such as the *Economist* and the *Statist* had been aimed less at the speculative public than those who were interested in a more analytical approach to the economic scene. The new money and capital markets required a more immediate service than that provided by weekly 'intellectual' publications. The emergence of financial dailies in the 1880s in London and New York signalled the end of the 'economic age' and the dawn of a new era when information and the market economy became more important than old ideas. If Wilson and Bagehot could be said to have revolutionized British economic journalism with their commitment to political economy, then, without doubt, it was one Harry Marks who was to have just as profound an impact in bringing the benefits of the information revolution to the financial news business in Britain. Marks set up the *Financial News* in 1884 after going to America to learn the tricks of the American journalistic trade: in the 1870s he worked on the *New Orleans Picayune* and *New York World*.

The American scene in financial and economic journalism was very different from that in Britain at this time. There was no equivalent of Bagehot or the *Economist*, and economic journalism – apart from market information – had a generally low editorial priority. As we have seen, like their British counterparts American newspapers evolved out of the demand for commercial

advertising and information. And, as was the case in Britain, a
new journalism – more dependent on circulation than advertising
revenue – evolved to represent emergent radical movements: in
Britain it was free trade in the 1830s and 1840s, in America in the
same period it was Jacksonian democracy opposed to the influence
of special interests. Whereas political economy led to the development of economic journalism of the quality of Bagehot, the
American reform movement led to the founding of a tradition of
'muckraking' journalism that was at its most sensationalist in
Bennett's *Herald* which had set the lead in American financial
journalism by announcing that his paper would go beyond the 'dry
quotations of the market' by reporting what was going on behind
the scenes. Later, in 1882, another milestone in the history of
American financial journalism was the setting up of a Wall Street
newsletter by Charlie Dow and Eddie Jones which proved so
successful that the following year they expanded their activities by
publishing a *Customers' Afternoon News Letter* which grew into
the *Wall Street Journal* in 1889. The *Journal* announced that its aim
would be:

> to give fully and fairly the daily news attending the fluctuation in prices
> of stocks and bonds and other commodities. It will aim steadily at
> being a paper of news, and not a paper of opinions . . . We believe that
> such a paper will be of use to operators, bankers, and capitalists who
> can find in its columns essential statistics compiled so that their pith
> and bearing can be readily remembered; also the events which have
> moved or are moving prices, together with the draft of opinion in the
> Street . . .[70]

The paper soon made good its prospectus and established a pre-
eminent reputation as the leading Wall Street newspaper – its
competitors being the *New York Commercial Bulletin*, *Daily
Financial News* and the *New York Daily Indicator*. The reasons for
its success were, apart from astute management, the fact that it
developed a reputation for sound judgement and, through Dow's
'Review and Outlook' column, an analytical style which had until
then been absent from the American scene. Dow's theory
attracted much academic interest and the Dow Jones averages,
which had made their first appearance in the afternoon newsletter,
became recognized as the most reliable measure of stock market
activity. Even so, notwithstanding the *Journal*, the American

financial press lacked the kind of tradition of economic commentary which had grown up in England. As Robert Sobel points out:

> economic analysis was a rare commodity. When this was required the reporter would peruse some columns by Walter Bagehot in the London *Economist* and try to paraphrase them for an American audience.[71]

The gap which Harry Marks endeavoured to fill in Britain was precisely the market which Bennett had begun to fill in the 1840s, and Down and Jones had identified in New York: authoritative daily financial journalism. On returning to England Marks had it in mind to profit from his experience of the American commercial newspaper industry by producing a paper that would:

> treat of financial subjects as the most thorough and most enterprising newspapers deal with political and general news topics, aiming to give the earliest, completest, and surest information upon all matters of public interest.[72]

American 'bounce' worked and the *Financial News* ushered in a new chapter in the history of British financial journalism. The paper employed all that Marks had learnt about layout and presenting news in an interesting manner. The *News* had no competition in the way in which it used telegraphic communications to bring 'American bounce' to a British scene that had been dominated by the staid City columns of *The Times* and the intellectualism of the *Economist*. Marks's paper was unashamedly 'devoted to the interests of the investor' and the growing speculative public that had thrived during the bull markets of the period, and in the railway and mining booms. The paper was involved in a number of scandals involving the use of the *News* to hype or 'puff up' shares and Marks died in 1916 with the paper which he founded still thriving but his personal reputation in shreds. Nevertheless, Marks had, through importing an American approach to journalism. totally changed the polite world of British financial reporting. The *News* was followed by the *Financial Times* which came out in 1888 as the *London Financial Guide* but within a few months changed its title so as more accurately to convey the authority at which it aimed. So as to differentiate the paper from its rival the *News*, the *Financial Times* proclaimed on its front page that it would be:

The friend of the honest financier; the bona fide investor; the respectable Broker; the genuine director; the legitimate speculator.

And:

The enemy of the closed Stock Exchange; the unprincipled promotor; the company wrecker; the 'guinea pig'; the 'bull'; the 'bear'; the gambling operator.

Needless to say, over the years it duly accused its rival of being in cahoots with all that was corrupt in British finance. Both papers delighted, until their merger in 1945, in casting doubt over one another's honesty and integrity. The truth of the matter was, however, that due to the condition of company and corporate law on both sides of the Atlantic, financial journalism was inherently on shaky ground when it came to being honest to their readers whilst serving the interests of their advertisers. The financial press inhabited a highly unregulated business world. It was not, for example, until 1908 that public companies were required in Britain to publish balance sheets: prospectuses were not stringently controlled by the stock exchange until the 1939 Prevention of Fraud Act. And it was not until 1948 that the Companies Act meant that more information had to be published as a legal requirement. In 1933 changes in US corporate law compelled listed companies to subject their financial statements to independent auditing. Subsequent legislation and stricter codes of journalistic practice have since then created the basis for a financial journalism less open to abuse than was the case in the late nineteenth and early twentieth centuries. Before such changes, even the most responsible of newspapers had to strike a balance between the need for honest reporting of the more unscrupulous activities of joint stock companies and the commercial necessity of attracting revenue from company advertising. Company prospectuses were invariably accompanied by rather doubtful comment. As Charles Duguid, advising those who would like to understand the money page, noted in 1901:

Providing it is thoroughly understood by the reader that his paper seldom, if ever, criticises a prospectus, be the company never so rotten, and that the colourless notice in its money article is merely to commend the prospectus advertisement to his attention and not to his favourable attention; if this is understood, then the abstention from criticism can do little harm. Nevertheless, it does seem that harm is done negatively; that a great opportunity of saving the investor from the trickery of the promoter is wasted by the powerful paper which is ready enough to express is opinion and advice upon almost every conceivable matter but company prospectus. Moreover, the great paper, in its silence, occasionally cuts a rather absurd figure when from the columns of some less dignified contemporary or contemporaries come indisputable and indisputed disclosures of an utterly condemnatory nature as to the flotation of a company.[73]

As the financial press became more and more reliant on advertising revenue, readers had to beware. Company news was, if not blatantly corrupted, invariably one sided. 'The system' was, as Duguid saw, not a conspiracy so much as an open secret.

As Harry Marks had realized in the 1880s, the growth of share ownership amongst the middle classes combined with the information and communications revolution had dramatically altered the whole social and cultural context of British capitalism. In the Bagehot era 'practical businessmen' concerned with the big issues of the day which would set the framework for commerce and industry were naturally in the market for theories; in the Marks era they were in the market for tips. As Duguid expressed it:

Whereas the literary and newspages of a newspaper are of some interest to the thousands – they read them for amusement – the City page is of intense interest to the few – they read it for their pecuniary profit.[74]

The new readership of the financial press wanted to understand the 'game of finance' all the better to make money, and were little bothered by the need for any intellectualization of the activity of making a profit. The *Economist* stood out as the last bastion of the old financial journalism and could only berate the way in which 'Financial journalism has altered not a little from what it was fifty or twenty years ago' (1 November 1913). The new journalism confronted a more complex investment world, a new scale of economic activity, and a new demand for notes and advice, rather than the kind of analytical, and by comparison the worthy, academic style of the *Economist*. For this reason, as for the fact that financial journalists were never really regarded as 'proper' journalists, the profession did not acquire a reputation for literary merit or high journalistic standards. Indeed, for this reason, in most accounts of the history of journalism, financial reporting is mentioned either not at all or merely *en passant*. As Kenneth Fleet notes:

> The role and status of City editors and financial journalists were not always considered to be important ... They were regarded as an inferior breed concerned with remote and esoteric subjects like the price of Consolidated Stock and the movements in the Bank Rate. Their literary efforts were consigned to a small corner which the vast majority of readers were expected to ignore.[75]

Clearly, the historical importance of the financial press does not lie so much in its contribution to the development of a literary form as in its role in defining a capitalist language and culture: free markets, individualism, profit and speculation. Not only did the publication of information facilitate the growth of the international-ization of markets, it also assisted in no small way in the promotion of capitalist culture. Lupin, Pooter's son in *The Diary of a Nobody* (1892), was, perhaps, all too typical an example of the up-and-coming new generation who seemed to have been 'born a capital-ist', riveted as he was to the pages of the *Financial News*. And Samuel Butler, for example, writing at a time when financial publications were booming (in 1884), commented that:

> If I had my way I would have a speculation master attached to every school. The boys would be encouraged to read the *Money Market Review*, the *Railway News*, and all the best financial papers ... If Universities were not the worst teachers in the world I should like to see professorships of speculation established at Oxford and Cam-bridge. When I reflect, however, that the only things worth doing which Oxford and Cambridge can do well are cooking, cricket, rowing and games, of which there is no professorship, I fear that the establishment of a professorial chair would end in teaching young men neither how to speculate, nor how not to speculate, but would simply turn them out as bad speculators.[76]

Bagehot would surely have taken a dim view of such attitudes towards the use of the financial press.

There was no successor to Bagehot in 1877, even though he has remained as a kind of patron saint of business journalism – as instanced by the fact that Columbia University's School of Journalism named its prestigious programme in Economics and

Business Journalism after him in 1975. The 'economic era' on which Bagehot had written so brilliantly had changed radically by the closing decades of the nineteenth century – as had the political system of the mid-Victorian era. At one level, the intellectual ferment which had brought the *Economist* into being had subsided into a conventional wisdom. At another, so had the scale and complexity of the British and the world economies. Just as it was possible for Bagehot's *English Constitution* to have been written in 1867, so too the relative stability and strength of the British economy in the mid-nineteenth century also facilitated the kind of economic journalism at which he and his journal excelled. Thus Bagehot's economic age – the 'age of discussion' – died with him, even though through his influence on Woodrow Wilson and the federal reserve legislation, and on generations of readers of his classic work, *Lombard Street*, his impact was still to be felt fifty years and more after his death.[77] The economic journalism of the subsequent decades saw the financial media quickly adjust to the changing economic climate, particularly in terms of its bias towards finance and speculation. There was both a lack of demand for economics and economists and, until after the Second World War, a lack of supply of the latter. Furthermore, as Sir Alec Cairncross has observed of the period before the First World War, there was also a lack of interchange between government and academic economists, and even less of an interaction as between business and finance and economists:

> in general the few economists who took an interest in policy had to content themselves with a letter to *The Times* if they wanted to bring their views to the attention of the public.[78]

Although newspapers had, by the First World War, developed into important disseminators of financial and business information and a channel of policy debate (leastways, by letters to *The Times*), there was, however, as Sir Alec adds:

> very little that could pass as economic analysis and nearly all the commentators with any detailed knowledge were interested in specific industries or specific problems. None of the financial journalists would have claimed any standing as an economist except possibly Sir Robert Giffen (who gave up financial journalism long before 1900), Hartley Withers, the editor of *The Economist* or his successor Walter Layton.[79]

The reality was that issues in economic policy and business which arose after Bagehot did not really call (or were seen not to call) for an *economic* analysis. The old controversies which had sparked off the public debates on political economy, currency, trade and income distribution were long settled. This is not to say, of course, that economic controversy vanished. The tariff reform issue, for example, was a matter which excited much political discussion in the two decades before the First World War: indeed, the 1906 General Election was largely fought around the whole question of free trade versus protectionism and the newspapers of the day were full of arguments for and against. Again, in the late nineteenth century bimetalism and the idea of a silver standard were also issues which stirred up debate – especially in the United States. The point that needs to be stressed is, however, that there was neither the demand for the kind of sustained economic commentary which had been such a feature of the age of Bagehot, nor was there any real source of supply. The professionalization and privatization of economics from the late nineteenth century onwards served to further ensure that economics had, when comparison is made with the first half of the nineteenth century, only a marginal role to play in influencing and informing public opinion. And as Giffen understood, the great absence of statistics – other than that which were produced for business men by the financial press – was a factor which made for economics as a purely academic and largely abstract form of inquiry.

In reflecting and disseminating this change, the financial media were a powerful force for shaping the operative economic agenda and ruling economic culture. Not the least of the consequences of this was the sense of confidence which reliable communications generated in the financial system. Shortly before the outbreak of the First World War the editor of the *Financial News*, Ellis Powell, could reflect with confidence that, thanks to the workings of the financial markets, war was an unlikely possibility:

> We have, up to now, been accustomed to think that the destinies of the world were, in the main, entrusted to the hands of politicians. But within the last few years it has dawned upon the most competent observers that this progress and contentment depend very much more upon financial than upon political factors. The financial and economic forces have become the predominant factors in our twentieth century life, while the political elements have receded into second place.[80]

44 *The Power of the Financial Press*

The war and the depression which followed did much to shake such confidence in the capacity of the economic and financial system to function as it had done in the past.

NOTES

1. G. Storey, *Reuters Century, 1851–1951* (Max Parrish, London, 1951).
2. J. J. McCusker, 'The Business Press in England before 1775', *Library*, vol. 8 (1986) p. 46.
3. Ibid.
4. T. R. Nevett, *Advertising in Britain: a history* (Heineman, London, 1982) pp. 10–11.
5. R. M. Wiles, *Freshest Advices: early provincial newspapers in England* (Ohio State University Press, Columbus, 1965) p. 151.
6. C. Wright and C. E. Fayle, *A History of Lloyds from the Founding of Lloyds Coffee House to the Present Day* (Macmillan, London, 1928) p. 6.
7. Cited in John Carswell, *The South Sea Bubble* (Crescent Press, London, 1960) p. 1.
8. On the role of coffee houses see A. Ellis, *The Penny Universities: a history of the Coffee Houses* (Secker and Warbug, London, 1957).
9. See McCusker, op. cit.
10. K. R. Middleton, 'Commercial Speech in the Eighteenth Century', in D. H. Bond and W. R. Mcleod (eds), *Newsletters to Newspapers: eighteenth century journalism* (School of Journalism, West Virginia, 1977) p. 282.
11. See Carswell, op. cit., p. 150.
12. C. Kindleberger, *Manias, Panics and Crashes: a history of financial crises* (Macmillan, London, 1978) pp. 88–9.
13. Cited in J. H. Plumb, *England in the Eighteenth Century* (Penguin, Harmondsworth, 1963).
14. *Idler*, no. 40, January 1759. Johnson was very interested in economic affairs and wrote widely on issues of public policy and business. See P. Mathias, 'Dr Johnson and the Business World', in S. Marriner (ed.), *Business and Businessmen: studies in business and accounting history* (Liverpool University Press, Liverpool, 1978).
15. W. Michinton 'Patterns of Demand, 1750–1914', in C. M. Cipolla (ed.) *The Industrial Revolution*, Fontana History of Europe, (Fontana/Collins, London, 1973) pp. 94–5.
16. J. Brewer, 'Commercialisation and Politics', in N. McKendrick et al., *The Birth of a Consumer Society: the commercialisation of 18th century England* (Hutchinson, London, 1983) p. 217.
17. Ibid.
18. R. Sobel, *Panic on Wall Street: a history of America's financial disasters* (Macmillan, London, 1970) p. 436.
19. G. A. Cranfield, *The Development of the Provincial Newspaper. 1700–1760* (Clarendon Press, Oxford, 1976) p. 98.
20. See E. A. J. Johnson, *Predecessors of Adam Smith: the growth of British economic thought* (Kelley, New York, 1965).
21. *Financial Times*, 12 November 1967.
22. R. Wilson, 'Newspapers and Industry: the export of wool and controversy in

the 1780s', in M. Harris and A. Lee (eds), *The Press and English Society from the Seventeenth to the Nineteenth Centuries* (Associated University Press, London, 1986).

23. J. Black, *The English Press in the Eighteenth Century* (Croom Helm, London, 1987).
24. J. Feather, *The Provincial Book Trade in Eighteenth Century England* (Cambridge University Press, Cambridge 1985) p. 142.
25. D. P. O'Brien, *J R McCulloch: a study in classical economics* (Allen and Unwin, London, 1970), p. 22.
26. Ibid, p. 402.
27. On the price of gold in 1809, see *The Works and Correspondence of David Ricardo*, ed. P. Sraffa (Royal Economic Society, London, 1951–5), vol. lll.
28. G. Gilbert, 'The *Morning Chronicle*, Poor Laws and Political Economy', *History of Political Economy*, vol. 17, no. 4, (1985) pp. 511–12.
29. F. W. Fetter, Introduction to *The Economic Writings of Francis Horner* (London School of Economics, London, 1957). Fetter makes the important point that:

    Horner's great contribution to economics was not a particular idea so much as an attitude: that economic problems were important and that they should be discussed in the light of facts, against the background of history . . . It was not primarily a systematic body of theory that Horner presented, but an orderly exposition of a problem, that gave the reader the feeling that economic problems were fit topics for an educated man to discuss in the light of analysis (p. 19).

30. In J. Shaddock and M. Wolff (eds). *The Victorian Press: samplings and soundings* (Leicester University Press and Toronto University Press, 1982) p. xiv.
31. Fetter, op. cit.
32. F. W. Fetter, 'Economic controversy in the British Reviews, 1802–1850' *Economica*, vol. 32, (1965) p. 426.
33. Ibid, p. 436.
34. In this connection see, for example, Barry Gordon, 'Criticism of Ricardian Views on Value and Distribution in the British Periodicals, 1820–1850', *History of Political Economy*, vol. 1 (1969).
35. B. Fontana, *Rethinking the Politics of Commercial Society: the* Edinburgh Review, *1802–1832* (Cambridge University Press, Cambridge, 1985) p. 182.
36. S. G. Checkland, 'The Propagation of Ricardian Economics in England', *Economica*, vol. 16, (1949) p. 42.
37. J. S. Mill, 'The claims of labour', *Edinburgh Review*, (1845).
38. See J. Ginswick (ed.) *Labour and the Poor in England and Wales 1849–1851: letters to the Morning Chronicle from the Correspondents in the manufacturing and mining districts of the towns of Liverpool and Birmingham and rural districts*, 3 vols (Frank Cass, London, 1983).
39. In Shaddock and Wolff, op. cit., pp. 351–2.
40. P. Steinfels, *The Neo-Conservatives: the men who are changing American Politics* (Touchstone Books, New York, 1979) p. 4.
41. E. V. Morgan and W. A. Thomas, *The Stock Exchange: its history and functions* (Elek Books, London, 1962).
42. B. A. Weisberger, *The American Newspaperman* (Chicago University Press, Chicago, 1961) p. 75.
43. On Bennett see Richard O'Connor, *The Scandalous Mr Bennett* (Doubleday,

New York, 1962) and D. C. Seitz, *The James Gordon Bennetts: Father and Son* (Bobbs Merill, Indianapolis, 1928). Another figure in the history of American economic journalism in the early part of the nineteenth century who should be noted was William Leggett, (1801–1839). His columns in the *New York Evening Post, Examiner* and *Plaindealer*, combined *laissez-faire* political economy with the ideas of Jacksonian democracy. See *Democratick Editorials: Essays in Jacksonian Political Economy By William Leggett*, edited by L. H. White, (Liberty Press, Indianapolis, 1984).

44.   R. Holt Hutton (ed.), *Economic Studies*, (Longmans, London, 1880) p. x.

45.   Memoir on the Right Honourable James Wilson, *Literary Studies*, vol. 1 (Dent, London, 1916) p. 348.

46.   Gordon Scott, 'The London Economist and the High Tide of Laissez Faire', *Journal of Political Economy*, vol. 63 no. 6, (1955) p. 465.

47.   W. D. Gramp, *The Manchester School of Economics* (Stanford University Press, Stanford, 1960) p. 13.

48.   *The Economist, 1843–1943: a centenary volume* (The Economist Newspaper, London, 1943).

49.   *Literary Studies*, op. cit., p. 349.

50.   *Economic Studies*, op. cit., p. 50

51.   J. M. Keynes, 'The Works of Walter Bagehot', *Economic Journal*, vol. 25, no. 99 (1915) p. 369.

52.   R. Giffen, 'Bagehot as an Economist', *Fortnightly Review*, vol. 27 (1880) p. 556.

53.   *Economic Studies*, op. cit.

54.   Ibid., p. 7.

55.   Ibid.

56.   Ibid., p. 55.

57.   W. T. C. King, in *The Economist 1843–1943*, op. cit., p. 112.

58.   Lucy Brown, *Victorian News and Newspapers* (Oxford University Press, Oxford, 1985). See also W. J. Fishman's *East End 1888: a year in a London borough among the labouring poor* (Duckworth, London, 1988).

59.   Ibid., p. 263.

60.   D. P. O'Brien and J. R. Presly (eds), *Pioneers of Modern Economics in Britain* (Macmillan, London, 1981). See also T. S. Kuhn, *The Structure of Scientific Revolutions* (University of Chicago Press, Chicago, 1970). Professionalism, he maintains, leads to an 'esoteric vocabularly', and an 'immense restriction of the scientist's vision' (p. 64).

61.   See Harriet Martineau's *Autobiography*, 3 vols (Smith, Elder, London 1877).

62.   See A. Birnie, *Single Tax George* (Nelson, London, 1939).

63.   A. Marshall, 'The "Old" Generation of Economists and the "New" ', *Quarterly Journal of Economics*, (January 1897).

64.   See R. V. Eagly (ed.), *Events, Ideology and Economic Theory* (Wayne State University Press, Detroit, 1968) p. 190.

65.   A. Kadish, *The Oxford Economists in the Late Nineteenth Century* (Clarendon Press, Oxford, 1982).

66.   T. W. Hutchison, *A Review of Economic Doctrines, 1870–1929* (Clarendon Press, Oxford, 1966) p. 427; see in this connection Fishman, *op. cit.*, p. 50.

67.   J. M. Keynes, *Essays in Biography* (Norton, New York, 1951) pp. 173–5.

68.   Scott, op. cit., p. 488.

69.   J. Benson, *The Penny Capitalists* (Gill and Macmillan, Dublin, 1983) p. 71

70.   *Wall Street Journal*, 8 July 1889.

71.   R. Sobel, *Inside Wall Street: continuity and change in the financial district*, (Norton, New York, 1977).

72. *Financial News*, 23 January 1904.
73. Charles Duguid, *How to Read the Money Article* (Effingham Wilson, London, 1901) pp. 38–74.
74. Ibid.
75. Kenneth Fleet, *The Influence of the Financial Press* (Annual Livery Lecture, The Worshipful Company of Stationers and Newspaper Makers, London, 1983).
76. Samuel Butler, *The Way of All Flesh* (Penguin Books, Harmondsworth, 1947) p. 317.
77. See R. S. Sayers, 'Bagehot as an Economist', *The Collected Works*, op. cit., vol. 9, pp. 42–3.
78. Sir Alec Cairncross, 'Academics and Policy Makers', in F. Cairncross (ed.), *Changing Perceptions of Economic Policy: essays in honour of the 70th birthday of Sir Alec Cairncross* (Methuen, London, 1981) p. 8.
79. Ibid.
80. Cited in David Kynaston, *The* Financial Times*: a centenary history* (Viking, London, 1988) p. 75.

2. Economics and persuasion

The expansion of the financial media and communications which continued apace in the early decades of the twentieth century and which was overwhelmingly aimed at the market identified by Samuel Butler in the late nineteenth century, tends to obscure the fact that the actual participation of the general population in speculation and investment remained small, despite the greater involvement of the middle classes from the 1880s onwards. It is estimated, for example that, even in the case of America (a country with traditionally a higher rate of participation), only 1.5 million people out of 120 million were active in the stock market in 1929.[1] The actual numbers in comparison to the scale of media coverage was, therefore, remarkable for its relatively smallness of scale. Indeed, as Galbraith comments in his classic study of the 1929 crash:

> The striking thing about the stock market speculation of 1929 was not the massiveness of the participation. Rather it was the way it became central to the culture.[2]

Undoubtedly, the existence of an extensive communications system, combined with the mass of publications geared to feeding the demand for more news and information orientated to gain and profit greatly assisted the process whereby the markets became so 'central to the culture' of twentieth-century capitalism. Brokers letters and bulletins, tipsheets and newspapers constituted powerful means of sustaining the somewhat distorted illusion of capitalism as a game for making money. The development of the telephone and transatlantic ticker services meant that 'casino capitalism', as Keynes described it, was a game that could be played by anyone, anywhere, whether it be on board an ocean liner or at home by the fireside. Even economists like Veblen were not immune to the speculative fever which spread through America. The advances in the technology of communications and the ready availability of news and information brought what was later to be termed 'popular capitalism' within the reach of a number of players which far exceeded that of the old and more intimate prewar financial markets. Newspapers and magazines were all eager to reap the advertising revenues and report the stories of spectacular profits just waiting to be made. As John J. Raskob expressed it in his oft-cited articles in the *Ladies Journal*: 'Everybody ought to be rich!'. It was the roaring twenties and, as the song went, everybody was doing it. Money made good copy. Thus, as Galbraith argues, 'By the summer of 1929 the market not only dominated the news. It also dominated the culture.'[3] And the news media obligingly reported the movements and discourse of the markets with the kind of uncritical eye that had, since the early days of financial journalism, come to characterize the greater proportion of the financial press. Eventually it all came out: respected journalists, working for respectable papers were found to have accepted money – in considerable amounts – to hype stocks in their columns. The list included reporters on the *New York Times*, including the financial news editor himself, F. J. Lowther: Messrs Comber and Edmondson of the *Wall Street Journal*: 'trader' Raleigh T. Curtis of the *Daily News*; William White of the *Evening Post*; Charles Storm of the *American* and Stanley Prensosil of *Associated Press*. Even when one discounts the blatant corruption of these journalists, it is still true to say that they were the most obvious manifestation of the role of the press in whipping up speculative mania. The whole of the financial press, and indeed the press and magazine industry in general, did very nicely out of carrying page after page of advertisements for new shares, which conveyed the impression that the stock market was indeed a game for all the family. There were, of course, some notable exceptions to the share puffers and those who jumped on the quick money bandwagon: the crash also showed the more responsible financial press in a good light. *Poor's Weekly Business and Investment Letter*, spoke out against the 'great common-stock illusion' and the *Commercial and Financial Chronicle* also refused to get caught up in the speculative madness that had taken grip of America. Above all, and notwithstanding the behaviour of some of his other colleagues, there was Alexander Dana Noyes, a financial journalist of the highest calibre who deserves more recognition in the history of American journalism

than he has generally received. Noyes was a consistent opponent
of the stock market hype and the way in which the finances of the
nation had been turned into a speculative game gone mad and his
columns were often critical of the part played by the press in
selling a new vision of capitalism to the American people.[4] In 1932
Noyes reflected that:

> The industrial breakdown of 1921 gave the coup de grâce to the
> illusion that the extravagant post-war rise of commercial prices was
> permanent. But it required the precipitous crash of October 1929, and
> the years of extreme depression that ensued, to put a final quietus on
> the propaganda which convinced a good part of the American people
> that financial practices which were utterly unsound before the war were
> perfectly safe and entirely advisable in the new financial era.[5]

Not unsurprisingly, Noyes's pessimism was discounted at the
time by the younger financial journalists as the views of an 'old
timer' who 'did not understand the new type of stock market'[6] To
his credit, when the Harrimans complained against Noyes's
gloomy reports on the grounds that his dismal observations might
lead to a fall in advertising revenue, Ochs replied: 'One of the
most rigid rules of the *Times* is that no editor must be interested in
or seek, or solicit advertising.'[7] Even after the crash, leading
financial journals (like *Business Week* and the *New York Times*)
still took quite a time to come around to accepting the view that
the party was well and truly over and that America and the world
was heading for a depression. Throughout late 1929 the press was
packed with optimistic statements: the general view was that there
would be a mild recession. *Business Week*, for example, on 3
November was predicting a mere 7 per cent drop in business. In
the new year the *New York Times* was predicting continuing
prosperity; by the autumn, and with the banking crisis of November and December 1930, the press consensus finally began to shift
into a more pessimistic frame of mind.[8] Of course, no one can say
that media can be blamed for causing the infamous crash, but as
we commented earlier in Chapter 1, the role of the press in feeding
speculative mania is something which had, by that time, sufficient
historical precedent: as in the past, they greatly contributed to the
mood of the times. Newspapers brought Wall Street to the
American breakfast table as they had brought the South Seas to
the coffee houses. And, combined with the existence of telegraph

and ticker tape, it meant that there was a far more effective medium for the diffusion of a speculative mentality than in the days of Defoe. As the payoffs to Wall Street journalists admirably demonstrated, those who were pushing stock knew only too well the value of the publicity which financial journalists could give.

It was not just the reputation of the financial media which suffered as a result of the crash: '1929' also came to epitomize what many believed to be the manifest failure of the capitalist system, and this low standing of the financial and business world was reflected in its subsequent treatment by the press. As Sobel notes:

> Finance in general and Wall Street in particular still made the front pages, but the stories were now written by political reporters. Once again liberalism was in vogue . . .[9]

The leading voice of this liberalism was that of an economist: John Maynard Keynes.

It was inevitable that Keynes's influence was far more immediate in Britain than in the US. His articles and ideas stimulated an unprecedented amount of economic controversy: they were news events in their own right. As in the nineteenth century, the existence of periodical literature gave Keynes the opportunity to make an impact where it mattered and to enter into an on-going dialogue with the opinion-forming community. The 1920s and 1930s were something of a golden age of the British weekly journalism. And there is a significant parallel to be drawn here between the role of literary journals in Britain in the 1840s – like the *Edinburgh Review* and other journals – and the weeklies – like the *Nation and Athenaeum* and the *New Statesman* – in the interwar period. Continuous public dialogue was a far more potent shaper of opinion than a single great book. This is particularly true in the case of the progress of economic ideas, as the formation of a public discourse involves a regular adaptation of theories, concepts and views in the light of prevailing circumstances and events. Like the Victorian periodical literature the *Nation* had the great capacity to sustain such a dialogue. For this reason, as Kingsley Martin observed:

> All the young writers who wished to make a reputation as literary figures or even budding politicians looked to the weeklies as the natural place where they could establish themselves. There was no competition from the Sunday magazines or television.[10]

The scale of Keynes's journalism in the *Nation* and elsewhere is, to those who consider him as primarily the author of the *General Theory*, most surprising. Keynes wrote around 300 articles for all kinds of newspapers and magazines; and it is true to say that he achieved his fame in the 1920s not as a 'professor', which he never was, but as an economic journalist and intellectual celebrity. That we see Keynes today more as an academic theorist than as a publicist is perhaps one of the less discernible outcomes of the Keynesian revolution and the publication of what Hayek (rightly) describes as a 'tract for the times': the *General Theory*.[11] Harrod, Keynes's biographer, may have been initially responsible for this perspective since he greatly underestimated Keynes's journalistic involvement and output. Yet, as the editors of the collected works of Keynes observe, Keynes wrote far more than he ever actually signed in the *Nation and Athenaeum*.[12] Harrod also tends to assume that Keynes was subsequently less involved with the *New Statesman*. But as Hyams points out in his history of the journal, Keynes continued to be closely involved throughout the 1930s.[13] Indeed, as Patinkin reminds us, it is important to keep this side of Keynes constantly in mind as we study his economic ideas since: 'for some periods of his life . . . it would be more appropriate to say that in addition to being a publicist he was also an economist'.[14] Keynes had an incomparable gift of getting into the news and of putting over his arguments across to a larger audience than could ever be reached via professional economic journals. His literary agents placed his articles in papers all around the world, and he diligently followed what the world's press said about him. As Elizabeth Johnson emphasizes:

> The point is that Keynes was a professional journalist as well as an economist, and regarded himself as such. He acted like a professional propagandist for whatever was his personal cause of the moment. He wrote regularly, and for money; during his earlier career, at least, he regarded the money part of it as important enough to bargain about. One could argue indeed that in a certain sense all his writing was journalism of one order or another.[15]

Certainly, it is the case that Keynes's views on economic policy actually predated the attempt to formulate a theoretical model which could win over academic economists. And, as far as Keynes was concerned, the activity of theoretical proof was closely related to that of convincing those who disagreed with him. (Here one is reminded of Bagehot's comment about Wilson being a person who 'discovered by convincing'. Such a description admirably fitted Keynes's own methodology of inquiry.) Thus he was not, as Johnson maintains, a man to be 'chagrined in the slightest to find his yesterday's winged words wrapping today's fish and chips'.[16]

Bearing such an assessment in mind, there is a sense in which it could be argued that all of Keynes's work was essentially journalistic; that is, concerned with current problems and events. This must include the *General Theory* itself. We may, for instance, recall Keynes's own observation that:

> Economists must leave to Adam Smith alone the glory of the Quarto, must pluck the day, fling pamphlets to the wind, write always *sub specie temporis*, and achieve immortality by accident if at all.[17]

He wrote to influence the times, rather than posterity or purely for money, confident in the knowledge that he had the answer to whatever problem was currently defeating those actually charged with dealing with their solution. Frustrated and depressed by the peace conference he resigned to write *The Economic Consequences of the Peace*. The book launched him into the limelight of press attention and established him as a major postwar opinion leader. Keynes soon realized that this fame (come by accident, if at all) afforded him the opportunity to communicate to a larger audience than could normally be expected for an 'academic scribbler'. Journalism thus allowed him to transcend party lines, national frontiers and, at a bound, to leap the confining walls of academia.

At the end of the war he felt that (as Harrod puts it) he had a 'vocation . . . to intervene actively in shaping public opinion'.[18] The *Economic Consequences* was widely reported and reviewed in the world's press more extensively than any book by an economist since Marshall's *Principles* and his reputation as a commentator and prophet was firmly established for the rest of the decade. In America Keynes achieved instant fame. Extracts from the book appeared in *New Republic*, and he also wrote for the *Baltimore Sun* and the *New York World*. By 1919 he was, largely through his prolific journalism, one of the better known figures in the western world outside the major politicians and Charlie Chaplin. His journalism was very extensive in this period. In the spring of 1921 he wrote a number of articles for the *Manchester Guardian*. His views were reported in other papers, and he was soon on a position to command a high price for his opinions. In the summer of 1921 alone he wrote five large articles for *The Sunday Times*. These journalistic activities through which he began to expound his economic and political opinions were contemporary with his more academic interests – for example, as editor of the *Economic Journal* – and were integral to what may be described as his 'theoretical' work. And, as Patinkin suggests, we do well, in interpreting the latter, to realize that his 'scientific' work which bears on policy evolved parallel, if not slightly behind, the views which he expressed in a journalistic form. Indeed, it is doubtful if Keynes himself would have made such a distinction since, like the early political economists, theorizing and persuading were part and parcel of the same activity. There were times when, as he expressed it in the *General Theory*, he had to speak in private to his fellow economists and on other occasions to influence opinion. It was an important distinction for Keynes. In 1921 he made an assessment which sheds some light on how he saw the relationship between public and private argument:

> there are, in present times, two opinions . . . the outside and the inside; the opinion of the public voiced by the politicians, the journalists and the civil servants . . . expressed in limited circles. Those who live in the limited circles and share the inside opinion pay both too much and too little attention to the outside opinion.[19]

The purpose of public debate was to influence and guide governing opinion. It took the form of a persistent attack on ruling ideas as articulated by those in authority through which its deficiencies could be exposed and laid bare. His aim was to shape the intellectual agenda; something which could not be settled on purely abstract grounds:

> We have to discriminate between what Bentham . . . used to term *Agenda* and *non-Agenda* . . . Perhaps the chief task of economists at this hour is to distinguish afresh the *Agenda* of government from the *non-Agenda*; and the companion task of politics is to devise forms of government within a democracy which shall be capable of accomplishing the Agenda.[20]

Keynes was aware that this was no easy matter. Ideas in themselves were powerful not least because of the degree to which they could be used to support and justify an existing social order. The victory of ideas was part of a wider struggle for power and legitimacy. This is the central theme of his comments on the Ricardian revolution at the beginning of the *General Theory*: economic theories could serve as powerful forms of political justification and thus 'attract the support of the dominant social force'.[21] For this reason, no doubt, as for others, Marshall and Pigou felt strongly that the economist should keep clear of politics and policy. Pigou, for example, comments in *The Theory of Unemployment*:

> While it is natural and right . . . that economists should seek to play a part in guiding conduct, that is not its primary business. They are physiologists not clinical practitioners; engineers not engine drivers. The main point of such contributions as they may hope to make must be indirect; in the study, not in the pages of a newspaper . . . [22]

Keynes wholeheartedly rejected this view of the economist as someone who passively watches the trains go by. He saw his role as pro-active and his influence as extending as it were on to the footplate of the state, and welcomed his theories being discussed by the leader writers and in the letter columns. Intellectual revolutions were not simply private or professional affairs: he wanted his theories to be news! Keynes believed that, in the end, such direct contributions to public opinion were necessary if the old orthodoxies, which permeated all aspects of ruling opinion, were to be toppled: in the battle of ideas victory would go to 'those who could speak with the greatest appearance of clear, undoubting conviction and could best use the accents of infallibility'.[23] Journalism thus provided him with the necessary involvement with events and a channel of communications which gave him the opportunity of intellectual exploration and of bringing economic opinion around to his economic theories. Journalism was thus both a mode of discovery and a medium of persuasion and dissemination. It was his way of making sure that the agenda which emerged was framed on his (and later *in* his) terms. He thereby could always use events to their maximum advantage. Keynes was, of course, in a unique position so to exploit both events and ideas: from 1911 he was the editor of the *Economic Journal* and from

1925, Chairman of the Board of the most important weeklies, the *Nation and Athenaeum* – later, the *New Statesman and Nation*.

From the early 1920s journalism was a major part of his literary output and although it diminished somewhat in the late 1930s and during the war it remained, throughout his life, a vital part of his work as an economist. As is well known, many of his books and pamphlets appeared in journalistic form prior to being collected or published in a more academic guise. These included, for instance, his ideas on the gold standard, deflation, and the multiplier. These articles were often syndicated in many different countries, and in numerous newspapers and magazines. And through them he became as well known a commentator to the American newspaper public as to that in Britain. He was, for example, quick to cable his views on the Wall Street crash to the *New York Post*, so that they appeared the following day!

His journalism did not confine itself to purely economic matters: he was a great book reviewer. Volume 28 of the collected writings, for example, contains some dozen notes and comments, and over twenty letters on literary and political issues, and a lengthy correspondence between himself and the editor of the *New Statesman*, Kingsley Martin. *Essays in Persuasion* (which was originally due to be called *Essays in Prophercy*) published in 1931, contains, as he put it, 'croakings of twelve years – the croakings of a Cassandra who could never influence the course of events in time'. These croakings include articles from the *Manchester Guardian Commercial Supplement* (1923); the *Nation and Athenaeum* (1926, 1928); and 'Can Lloyd George Do It', (originally, 'The Cost of the Liberal Scheme'); as well as articles for the *Listener* and the American monthly magazine, *Vanity Fair* (1931). It also included material from the *Evening Standard* – which later became the *Economic Consequences of Mr Churchill* – and his controversial article which appeared in the *New Statesman* in 1931 on 'Proposals for a Revenue Tarriff'. Other volumes of the collected writings are replete with examples of economic journalism which, if they did not have the kind of immediate impact on affairs that he would have liked, nevertheless came to define, in a relatively short time, the parameters of liberal opinion and a community of discourse. His views were, throughout the interwar years, reference points for political opinion: Keynes was news. His arguments, whether pitched at the President of the United States, as in his famous open letter to Roosevelt in the *New York Times* (1933), or at the ordinary American, were always expressed in elegant and convincing prose. He was, above all a master of economic writing, if not always of economic logic. Here he is answering the question of could 'America spend its way into recovery', which appeared in the magazine *Redbook* in 1934:

> Why, obviously! – my first reflection when I am faced by this question. No one of common sense could doubt it, unless his mind had first been muddled by a 'sound' financier or an 'orthodox' economist. We produce in order to sell. In other words we produce in response to spending. It is impossible to suppose that we can stimulate production and employment by *refraining* from spending. So, as I have said, the answer is obvious. [24]

Keynes was a great controversialist: he loved nothing better than expounding a general principle, or evolving a theory from engaging in current events and issues.

We may conveniently date the commencement of Keynes's journalistic activities in 1920, the same year as C. P. Scott launched the *Manchester Guardian Commercial* as a weekly economic review. The paper provided what was unquestionably one of the most important sources of economic information during the inter-war period. The standing of the *Commercial* was confirmed by the decision to ask Keynes to edit a series of 'Reconstruction' supplements. Keynes immediately took to the idea with the proviso that he should have editorial control of the enterprise; (though the 'Reconstruction' series carried on into 1923 'New Series' – but not under the general editorship of Keynes). The twelve supplements on 'European Reconstruction' are a truly massive and significant collection of opinions and data and they constitute a landmark in the history of financial journalism. Published to coincide with the Genoa conference, they aimed to 'do for the businessman what the high placed economics experts do for the statesman', and provide an authoritative survey of the world economy and economic opinion. Their aim was not to propagandise, but 'state simply; to indicate without bias on what lines relief and reform may come'. [25] The contributors came from all over the academic, financial, business and political world, and the supplements gave detailed analysis, over many hundreds of pages, of the economic and political aspects of recovery. Introducing the series, Keynes argued that it represented an 'assemblage of opinions and facts' whose 'collective wisdom' might play a part in remedying the man-made difficulties in Europe. 'The intellectual forces of Europe will here assemble in order to reinforce those of generous impulse'.

Keynes's aim was to provoke public controversy. He believed that such was the natural and only arena wherein new ideas could be fashioned. As he stated at the outset of his first article, on 'The Stabilization of the European Exchanges':

> How happy are chemists, mathematicians, physicians and astronomers that the world holds the craft of each to be an unsearchable mystery, and it does not seek or pretend to understand it! If it were crypton, harmonics, kidneys of nebulae we sought to stabilise, we could contemplate the best plan and carry it out in scientific seclusion without ever troubling to make it clear to you my intelligent but unscientific friends, the readers of this article. But an economist must be humble; – his field of thought lies in the public sphere. He cannot accomplish, except by persuasion – and by simplifying.[26]

Public debate had to be stimulated by economic education in order, so he argued, to bring those in authority to the point of rethinking their ideas for:

> Even if economists and technicians knew the secret remedy, they could not apply it until they had persuaded the politicians, and the politicians, who have ears but no eyes, will not attend to the persuasion until it reverberates back to them as an echo from the great public. Instructed opinion is already far in advance of public policy.[27]

What is most significant about the *Manchester Guardian* articles was that Keynes used them to assert unequivocally that the new age was one in which economic ideas, and economists, were destined to take the leading part in setting the political agenda. The debate on the future of Europe – and the world – was perforce an essentially economic one, and the role of the economist as an interpreter and guide was consequently, as Keynes predicted, pre-eminent.

Interestingly enough, Gabriel Hanotaux (a former Minister of Foreign Affairs for France) took exception to the pre-eminence of economics: as 'it has no soul it lacks humanity'. This in turn prompted Keynes to observe, rather grandly, that:

The economist is not king. But he ought to be! He is a better and wiser governor than the general or the diplomatist or the oratorical lawyer. In the modern over-populated world, which can only live at all by nice adjustments, he is not only useful but necessary.[28]

Right from the first issue, Keynes advanced ideas for economic reform, with articles on 'The Theory of Purchasing Power Parity' and 'Forward exchanges'. Later on, of course, these were incorporated in the *Tract on Monetary Reform*. In the eleventh number Keynes launched an attack on the theory and practice of deflation arguing, as he was to throughout his life, that deflationary economic policies were a recipe for economic depression and mass unemployment. Keynes contributed, in this spirit of philosopher–king, some thirteen articles to the series. They were published in French, German, Italian and Spanish and the *New York Journal of Commerce* published the supplements in America. Taken together they amounted to some 810 pages! Whilst this venture into journalism was proceeding, the *Guardian* asked him to go to the Genoa conference. He was also the correspondent for the *Daily Express* and had an arrangement with the *New York World* and with papers in Italy, France, Spain, Germany, Austria, Czechoslovakia, Holland and Sweden. All of which served to enhance his status as the first economist to have achieved the status of international media celebrity.

At this stage in his career journalism gave him a personal influence which far exceeded anything which could be attained in active politics or by purely academic scholarship: the journalist's pen was mightier than the power of a party or the impact of big books. In keeping with the views he had enunciated in the reconstruction supplements and in his essay on Marshall (1924), that the economist should fling his thoughts to the wind, in 1923 Keynes, together with a group of Liberals, bought the *Nation and Athenaeum*. This paper was to be his main avenue of communicating his ideas until the early 1930s. The *Nation* proclaimed that economics would inevitably take the centre stage in world affairs. To this end it intended to play 'a part in forming and expressing the new thought'! Overcoming his doubts about his lack of journalistic experience, Keynes recruited the young Cambridge economist, H. D. Henderson as editor. Henderson remained its editor until 1930, when he became secretary of the Economic Advisory Council.[29] He later became disenchanted with Keynes and as a fellow of All Souls he attacked the *General Theory*. (He was replaced, for a few months, by another economist, Harold Wright.) As chairman of the board, Keynes was to devote a good deal of his time to the paper, although he was not in the habit of interfering with the editorial policy. At first, his main interest was in the reparations problem – on which he was naturally an acknowledged authority. Later on, his interests broadened to take in the wider economic issues when, on 7 July 1923, bank rate was raised from 3 per cent to 4. This set Keynes off in a more specifically economic direction. On 14 July he judged the decision as:

> one of the most misguided movements of that indicator that has ever occured. The Bank of England acting under the influence of a narrow and obsolete doctrine has made a great mistake.[30]

In November 1924 he published his *Tract on Monetary Reform* which drew on arguments which he had advanced in his earlier journalism. Again, in May 1924, following a long debate in the pages of the *Nation* on Lloyd George's proposal for public works, Keynes put forward his own ideas. Keynes's journalistic theorizing during the 1920s was prolific. There were articles in the *Nation* (21 February, 7 March, 4 and 18 April 1925) and three articles for the *Evening Standard* which were later published as *The Economic Consequences of Mr Churchill*, and an important letter to *The Times* on 4 September 1925. In all of this Keynes was endeavouring to drag economic issues off the 'back page' – the City page – into the 'limelight of the big world'.[31] For this reason his involvement with the *Nation* (and subsequently with the *New Statesman* when the two papers merged in 1930) was deeply important to his strategy of putting economics into the headlines and bringing himself to the fore on the debate about economic policy. Martin himself was Keynes's preferred choice as editor for the merged publications – the *New Statesman and the Nation*. Martin came to the paper after reading history at Cambridge, a Princeton Fellowship, a lectureship at the London School of Economics and a few years' experience as a leader writer on the *Manchester Guardian*. The Scotts, however, found him a little too radical for their taste and so he was recommended for the *New Statesman* with some relief. From the start of their relationship he enjoyed Keynes's absolute confidence. It was a trust which he executed brilliantly and for which he was well equipped. Martin, more than any other journalist, managed to give a coherent voice to the new economic and political consensus that emerged in the 1930s and which was to triumph so completely in the postwar era. As an historian he was preoccupied with the notion of 'public opinion'. And, like Keynes, he was pulled between the lure of academic life and the excitement of actually being involved in events and moulding opinion. At one stage, for instance, Martin seriously considered taking up a chair in international politics at the University College of Wales, Aberystwyth. Keynes was pleased when he decided against the move from journalism to academia. In a letter, which is as revealing about his own frame of mind as about Martins', he wrote in 1936, the same year as the publication of the *General Theory*:

> Your subject is one which is best done *not* academically . . . the only point is to get leisure for writing a large book. But is a large book so much to be preferred to the daily task of persuasion?[32]

It was a question which Keynes himself never resolved: perhaps his own 'large books' were, in essence, part of his own 'daily task of persuasion' rather than exercises in pure economic theory. As he was aware, however, public discourse and well-argued economic opinions required an additional buttress of economic theory. A revolution needed a textbook as well as rhetoric. There was thus no substitute for a more private conversation aimed at winning over professional economists and establishing a body of economic theory and language which would serve the cause in the longer run. In his own mind Keynes was very clear about the distinction between persuasion and theorizing. But the relationship does lead to problems for those who wish to study the development of his ideas. At heart Keynes was motivated primarily by a desire to employ economic theory for practical ends. He was concerned with the here and now and thus he adapted his arguments to fit the particular circumstances pertaining at the time. He was activated by what was happening in the pages of *The Times* rather than the world of academic economics. This fact goes some way to explaining Keynes's apparent contradictions (and later mythologies): as, for example, between the monetary policy contained in the *Treatise* and what came to be seen as the fiscal preoccupations of the *General Theory*. That Keynes can be seen as advocating different solutions at different periods of his life is, as Patinkin suggests, a reflection of the 'different roles that Keynes was simultaneously playing':[33] journalist, world figure and economist. The *General Theory* was, therefore, as Schumpeter describes it, the final result of a long struggle to make the vision which he had advanced in public arguments and in his journalism 'analytically operative'.[34] Keynes's 'large books' dressed up in more esoteric academic discourse arguments which had been tested in public controversy first, as opposed to the slower and more private route of academic publication. And it was a form of testing which Keynes did not think to be less demanding than that of engaging in debate in the professional journals or keeping up to date with other developments in economic theory. For as Harrod notes: 'His recipe for the young economist was to know his Marshall thoroughly and to read his *Times* every day carefully, without bothering too much about the large mass of contemporary publication in book form. His own reading after 1914 was probably not much more extensive'[35] His enormous journalistic output, and the close relationship between his literary and economic work, well illustrates that he envisaged theorizing as something driven by outside events and problems and not internal private professional nitpicking. His journalism was a way in which theories *qua* policies and solutions could garner facts and support in a policy community wider than academia. A sense of this comes out, for instance, in his discussion, in 1923, of monetary reform when he maintains: 'A new theory can never win its way in the field of practical affairs unless it is illuminated by vivid facts and supported by events.'[36] In retrospect, and with the benefit of the experience of the 1970s and 1980s, the argument that Keynes's concern – as an economic journalist and propagandist – with *events* which at the time supported his interpretation of monetary policy and investment, meant that his work as an economic theorist lacked the necessary distance and objectivity.[37] Equally deficient was his assessment of the political consequences of his ideas. Apart from the odd essay, especially *The End of Laissez Faire*, Keynes – unlike Hayek or the journalist Walter Lippman – did not trouble himself too much about the implications of economic management. Keynes's most famous remark was: 'In the long run we are all dead'. It is an observation which reflects much about Keynes's own attitudes

towards his economic theories as being less academic quartos than
'*sub species temporis*'. An intimate and inside knowledge of events
and an ability to sway public opinion may have been just the recipe
for powerful economic journalism, but it was somewhat inadequate to the task of articulating more long-term statements of
political economy and methodology. To students of Keynes's
social and political thought this neglect is somewhat puzzling. He
avoided the construction of a philosophical or methodological
'general theory' although to some degree it is imminent in the
Treatise and in unpublished letters and notes. And he devised, as
Hayek has pointed out, a theoretical system based upon 'scientis-
tic' assumptions of knowledge which subsequently lent itself to the
development of models of economic behaviour of a highly mathematical and statistical form.[38] Yet he was, as his criticism of
Tinbergen shows, manifestly ambivalent towards the kind of
pseudo-scientific economics that was beginning to emerge.[39] From
Keynes's point of view, however, as one primarily determined to
influence the political agenda, to have included his philosophical
ideas about economic knowledge in the body of his theory would
have made for a richer academic theory, but for a poorer, and in
practical terms less influential, polemic. The antipathy Keynes
displayed towards the scientific pretensions of economics, when
set against the subsequent 'scientism' of his followers, is perhaps in
part due to his failure to explore and expand his philosophical and
epistemological position, but is equally an outcome of what
Fouraker identifies as his didactic style:

> When faced with a subtle, yet complex, problem in the development of
> a concept, both pupil and master [Marshall] would assault it with all
> the resources at their command: logic, mathematics, statistics, in-
> tuition. Having satisfied themselves, however, they employed a curious
> device when it came to recording the results of their pursuits. Instead
> of leading the reader through the intricate analytical processes that
> their own mind had recently traversed they would provide a short cut,
> in the form of an assumption whose purpose was to eliminate
> consideration of the difficult problems they had faced and solved.[40]

It was, as Fouraker argues, a highly successful form of changing
opinion, if not of scientific method. And, we may add in the
context of this present study, it was also a style which well fitted
Keynes's approach to the public role of the economist, which was
not something shared by Marshall. Keynes's articles in the *Nation*

and elsewhere would frequently use the device of short-cutting the argument and taking the reader to an ultimate conclusion or recommendation without the burden of complex arguments. Journalism enabled Keynes to have a ready command of public (outside) and policy-making (inside) opinion. Notwithstanding the *General Theory*, it was *opinion* which Keynes aimed at until his wartime official involvement precluded publicity seeking, and by that time, anyway, it was no longer as necessary. Even so, Keynes continued with the business of the 'daily task of persuasion' after the publication of the *General Theory* with, for example, his letters and articles to *The Times* in 1937 on the need for public works and later, in his correspondence on postwar economic policy. This passion to persuade and his preoccupation with problems of policy and national and international events, or what was in the morning's newspaper was, as we shall discuss in Chapter 3, a vital part of the Keynesian intellectual inheritance. Little wonder, then, that journalists were to be amongst the first converts to Keynesian economics. In the end, Keynes's emphasis on the need to persuade was, perhaps, just as influential a notion as that of his actual theory. Keynes put 'personality' into economics and the success of the *General Theory* ultimately owed much more to Keynes the man of affairs than it did to Keynes the economist. As Galbraith admits:

> The *General Theory* owed much of its acceptance to the Great Depression and to the failure of classical economics to contend with that persuasively unsettling event. But it also owed much to Keynes's assurance in economic argument and analysis, the confident expression of his expression and mood. This confidence should especially be stressed. No economist is ever more highly regarded than he regards himself or followed with more certainty than that which he himself manifests. And Keynes's influence also owed much to his personal background, reputation and prestige. Had the *General Theory* come from someone who lacked these qualifications, it might well have sunk without trace.[41]

No doubt the lesson that fame spurred on the advance of economic ideas was not lost on those who endeavoured to follow in the footsteps of Keynes.

By the time of the publication of the *General Theory* much had altered in the financial press to facilitate the spread of the kind of economic discourse which Keynes had promoted since the 1920s.

Despite the fact that the main organs of the British financial press
– the *Financial Times* and the *Financial News* – were vigorous in
their defence of orthodox economics and the gold standard, there
were by 1936 a number of prominent journalists who were pressing
for the abandonment of the old 'Treasury orthodoxy' and greater
economic expansion led by government spending. In America
Keynes's most distinguished convert was Walter Lippman. He
proved very sympathetic to Keynes's arguments in the early 1930s,
particularly with regard to the Gold Standard and managing
currencies. After a meeting in London with Keynes in 1933 he also
became convinced that Keynes was right about the need for the
state to take a more active role in managing the economy. As
Lippman's biographer records:

> With Keynes's guidance Lippman grasped what he and many others
> had been groping for instinctively. For the first time he understood why
> a balanced budget not only was unnecessary, but might actually stand
> in the way of recovery . . . Keynes's prescription for countercyclical
> spending seemed to provide a compromise between laissez-faire
> capitalism and Marxist socialism. It removed the sense of helplessness
> in dealing with the depression and offered a middle way for those, like
> Lippman, who wanted to use the power of the state to achieve
> economic stability[42]

However, his conviction about the use of the state so to implement
Keynes's ideas was soon overtaken by a more urgent concern
about the dangers of central control and he came to fear that the
New Deal might lead to a planned economy. Lippman therefore
made a distinction, which eluded Keynes himself, between the
measures necessary for economic recovery and wider political
reforms which might, in the longer run, transform democracy and
the free-market economy. Thereafter, as his *The Good Society*
(published the year after the *General Theory* in 1937) demon-
strates, Lippman attempted to carve out a section of middle ground
between Keynes's economic theory and Hayek's political liberalism. Thus, although his writings in this period argued a largely
Keynesian case for public works and countercyclical spending, he
continuously stressed the need to ensure that measures of economic stimulation and social progress should be closely monitored.
Lippman's highly sophisticated brand of economic and social
liberalism allied with an abhorrence of the slightest shift towards

collectivism and a firm adherence to a free-market society had no parallel in Britain. As was true of Keynes himself, the political dangers which Lippman had seen as inherent in the extension of the state in managing the economy were not issues which bothered his supporters in the British press. Amongst the most prominent of these followers were Nicholas Davenport, in the *New Statesman*; Francis Williams, in The *Daily Herald*; Douglas Jay, in the *Economist* and the *Daily Herald*; Geoffrey Crowther, in the *Economist*; and Paul Einzig, in the *Financial News*.

Davenport began his journalistic career by writing two articles on oil for *The Times* and subsequently became the oil correspondent for the *Manchester Guardian* under Oscar Hobson, who later became editor of the *Financial News*. Davenport was asked to contribute to Keynes's 'Reconstruction' supplements, and in 1923 when Keynes and other Liberals acquired the *Nation*, Keynes recruited him to the City page, along with another disciple, Sidney Russell Cooke – who had also contributed to the 'Reconstruction' supplements. Davenport saw himself as very much Keynes's City correspondent, and his constant theme was, as he described it in his autobiography, 'exposing the shortcomings of the financial machinery of the capital market'. He wrote under the pseudonym of 'Torreador', presumably because he was assisting the matador, Keynes, in contributing to the campaign that he and 'other socially minded economists were making to reform and civilize the capitalist system'. As a 'City radical' he was, naturally enough, suspected, but he was nevertheless not regarded as a rampant red intent upon overthrowing the system. He was tolerated and respected within the stockbroking firm for which he worked and by the City establishment. In 1930, when the *Nation* was merged with the *New Statesman*, Davenport was brought in as the City correspondent to replace Emil Davies as Keynes's man in the City. He was also a contributor to the *Economist* where, under Walter Layton, he assisted Hargreaves Parkinson in starting a stock exchange section. He also wrote occasionally for the *News Chronicle*, *Financial Times* and the *Investors Chronicle*. In the *Investors Chronicle* he wrote under the pseudonym 'Candidus'. The column, with the blessing of its proprietor, Brendan Bracken, developed a racy critical style which was later taken up by his successor, someone much less ideologically opposed to the City and all its works – Harold Wincott. Davenport's Keynesian inspired journalism

(Keynes was, he says, his 'guru') well reflected the new economic morality which was gaining ground in British middle opinion in the 1930s. Davenport actually made his (very good) living out of the City, but found it ethically upsetting: he thought of his journalism as his 'weekly good work' and his penance for being well off:

> During [a] phenomenal boom in the gilt-edged market, which allowed the market traders to make a lot of safe money, 2½% Consols rose to 77 in 1933, to 93 in 1934 and to 94 in 1935. We Keynesians were delighted, but again the unpleasant side of the City stirred one's conscience. While the quite innocent investors were making a lot of money out of their shares and bonds, the wretched unemployed and half-starved workers were having a miserable time.[43]

Davenport's attitude to the workings of capital markets, which was not shared by Martin – perhaps because he did not understand them – was presupposed on the fact that, as he put it:

> We Keynesians did not want to destroy the capitalist system, but to make it more humane and withal a more dynamic instrument for the creation of wealth.[44]

It was a sign of how the British economic consensus was shifting into a Keynesian mode during the 1930s and 1940s that Davenport, who had contributed much to the Labour Party's (1933) programme, *Socialism and the Condition of the People*, was to write for the conservative weekly, the *Spectator* after the war. Davenport, with Douglas Jay, Francis Williams and Cecil Sprigge (City editor of the *Manchester Guardian*) were members of a group that was a major influence on the Labour party's economic policy – the XYZ club. As Williams recounts in his memoirs:

> It has . . . some claim to have exercised in a quiet sort of way more influence on future government policy than any other group of the time and to have done so in the most private manner without attracting publicity to itself.[45]

Francis Williams's financial journalism was, of course, another example of the way in which radical ideas began to widen the parameters of acceptable opinion from inside the bastion of free market capitalism. Williams was appointed by Beaverbrook to write on the City after reading a piece which he had written on

Epstein in the *Sunday Express*. As Beaverbrook's man in the City, Williams had access to a considerable cross-section of the financial and business élite. Beaverbrook gave him personal introductions to bankers, Directors of the Bank of England, former Chancellors of the Exchequer, and he learnt about 'finance from the best tutors': but in the end, Beaverbrook's gods were not Williams's. In political terms they were on 'opposite sides of the barricades'. [46] It was not until he was appointed City editor of the *Daily Herald* (a Labour party paper) that he could have as free a range as he would have liked. As he explained in his memoirs:

> I was determined . . . not to have not merely a traditional City page dealing with investments and kindred matters. I headed my own column . . . and so far from confining myself to the City took the whole world for my province. I aimed in fact, to link finance with economic and political policy in the way that although now common was little done on the City pages then. [47]

Williams was, without doubt, one of the most respected financial journalists of his day. He was much sought after, as he recounted,

> [by] the penguins in the City and eventually by the Chief penguin himself – Mr Montague Norman, governor of the Bank of England. I had for a time, indeed, the curious priviledge of being almost the only City editor Mr Norman could bring himself to see. [48]

As far as Keynes was concerned, Williams was, in his own words, 'wholly convinced by him', and regarded him as a 'genius with solutions that could save the world'. [49] In his columns and numerous pamphlets – *Democracy and Finance, The Bank of England and the Nation*, and so on – Williams was a prominent advocate of Keynesian remedies and ideas. As a 'Labour' City journalist he was also in an important position from which he could bring Labour intellectuals and leaders into contact with sympathetic financial opinion and expertise.

When, in 1936, Williams became editor of the *Herald* Douglas Jay took over his City desk. Like Davenport and Williams, Jay was also a campaigning journalist determined to propagate his views on fighting unemployment. [50] As one of the financial journalists active in the XYZ club, Jay was the man most involved, at an intellectual and personal level, with the development of Labour thinking. He had worked on *The Times* in 1929 after coming down from Oxford, but disillusioned by the paper's pro-Hitler bias, Jay left the paper in 1933 to take up a job on the *Economist*, which was at that time edited by Walter Layton. Together with Graham Hutton, a Fabian who subsequently recanted and moved to the right, Jay shared a flat with Kingsley Martin, and Geoffrey Crowther. It was through Martin that he was introduced to Thomas Balogh and Nichlas Kaldor, who later became prominent Labour economic advisors. Jay and Crowther wrote a good part of the *Economist* in the 1930s and were constant advocates of more expansionary economic policies. His book, *The Socialist Case*, is an acknowledged landmark in Labour party economic thinking and was, as Trevor Smith observes, a 'foretaste of the kind of rationale for the mixed economy that moderate Labour party opinion was to put forward in the postwar period'.[51] Jay moved to the *Daily Herald* in 1937, the same year as his book was published, and was, in his words, more concerned with 'Labour party propaganda'[52] than financial scoops. He was a persistent and perceptive critic of Montagu Norman's deflationary measures, a keen advocate for the New Deal, and a campaigner for economic expansion on Keynesian lines. During the War he went into government and was largely responsible, with Hugh Dalton, for developing distribution of industry policy as a major component of the 1944 White Paper on Employment. After the war, he became a Labour MP and a Cabinet minister. His son Peter was to follow in his father's footsteps and become an economic journalist of some note.

The *Economist* itself had supported reflation from the early 1930s onwards with all the vigour with which it traditionally supported free trade – notwithstanding Layton's reservations. As Jay argues: 'Crowther and I were even permitted to introduce the phrase "full employment" ' – which in itself constituted a minor revolution since until this time such terminology was not in common usage. Furthermore, as Jay argues, the *Economist*'s wholehearted advocacy of reflation in the years before the publication of the *General Theory* helped in no small way to make the idea 'respectable'.[53] Crowther later argued that the shift towards a

Keynesian position was entirely in keeping with the traditions of the paper on the grounds that:

> The *Economist* gives an ungrudging blessing to certain wide extensions
> of state control for precisely the same fundamental reasons as led
> Wilson and Bagehot to advocate the maximum of lassez-faire a
> hundred years ago, because that seems to be the surest way of serving
> liberty and the common good. [54]

It was still quite a U-turn for a paper which had had so much responsibility for propagating the ideas of *laissez-faire* political economy. But it signified the way in which the opinion formers of the financial world were, by the 1930s, really in advance of the so-called Keynesian revolution in government and academia. Amongst Keynes's most whole-hearted supporters was Paul Einzig, someone who was recognized to be, as Jay observes, 'the best-informed financial journalist in the City'. [55] Einzig, though not moving in Keynes's circle, like Davenport, or involved in XYZ, like Jay and Williams, was a free and radical voice on the *Financial News*, and it was one which was listened to and respected. Like so many other economic journalists before and since, it was true to say that his 'journalism was not so much of a profession as a crusade. He was always seeking not simply to record events, nor simply to comment on them, but to shape and influence them'. [56] His contact with Keynes had begun when Keynes published an article of his in the *Economic Journal* and recommended one of his books for publication, but he did not actually meet him until 1936. As he notes in his autobiography:

> During the 'twenties and the early 'thirties, when hardly any financial
> editor had a good word for Keynes or the policies he was advocating,
> he probably received more support from me than from the rest of the
> financial Press put together. Having been allowed a fairly free hand in
> my column, I managed from time to time to get in a word of support
> for his ideas, even though this was not in accordance with the editorial
> policy of the *Financial News*. My own self appointed role in regard to
> those of his theories and policies with which I was one of the clearest
> writers of our generation on economic subjects, a large proportion of
> his writings were above the head of the layman. I conceived it to be my
> task to familiarize my readers with some of his ideas . . . Keynes told
> me on the occasion of our first meeting that he had read most of what I
> had written . . . From that day onward whenever I was writing

something that was likely to be of interest to him it was always at the back of my mind: 'What will Keynes think of this'. It spurred me on to be at my very best in order to interest him and to earn his approval.[57]

Keynesian ideas had, therefore, made considerable headway by the middle of the 1930s. Einzig *et al.* were powerful spokesmen for the idea that the age of market capitalism had come to an end. It was also a view that was effectively organized and articulated via the *Nation*, the *New Statesman* and the XYZ club, and one which was to come into its own during and after the war when these radical journalists were, in many cases, to be found in positions of some power and influence. Indeed, their belief in the efficacy of government planning could only have been confirmed by their experience of wartime administration. Davenport and Williams worked as temporary civil servants during the war, and after the war the latter was to become Attlee's Public Relations Officer. Richard 'Otto' Clarke, the man who was responsible for devising the index of ordinary share prices in the *Financial News* and which later became the famous FT Index, became a prominent civil servant and wrote what is generally considered to be one of the landmarks in British macroeconomic policy, the *Economic Survey* of 1947. Sir Richard later went on to be Permanent Secretary at the Ministry of Aviation and Permanent Secretary at the Ministry of Technology. (Lord) Geoffrey Crowther held positions in the Ministries of Supply, Information and Production, and held the post of editor of the *Economist* until 1956. Douglas Jay went into the Ministry of Supply and the Board of Trade during the war and was personal assistant to Attlee as Prime Minister. He became President of the Board of Trade in 1964 under Harold Wilson.

What Keynes and those who were (or who became identified as) his disciples in the press had achieved in the 1930s was a subtle shift in the discourse of economic policy. This shift ensured, perhaps more effectively than what was happening in the universities, that the context within which policy and events took place would be largely Keynesian in inspiration or inclination. This revolution in communicating the capitalist system was far more significant than is generally recognized by students of economic theory and policy who have tended to analyse the 'Keynesian revolution' from the point of view of what happened in government and academia. But the fact that journalists like Jay, Crowther and Einzig were setting out ideas and terms which came to structure the policy-making environment must be accounted as a key component of the change in opinion in the years preceeding and following the *General Theory*. As we have seen, Keynes himself was in great part responsible for this in the manner in which he had conducted his campaign of persuasion. From being largely a propaganda sheet for orthodox economic doctrines, British financial (and increasingly by the early 1930s, more specifically 'economic') journalism had evolved a more 'macro' rather than 'market' economic perspective. Jay, Einzig, Davenport and Williams represented a body of opinion in the media which was, with a few exceptions like Harold Wincott and Oscar Hobson, highly critical of market forces and sympathetic to the idea that government could and should take responsibility for dealing with those problems which the market, if left to itself, was inherently incapable of solving. At the same time, by presenting those ideas within the context of established and 'establishment' organs of the financial press – like the *Economist* and the *Financial News* – financial journalism also contributed to bringing about the most radical change in the locus British economic consensus since Wilson set up the *Economist* in 1843.

Underpinning all this there were other changes in the financial media which were really a necessary precondition of reforming journalism: a rise in the technical quality and editorial independence of the press. This was not peculiar to Britain: in America a new generation of business magazines had appeared by the mid-1930s, notably *Business Week, Fortune* and *Barrons*. Although these papers were not exactly eager to see more state intervention, they provided a more in-depth analysis of business and economic conditions than could be given by dailies, even of the quality of the *New York Times* and the *Wall Street Journal*. *Fortune*, in particular, started in 1929 by Luce, quickly established itself as a fiercely independent and critical voice. It supported the New Deal – until the economic recovery was on its way – and antagonized both liberal and conservative opinion. *Fortune* by the end of the 1930s became obligatory reading for all interested in American economic affairs. It was manifestly a business paper, but it steadfastly refused to compromise its journalism for the sake of commercial advantage. Luce once said, for example, that the price of planting a story in *Fortune* was $3million – and for that the industrialist concerned could also have the paper!

As Einzig noted with respect to the British scene, the fact that he was allowed to use his column to persuade readers to take Keynes's ideas seriously, even though it went against the economic philosophy of the proprietor and the editor, meant that, by the late 1930s, financial journalists were being given a new independence, and a chance to express their own ideas even when they cut across the grain of proprietorial interests. Such freedom was naturally to be expected in the *New Statesman* or the *Daily Herald*, or the anonymous columns of the *Economist*. What was revolutionary about Einzig's position was that it was being taken by the leading organ of the financial press, Harry Marks's *Financial News*. The foundations for this more independent and opinionated financial journalism had been laid in the 1920s by two men above all: Walter Layton and Hilton Young. Layton, who had a passionate belief in the free-trade principles of Bagehot and Hirst, had revived the fortunes of the *Economist* after the years when the journal seemed to have lost the reputation for ideas that it had established in the nineteenth century under Wilson and Bagehot. Layton recruited bright new people – like Jay and Crowther – with something to say and the technical training to be able to say it convincingly and, whilst also the editor of the *News Chronicle*, he allowed his young men considerable freedom to express their (mostly Keynesian) views. Hilton Young – later Lord Kennet – a former financial secretary to the Treasury under Lloyd George, a former financial editor on the *Morning Post* and an assistant editor on the *Economist*, took over the *Financial News* in 1924, and began a tradition of recruiting bright new graduates to improve the quality of its coverage – the 'Lombard Street' column which was one of the great features of the new financial journalism was started under his editorship. Young was, like Layton, eager to let his new recruits think their own thoughts, and when he left the paper in 1929 he left a newspaper with a standing very much higher than when he had come to it. Young was succeeded by Oscar Hobson, who had previously worked on the *Manchester Guardian* and was imbued by its spirit of free expression. Even though Hobson was hostile to the ideas which Einzig put forward in his columns, he steadfastly defended the independence of his paper against the challenges occasionally issued from the proprietor

– Brendan Bracker – and held true to his belief that the economic journalist had a role to educate the public as much as to inform investors. As he pointed out in 1938:

> it is, in these tense and difficult times, almost a matter of vital national interest that every good citizen of a democratic country should have some understanding of the economic principles which govern the production and distribution of wealth.[58]

What marked out Hobson and his successors – Maurice Green and Hargreaves Parkinson – from earlier financial journalists was their passionate commitment to their profession and a real interest in economics combined with a tough determination to be independent in their comments, and free from those commercial pressures and temptations which had done so much in earlier decades to lower the standing of financial journalism. They were also men who had, like Bagehot, a deep intellectual involvement in their subject and a practical knowledge of economic affairs. Hobson, for example had a sound academic background in economics – his father, J. A. Hobson, had taught Keynes mathematics at Cambridge. Hobson gained practical experience of the City by working in a bank after coming down from university. In the 1930s men like Hobson, and G. J. Holmes and Harold Wincott on the *Investors Chronicle* were quick to realise that the world of financial journalism was changing fast. As Hargreaves Parkinson explains, by the 1930s investment had 'been extended and democratised': there was scarcely one reader or potential reader of the *Economist* who did not hold at least a few thousand pounds of stock or a few hundred company shares.[59] One sign of this 'democratisation' of capitalism was the import of the American idea of unit trusts and their launch by Ian Fairbairn of the M and G group in 1931. Unit trusts brought in a new kind of investor, whose numbers were greatly to increase after the war. Oscar Hobson, when he retired from the *News Chronicle* was to become the first chairman of the Association of Unit Trust Managers in 1959. Alongside this 'popular' investment was also the expansion of corporate investment and, as Berle and Means had identified, a new class of 'managers' – often trained in economics – who now required a daily and weekly digest of the vastly increased information which was by then emanating from government, industry and commerce. To be successful in this market the financial press had to be totally above suspicion of the sort of practices which were notorious in the 1890s and the 1920s, and they also had to be technically much better. As Charles Anderson argues, at this time:

> Contacts with the market were still extremely valuable ... but financial, economic and business data had become so much more plentiful and their significance better appreciated. As a result a new and more scientific investment approach was developing: stories gathered in the market were being put through a finer sieve, and more original effort was being applied to interpretation and forecasting. A better equipped generation was making its arrival felt in the Stock Exchange and in the offices of the institutions.[60]

Financial editors realised that honest and technically informed journalism was vital to the survival and prosperity of financial journalism. As PEP's report on the financial press pointed out in 1938, the advertising pressures on financial journalism had, if anything, greatly increased in the 1930s.[61] It was a testament to the professionalism of men like Hobson – a journalist possessing what Paul Bareau described as 'pedantic integrity'[62] – that the pressures were resisted. And, to his great credit, Brendan Bracken was prepared to respect and defend that professional judgement. Indeed, as Hobson, who had himself had disagreements with Bracken over editorial independence, commented after his death: 'He always stood for the highest standards in his papers and the financial journalism of today owes him much.'[63] There can be little doubt that Brendan Bracken's proprietorship of the leading British financial newspapers was instrumental in creating the conditions within which new standards in financial journalism could be established. As Lysaght observes in his biography of Bracken:

> The most indispensible of all Bracken's qualities was his vision. It was not just that he had a sense of news values and an appreciation of good writing not only found in every newspaper proprietor. He ... grasped the essential truth that the only long-term future for quality and specialist papers lay in maintaining the highest standards. His central achievement was that he fired a team of able young men with enthusiasm for this vision. They found him ruthless when his papers' prestige was at stake ... Financial journalists had, in the past, been prone to corruption ... From the time he took control, Bracken spelt out the message that ... advertisements could not purchase immunity from adverse comment in his papers.[64]

And what papers they were! By 1945 Bracken had brought all the major financial newspapers – the *Financial News* and the *Financial Times*, *The Banker* and the *Investor's Chronicle* – under one unified management structure. In so bringing about a reorganization of the financial press Bracken undoubtedly helped considerably in preserving its financial viability whilst at the same time ensuring that the principle of journalistic independence would not be compromised. Though it sold to the market and was manifestly dependent on the market for its revenues and very existence it did not sell out to the market. In organizing a formidable assembly of financial papers and in fighting off any attempts to compromise journalistic standards of integrity Bracken the Conservative thus paved the way for an era of radical change in the notion of capitalism which was disseminated by the financial media.

The new financial journalism which grew up in the 1930s and 1940s adjusted quickly to the emergence of a very different readership to that which had for so long been the main audience for its product: for the first time it began to write about *the economy*. And this enunciation of the notion of 'the economy' is, as the following chapter discusses, a most important aspect of the 'Keynesian' revolution which, thanks to the growing editorial independence and intellectual integrity of the press, leading economists *qua* journalists were being allowed to promote and reflect. It is one of the more interesting aspects of economic discourse that, until the efforts of Keynes to persuade public opinion, the concept of there being an 'economy' was itself alien to the language, not simply in the financial media, but amongst society at large. The idea of 'economy' up to the 1930s was primarily related to the notion of *economising*. Keynes himself argued that his theory needed new terminology that would be more appropriate to describing the 'problems of the economic system as a whole'.[65] And Emmison has shown in a detailed examination of the idea of 'the economy', in the use of the term in *The Times*, *New Statesman*, *New York Times*, *Time* and the *Economist*, that it is not until the mid 1930s (that is, from the appearance of the *General Theory*) that the term 'the economy' comes into general usage in the press.[66] This adoption of the idea of 'the economy' marked not merely a semantic or linguistic change but was a sign of the fact that, by the outbreak of the Second World War, the precepts of neo-classical economics were, as Schumpeter and

Berle and Means demonstrated, being transformed by the behaviour of the state, entrepreneurs and the big corporations. Thus, it was not just academic paradigms which were being revised: 'popular business philosophy'[67] was also changing. As Leslie Hannah shows, the business community in the 1920s and 1930s was coming to question the 'wasteful' and 'destructive' system of competition and there was considerable interest in the issues of 'rationalization', 'economies of scale', 'mergers', 'mass production' and 'scientific management'. The business press remains for historians of the period a prime source of evidence for understanding the way in which the tenor of business opinion was evolving into a more corporate and managerial frame of mind: a process which was, although related, quite distinct from the 'Keynesian revolution'.[68] The changing language of commerce reflected the growing awareness of the economic forces at work in capitalist society as well as the more subtle impact of 'Keynesian' terminology.[69] In addition to this modification (in the scale) of business language and economic terminology – 'mass production', 'management' and 'the economy' – a new relationship was being forged between the state and modern capitalism. In the interwar period, the state in both Britain and the US was, in the face of rhetoric to the contrary, taking an increasingly active part in bringing public policy to bear on social and economic problems. So much so that, in Samuel Beer's words: 'government decisions of these years endowed Britain with a pattern of economic policy that was comprehensive and radically different from that of previous generations'.[70] Inevitably, the financial press was drawn into the process whereby such pragmatic interventionism was communicated, debated and ultimately endowed with a wider social and political currency, respectability and legitimacy. The present author, for example, has shown elsewhere how the bastion of economic orthodoxy, *The Times*, was in 1934 largely responsible for igniting the political controversy over the depressed areas which led to the government introducing the Special Areas Act – a measure that constituted the beginning of British regional planning policy.[71]

The notion which was disseminated by the press in the 1930s that there was a *national economy* and that there were such things as *economic problems* and *managerial problems*, from which it followed that there were *national* and *managerial* solutions

– signalled that, whether by persuasion or because of the changing nature of capitalism itself, or a combination of both, there had come about a revolution in the cultural or popular context of capitalism. In the next chapter we examine how this transformation in economic opinion was mediated through the press in the wake of the Keynesian revolution.

NOTES

1. See J. K. Galbraith, *The Great Crash 1929* (Penguin, Harmondsworth, 1984) p. 102.
2. Ibid., p. 103.
3. Ibid., p. 99.
4. In general, see his *The Market Place: reminiscences of American finance* (Little Brown, Boston, 1938).
5. A. D. Noyes, 'Present Value of Past Economic History', in *Addresses and Discussion at a Conference of Universities under the auspices of New York University at the Waldorf-Astoria, New York, November 1932* (New York University Press, New York, 1933).
6. R. Sobel, *Inside Wall Street* (Norton, New York, 1977) p. 355.
7. Cited in Martin Walker, *Powers of the Press: the world's great newspapers* (Quartet Books, London, 1982) p. 220.
8. See P. Temin, *Did Monetary Forces Cause the Great Depression?* (Norton, New York, 1976) pp. 76–9.
9. Sobel, op.cit, p. 250.
10. Kingsley Martin, *Editor: a volume of autobiography, 1931–1945* (Hutchinson, London, 1968) p. 12.
11. F. A. von Hayek, *Studies in Philosophy, Politics and Economics* (Routledge and Kegan Paul, London, 1978) p. 287.
12. See J. M. Keynes, *The Collected Writings*, vol. 19 (Macmillan, London 1971–) p. xiii.
13. Edward Hyams, *The New Statesman: the history of the first fifty years, 1913–1963* (Longmans, London, 1963).
14. D. Patinkin, *Anticipation of the General Theory* (Blackwell, Oxford, 1982) p. 33.
15. E. S. Johnson, 'Keynes as a Literary Craftsman', in E. S. Johnson and H. Johnson, *The Shadow of Keynes: understanding Keynes, Cambridge and Keynesian economics* (Blackwell, Oxford, 1978) p. 30–1.
16. Ibid.
17. Alfred Marshall, *Essays in Biography* (Norton, New York, 1951) p. 174.
18. R. F. Harrod, *The Life of John Maynard Keynes* (Macmillan, London, 1951) p. 254.
19. J. M. Keynes, 'The Change of Opinion', in *Essays in Persuasion*, Collected Writings, op.cit., vol. 19.
20. J. M. Keynes, 'The End of Laissez Faire', in ibid., p. 288.
21. J. M. Keynes, *The General Theory of Employment, Interest and Money* (Macmillan, Cambridge, 1973) pp. 32–3.
22. A. C. Pigou, *The Theory of Unemployment* (Macmillan, London, 1933).
24. J. M. Keynes, *Collected Works*, op.cit., vol. 21, p. 334.

25. *Manchester Guardian Commercial*, 20 April 1922, p. 519.
26. *Reconstruction in Europe*, no. 1 (1922) p. 3.
27. Ibid., no. 2, p. 67.
28. Ibid.
29. See H. Clay (ed.), *The Inter-War Years and Other Papers: a selection from the writings of Herbert Douglas Henderson* (Clarendon Press, Oxford, 1955).
30. *Nation and Athenaeum*, 14 July 1923.
31. Ibid., 4 August 1923.
32. Cited in C. H. Rolph (ed.), *Kingsley: the life, letters and diaries of Kingsley Martin* (Gollancz, London, 1973) p. 207.
33. Patinkin, op.cit., p. 206.
34. J. A. Schumpeter, *Ten Great Economists – From Marx to Keynes* (Oxford University Press, New York, 1951), p. 268.
35. Harrod, op.cit., p. 324.
36. *Nation and Athenaeum*, 19 July 1923.
37. See, for example, M. R. Darby and J. R. Lothian, 'Events and Ideas: 1930s and 1970s', in J. Burton (ed.), *Keynes's General Theory: fifty years on: its relevance to modern times* (Institute of Economic Affairs, London, 1986).
38. Hayek, op.cit., p. 287.
39. See J. M. Keynes, *General Theory and After*, Part 2, The Collected Writings, op.cit, vol. 14. p. 285–95.
40. L. E. Fouraker, 'The Cambridge Didactic Style', *Journal of Political Economy*, vol. 61. (1958) p. 66.
41. Galbraith, op.cit., p. 228.
42. R. Steel, *Walter Lippman and the American Century* (The Bodley Head, London, 1980) p. 305.
43. N. Davenport, *Memoirs of a City Radical* (Weidenfeld and Nicolson, London, 1974) p. 112.
44. Ibid., p. 65.
45. F. Williams, *Nothing so Strange: an autobiography* (Cassell, London, 1970) p. 112.
46. Ibid., p. 92.
47. Ibid., p. 95.
48. Ibid.
49. Ibid., pp. 108–10.
50. See Douglas Jay, *Change and Fortune: a political record* (Hutchinson, London, 1980).
51. T. A. Smith, *The Politics of the Corporate Economy* (Martin Robertson, Oxford, 1979) p. 40.
52. Jay, op.cit., p. 65.
53. Ibid., p. 53.
54. *The Economist, 1843–1943* (*The Economist Newspaper*, London, 1943) p. 15.
55. Jay, op.cit., p. 67.
56. *Times Literary Supplement*, 30 September 1960.
57. P. Einzig, *In the Centre of Things: the autobiography of Paul Einzig* (Hutchinson, London, 1960) pp. 166–7.
58. Preface to Oscar Hobson, *How the City Works* (*News Chronicle*, London, 1938).
59. *Economist*, op.cit., p. 130.
60. *Investors Chronicle*, 10 June 1960, p. 33.
61. Political and Economic Planning, *Report on the British Press* (London, 1938) pp. 198, 128, 172.
62. In Adrienne Gleeson, *People and Their Money: 50 years of private investment* (Hobsons Press, for M and G group, London, 1981) p. 3.

63. Cited in Charles Lysaght, *Brendan Bracken* (Allen Lane, London, 1979) p. 120.
64. Ibid., p. 125.
65. Keynes *General Theory*, op.cit., p 37.
66. Mike Emmison, 'The Economy: its emergence in media discourse', in H. Davis and Paul Walton (eds), *Language, Image and Media* (Blackwell, Oxford, 1983) p. 145.
67. Leslie Hannah, *The Rise of the Corporate Economy* (Methuen, London, 1976) p. 29.
68. Hannah makes the important point that:

    The effect of the depression in increasing political consciousness and stimulating the growth of the Labour Party, and its impact on the collapse of the classical paradigms of economic theory in the Keynesian revolution, have often been analysed by historians. Less well covered, but no less important, was its impact on the level of popular business philosophy, as more businessmen began to question the desirability of the configuration of firms and markets which they had inherited from the prewar era (ibid., p. 29).

69. As examples of the coverage of corporate affairs by the press see H. Quigley, 'Large Scale Organisations of Production', *Manchester Guardian Commercial*, 28 October 1926; 'S. R', 'Advantages and Disadvantages of Rationalisation', *Manchester Guardian Commercial*, 18 October 1928; *Economist*, 7 December, 1929.
70. Samuel Beer, *Modern British Politics* (Faber and Faber, London, 1965) p. 179.
71. D. W. Parsons, *The Political Economy of British Regional Policy* (Routledge and Kegan Paul, London, 1988).

3. The press and the Keynesian revolution

The main focus of the large and ever increasing literature concerned with the 'Keynesian revolution' has, naturally enough, been on its theoretical dimension; more specifically, on the influence of 'Keynesian' ideas on the academic community and on the policy-making process. However, as we have seen in the previous chapter, the impact of what passed for 'Keynesian' ideas and discourse on the general context of economic opinion, 'popular business philosophy' and the financial media, was equally important for the ultimate success of the discourse of national economic management. It was not just in the classroom that the 'Keynesian revolution' was propagated. Indeed, it is just as central to an understanding of the development of economic opinion to stress that Keynesian discourse had an impact far wider than the world of theoretical paradigms. And this translation of Keynesianism into a more popular language was no less vital an aspect of the 'revolution' than the theoretical changes themselves: indeed, in the end it may have proved more vital to this political impact.

No doubt because of the success of economists in establishing a scientific and technical reputation, as a group they have tended to be intellectually more introspective and less eclectic than other social scientists. As a consequence, discussions about the impact of economic theory invariably concern themselves with the analysis of policy in relation to its theoretical environment. Such a perspective was itself explicitly bequeathed by Keynes to his followers in the famous declaration at the end of the *General Theory*, with regard to the influence of 'academic scribblers' on 'madmen in authority'. Many economists have dismissed the notion as being naïve and improbable, but it is still the case that, when it comes to analysing the development of economic policy, economists of all varieties find it very difficult not to employ Keynes's statement about the influence of ideas as the basis for their explanation of how governments come to accept new policies.[1] Economists have thus been over-concerned about the 'message' to the great detriment of comprehending the medium of its dissemination. And yet, all too often, as Marshall McLuhan once observed, the medium has a habit of becoming the message! We now know (thanks largely to the publication of Keynes's *Collected Writings* and its attendant critical scholarship) that there has oftentimes been little correspondence between Keynes and the doctrines implemented or spread by his academic and political disciples. Such has been the not unusual fate of those whose name and ideas are invoked by a social or intellectual movement. Whatever the relationship between Keynes and the actuality of the Keynesian revolution, the essential political point to grasp is that it constituted a shift in the discourse which served to legitimate and articulate the formulation, implementation and explanation of economic policy. This process must, as Keynes says with reference to the Ricardian revolution, 'have been due to a complex of suitabilities in the doctrine into the environment into which it was projected'.[2] Manifestly, part of that 'complex' was, for Ricardian economics as for Keynesianism, the fact that it acquired the support of newspapers and economic journalists who could publicize and apply the ideas and language to daily events. And, as in the case of Ricardo and McCulloch, the fact was that, as is the way of communications, the message was somewhat distorted by the process of popular translation, dissemination and mediation. Keynesianism, like Ricardianism, also attracted the attention of the communicators and was an inspiration to a generation of journalists who would largely be responsible for popularizing Keynesian views in the postwar era.

The tradition of scholarly economic journalism which had grown up under Layton and Hobson in the 1930s was to continue in the postwar era nurtured in two great schools of British economic journalism: the *Financial Times* under Gordon Newton, and the *Economist* under Geoffrey Crowther, both of whom were, like most of their contemporaries, Keynesian in outlook. As Fred Hirsch, himself a former journalist on the *Economist*, observed in his *Social Limits to Growth*:

> Keynes's writings influenced a generation of economic journalists in Britain perhaps still more than academic economists. The campaigning journalists would have been less than human not to have been attracted by Keynes's insistence that it was the leaders of opinion and

the masters of pragmatic intellect rather than the men of party or the men of business – or even academics who remained in their ivory tower – who ruled the world.[3]

In America, too, where the impact of Keynes on the press was not as immediately obvious as in Britain, the acceptance of the Keynesian framework and vocabularly was, if not as complete, then certainly widespread: Galbraith, for instance, was employed by *Fortune*. As Henry Hazlitt, an American business journalist who steadfastly opposed the encroachment of Keynesian theory and policy, protested in 1959:

> Open any issue of almost any of the scholarly economic journals, and you will find [Keynes's] name and the phrases he coined or popularized sprinkled generously through its pages. Open any newspaper, and you will find interpretations of current economic events, or proposals for economic and monetary policies, that owe at least their ubiquity, if not their origin, to his writings.[4]

The process of, if not 'Keynesianization' of American journalism then of taking account of 'Keynesian' policies and theories had begun in the 1930s with Walter Lippman's reluctant and ambivalent conversion to Keynes's ideas. Keynes – the man – had not a little impact on the American newspaper scene through his syndicated journalism and in his famous open letter to Roosevelt in 1933. However, with the exception of individual commentators like Lippman and the liberal journals like the *Nation* and the *New Republic*, Keynes failed to win over the sort of committed converts in the US financial media that he had made in Britain. Even the *New York Times*, for example, a paper which had given him the platform to address the President in 1933, did not even bother – like many other papers – to review the *General Theory* when it was published in America, and with the New Deal on its doorstep was generally highly critical of Keynes and his ideas. And the *New Republic* itself did not exactly go overboard in praise of the book. Its review said:

> Mr Keynes undoubtedly will write other books as correctives to this one. In this present study he apparently has taken a step towards the positive position he will finally come to occupy in economic theory. But since it is presented in a highly abstruse and mathematical fashion, 'The General Theory of Employment' probably will not add directly to his popular prestige.[5]

Notwithstanding the 1933 letter to Roosevelt and the respect
with which he was held in America, dating from *The Economic
Consequences of the Peace*, Keynes's ideas – as opposed to his
personal prestige – made much less popular progress in America
than was the case in Britain. As Galbraith has noted, Keynes came
to America via *Harvard*:[6] he never built up the kind of journalistic
constituency in the US in the 1930s that he had so successfully
managed to assemble in Britain. As far as Britain was concerned,
what was remarkable about the acceptance of Keynesian ideas in
the press was the extent to which they successfully supplanted
existing ideas in several key journals. Indeed, Walter Layton, the
editor of the *Economist*, was so concerned about the way in which
his paper was becoming, in the eyes of the City, so closely
identified with Keynes, that he made a point of printing the name
of the reviewer of the *General Theory* – Austin Robinson – at the
end of the review: a rare exception to the century-old rule of
anonymity! Even so, until his resignation in 1936, Layton was
always ready to defend the *Economist*'s radical economic stance
against its critics.[7] As in the nineteenth century, the paper was in
the forefront of disseminating new economic ideas. Layton's successor, Geoffrey Crowther was to preside over a period which saw
an interventionist and largely managerialist consensus virtually
replace the old *laissez-faire*, free-market principles that the
Economist had done so much to spread a hundred years before. As
he remarked in his final editorial:

> Both parties seem to accept without demur their responsibility for
> maintaining the economic health of the community ... The new
> doctrine is so universally accepted that one would be thought very
> eccentric, and very reactionary even to question it.[8]

His successors, Donald Tyerman and Alastair Burnet also assented
to the belief, that, as the former expressed it:

> It is not the mixed and managed economy that holds back what
> Bagehot called the 'march of improvement', but the kind of mixture
> and the kind of management.[9]

Another sign of the degree of intellectual hegemony acquired by
Keynesian discourse in the British press was that Nicholas Davenport, who had been so closely associated with Keynes in the 1930s,

wrote a City column for the leading conservative weekly the *Spectator* in the 1950s and 1960s. His articles were consistently critical of the domination of the City in the economic life of the country and of the failure of the government to take more account of the financial aspects of economic policy. In 1964 his book *The Split Society* was well received by all shades of opinion with its argument that Britain was divided by class interests, that economic policy was over-influenced by the City and that there was a need for a more 'humane' financial policy which put 'men before money'. It was, as the *Economist* review concluded: 'Full of good stuff and rich in its denunciation of finance capitalism'[10] But it was the capture of the *Economist* itself which was, perhaps, the most significant victory of the Keynesian revolution in the media. As in the 1840s, when the journal greatly facilitated the propagation of contrary economic ideas, the *Economist* ensured that the Keynesian belief in managing the market economy through doses of government intervention was incorporated into a form of discourse acceptable to the postwar financial community. Furthermore, thanks to the emphasis which Crowther and successive editors placed on expanding the American and international sales of the paper, its role in spreading the notion of the 'managed economy' beyond British shores should not be underestimated. The contrast between the broadly Keynesian line adopted by the *Economist* and other leading British financial papers – although not oftentimes by their City editors – and the *Wall Street Journal* was expressed graphically in 1962 when the *Economist* explained to its readers that: 'Editorially, the *Journal* espouses a Simon-pure (sometimes simple-Simon pure) doctrine of *laissez-faire*'. Coming from the leading organ of nineteenth-century economic liberalism, that was some criticism! Unlike the British press, the postwar editorial stance of the *Journal* was what it had long been: consistently anti-government and anti-interventionist and anti-deficit spending. The *Journal* was, at a time when the *Economist* was eagerly proclaiming the new consensus, an outspoken critic of the ideas of the 'neo-Keynesians', as Vermont Royster termed them. Again, the *Journal* was, unlike comparable British publications, of no doubt that American economic ills were largely the product of the Keynesian economic virus.[11] When Richard Nixon proclaimed (in January 1971) that he was now a 'Keynesian', the paper became ever more vigilant in its defence of free-market principles.

As Lloyd Wendt explains in his history of the *Journal*, it maintained that:

> while Keynes's ideas may have been effective in an emergency, they
> had been perverted by the neo-Keynesians in the next half a century
> into wasteful government spending on a seemingly permanent basis.
> This policy would create a trillion dollar deficit, resulting in diminished
> investment in productive facilities, high taxes, high interest rates,
> soaring inflation, and continuing unemployment. [12]

The Keynesian revolution in America did not find the *Journal* or
Forbes as conducive a medium for the dissemination of its message
as the *Economist* and the *Financial Times* in Britain. Nevertheless,
the economic news agenda was moved inexorably in a Keynesian
direction in both countries not primarily because of the impact of
ideas but because of the changing context of economic *news* itself.
This was recognized even by the *Journal* in the way that, from the
Roosevelt era onwards, Washington became an *economic* news
centre that rivalled the pre-eminence of the financial district: from
the 1930s onwards *governments* were making *economic* news.
Roosevelt himself was a master of the art of manipulating the press
so as to make the overwhelmingly hostile business press actually
report his administration's policies on his terms. The press –
particularly the financial press – were naturally antagonistic to the
New Deal. Roosevelt, however, still got his message across in his
conferences. As Schlesinger comments:

> the conference enabled him to some degree to guide the whole
> movement of public discussion, spotlighting some issues, minimising
> others . . . And while he had pretty well lost the editorial pages by 1936
> and suffered an undue amount of distortion and misrepresentation in
> the news columns, he succeeded nonetheless in using the press much
> more than it succeeded in abusing him. By the simple trick of making
> news and *being* news, Roosevelt outwitted the general hostility of
> publishers and converted the press into one of the most effective
> channels of his public leadership. [13]

Keynes was, as Chapter 2 showed, adept at using the same trick:
making news by being news! During the 1930s and 1940s, and
especially during the war, the British and US governments continued to extend their ability to manage the presentation of
economic news and events. this was accomplished, first, through

the increased use of official statistics and reports; secondly, by the way in which government more generally became the focus of economic news and a source of information and opinion; and finally, through taking the press more fully into its confidence in off-the-record, and on-the-record briefings and conferences. During the war the press became more dependent on government as a source of economic news. As the *Economist* has noted:

> The second world war left a permanent mark on Britain's financial journalism. Financial markets became tightly regulated. Instead of the daily round of banks, brokers and bond dealers, journalists began to call on government departments to ask how the civil servants expected to keep the economy going and raise the money to pay for the war. The habit of looking largely to the government for material survived the war: to be on speaking terms with the chancellor was an asset worth striving for. For their part, ministers were suspicious of their civil-service advisers and liked to try out ideas on a friendly columnist. The senior civil servants knowing this, built up their own good relations with intelligent journalists.[14]

This revolution in the relationship of the economic media to the governmental machine was in many ways just as important to the way in which the economic agenda developed as the intellectual process associated with the victory of Keynesian theory.

What altered in the decades after the Second World War was that the news agenda came more under the influence of the activities of government than had previously been the case. Furthermore, after the war the state, had a more central role in 'the economy', and the management of economic *news* – if not of the economy – became more accomplished. As Peter Hennessy comments, for example, in his case study of the 1949 devaluation, the press

> had no idea, beyond the managed trickle of news from lobby briefings, what the real position was or what the options were. Even . . . a critical event [received] the most crass and non-inquisitorial explanation . . . The quality papers, with the exception of the *Financial Times*, were little or no better . . . The main channels of communication between government and the governed offered at best fragmentary and at worst, misleading coverage.[15]

In the postwar era the 'nation' and the national economic interest became a point of reference for economic news alongside

the City or Wall Street: this in turn underlined the fact that the
pragmatic interventionism of the interwar period, the growth of
big business and, most especially, wartime economic administration, had shifted media attention away from the stock market and
investment to the economy as a whole. As Hedley Donovan,
managing editor of *Fortune* during the Eisenhower years, has
commented, in the 1950s the *economy* was news, 'the biggest story
in America', and the magazine 'analysed and celebrated the
phenomenon in almost every issue'.[16] In the midst of this extension of government in to the economy the old City and Wall Street
journalism became something of an anachronism. As Kenneth
Fleet notes, during the war years and until the recovery of the
markets in the 1950s, finance and investment 'virtually disappeared from newspapers'.[17] The move towards reporting macro
– national – economic events and government policies was therefore not simply because of *Keynes*, or '*Keynesianism*', although
clearly, as Hazlitt noted in the 1950s, the fact that Keynesian
terminology rapidly became the accepted discourse through which
economic events were reported was of great significance. More
important than this was that, as Burnham had identified in 1941
(perhaps a better point in time to consider where Western
capitalism was going than 1936), the criterion of success had
altered, and the locus of power had shifted, or so it was supposed,
from market forces, to *managerial* capitalism. The impact of the
war economy and the consequent demise of the stock market and
private investor was not lost on those like Hargreaves Parkinson
who had closely observed the changing climate of opinion over the
years and the consequences that this would have for the market for
information and news. As he argued in 1944:

> There is no suggestion whatever that private enterprise, as we have
> known it, will disappear in any post-war regime. What is clear is that
> public and private enterprise will exist side by side, with rather less
> private and more public than before.[18]

This fact, he reasoned, would have profound effects on the market
for financial news and information. The shareholder class, who in
the past demanded information and tips in order to make money,
would inevitably give way to a managerial class demanding more
wide-ranging information on economic conditions, exports,

unemployment, international affairs and government economic policies. The readership of the financial press would no longer be confined to the old investing community, for, as Parkinson noted in the first number of the newly merged *Times* and *News*:

> The growing class of business managers and professional advisors whose function is destined to be decisive in every branch of industry and trade, under any form of capital ownership, calls for increasingly specialised service on matters bearing directly on the daily conduct of its affairs. Above all, a great body of readers, men and women in every walk of life, find that, in this difficult mid-twentieth century world, questions which used to be the exclusive concern of the economist and the businessman exert a profound influence on their daily work and happiness. Never have readers been so avid for guidance on everything bearing on full employment, taxation, the future of government controls and similar problems.[19]

Editors on both sides of the Atlantic, ever sensitive about their own readership market, responded to this change more rapidly than most sections of society by becoming more concerned with presenting news in a form which was acceptable to a more (national) community far wider than the financial districts which had been their principal target before the war. The *Wall Street Journal*, like the *Financial Times*, also realized that the future market for information would be far less parochial than the very title of the paper implied:

> We think that so far as information wants is concerned business is universal. The information on which the great automobile manufacturer acts is the same information which influences the man who buys trucks . . . we think we have pretty strong evidence that business is a national community . . .[20]

The transformation of the *Journal* from a Wall Street newsletter to a truly national newspaper printed in four cities and meeting the demand for economic information in the broader sense, rather than just the stock market and the Street, was like the changing policy of the London *Financial Times*, a sign of the fact that the war had brought into focus the emergence of a different structure of business, ownership and state–industry relations. At the same time, economic reality itself appeared to be behaving in a 'Keynesian' way after the war. As *Time* commented in 1965: we were 'all Keynesians now' because, as the magazine editors saw it:

> even his severest detractors . . . use his macro economic terms and framework that he devised, and concede that his main theories have worked out in practice . . .[21]

The point that needs to be stressed is, then, that the Keynesian revolution in economic theory was but part of a larger revolution: the context of economic news confirmed and reinforced the progress of economic knowledge and its attendant rhetoric. As Samuelson commented in 1958, so well charted was that state of the national economy that:

> the casual reader of the newspaper has today an awareness of contemporaneous economic events that was just a few decades ago unavailable even to the most energetic scholar. And beyond this knowledge of the facts of the case there is a calculated confidence in our ability to battle this scourge of depression.[22]

Knowledge – or leastways, information – was power. The financial press were ready to respond to the demand for such news since, as the *Financial Times* reasoned in 1969, because:

> Economic events are no longer regarded as unpredictable and uncontrollable like the weather: men, especially men elected or appointed to positions of power, are held to be at least partially responsible for them . . . The modern business man has to take the possibility of government action into his calculations much more than before the war. He has to understand a new economics and familiarise himself with a new jargon and mass of statistics. The specialist press has grown up to help him.[23]

In Chapter 1 we were critical of the way in which the Victorian press – and politicians – seemed to pass over economic events that did not have a City implication. But, as Brown noted, actually discerning those events was by no means an easy task, given the paucity of economic statistics available for public debate in the nineteenth century. Thanks to the developments of financial journalism in the *Economist* and the *Statist*, there were accurate 'facts' and figures available on the City but not much else. As the availability of more national economic data made itself felt in newspapers, so the possibility of arguing a case from the sort of figures which, by the 1930s, could be accessed by Keynes and his followers became possible. (Keynes's own technique, for instance, was to make a point one week in an article and then follow this up with a mass of government and other statistics to drive home, and usually win, his case.) Information manifestly shaped knowledge, but it also refashioned the intellectual context of the economic agenda – as that great advocate of statistical journalism, Sir Robert Giffen, had argued when setting up the *Statist*.

After the war this expansion of information about the 'economy' as a whole continued at a greater pace than ever before. It was fuelled by the growth of the wartime civil service, by the increase in the number of professional economists and statisticians, and also by the changes in company and corporate law which required that more information be made public. Coupled with this was the establishment of international agencies and organizations, such as the International Monetary Fund, the Organization for Economic Co-operation and Development and the European Economic Community which all contributed to the volume of data available to the academic and the journalist. This vast output of national and international economic information, combined with growing interest in equity investment created, on the one hand, a demand for more economic news, and on the other, financial advice: the former being concerned to report economic events and government policies which affected the nation and the latter to provide news and comment for the investing public. The balance between these two kinds of journalism was, given the higher level of government involvement in the economy in Britain, very different to that of America. The differences of approach reflect as much upon the nature and extent of economic management in both countries as upon the structure and position of their respective news industries and, not least, the public status accorded to economists in Britain and America.

The financial journalism which developed in the decades following the end of the war was, therefore, geared to informing what was believed to be a very different market from that which had existed before the war. It is interesting to note that the financial press were quick to adapt their marketing strategies to the arguments of Schumpeter, Berle and Means, Burnham *et al.*, that postwar capitalism had fundamentally changed: old fashioned free-market capitalism and the individual entrepreneur were dead.

The decision taken by the financial media to aim their product at a more *national* audience and specifically at the up-and-coming managerial class was a significant cultural reinforcement of the intellectual and material changes taking place at the time. The role of the postwar press thus evolved to incorporate teaching as well as tipping. In America this view of the need for the business press to *educate opinion* was most noticeably developed by the news magazines. Kenneth Kramer, former editor of *Business Week*, has noted, for instance, that he was proud that his magazine was a pioneer in 'improving economic awareness in business' and in 'writing about the development of economic ideas as 'news events'.[24] The man who was at the forefront of this development of American economic journalism was Leonard Silk. Much to their credit, publications like *Business Week, Time* and *Newsweek* set out to increase the level of economic understanding as well as report economic news. As we shall discuss in the following chapter, *Newsweek* had a particularly important role in providing a platform for economic debate in the 1960s and 1970s.

In the postwar period, leastways up until the mid-1970s, economic events apparently supported Keynesian ideas. Economies were booming and unemployment was low: economic growth – something about which Keynes himself had been vague – powered along at an unprecedented rate. It was difficult for those who were critical of the 'Keynesian revolution' to win the arguments when the whole context of economic news seemed to point to the fact that it was all working wonderfully well. Thus, as Hirsch and Gordon argue, the British press in the 1950s and 1960s greatly assisted in the articulation of a very narrow and largely macroeconomic agenda predicated on the assumption that the economic order itself was sound and the issues that remained were largely those of technique. The British press, they maintain, propagated a narrow band of managerialist opinion. And, as they demonstrate in their analysis of the coverage of budgets in the British press from 1964 to 1973, the financial pages and editorial comment were overwhelmingly preoccupied with the problems of economic management to the exclusion of discussing other issues. The press, they conclude, did not

form an independent body of criticism. It did not draw, as it could have done on work being done at least peripherally in the universities indicating the limitations of economic growth in solving the problems of the worst off . . . The press did not act as a check on the instincts, rationalisations and self delusions of Britain's all party establishment. It reinforced them.[25]

Hirsch and Gordon contend that the critical constraints on the press stem from the very economics of the newspaper industry, namely, their need to attract the readership necessary to win advertising revenues. The press was therefore inherently limited in its intellectual horizons due to the narrow base of their readership market. Undoubtedly, the fact that, by definition, the financial press is geared to an up-market audience is a major factor in determining the editorial line. A business-orientated paper would not last too long if it came out advocating an economic policy that merited the support of the Communist Party! However, the fact that the financial pages and economic comment are aimed at a narrow class base does not go far in explaining the differences between, say, the *Financial Times* and the *Wall Street Journal*. Whereas the London paper took from the outset under the editorship of Gordon Newton a very pragmatic attitude towards Keynesianism, the *Journal* maintained a highly antagonistic stance, viewing with considerable distain its adoption by politicians and academics. The problem with the British press was not that they took such a narrow line, but that it was, if anything, too broad and eclectic and too ready to direct its attention to the experience of other countries and new techniques than suggest real alternatives.

The pronounced Keynesian ethos of the British press soon became a target of the Institute of Economic Affairs (IEA) set up in 1957 and inspired by Hayek's *Road to Serfdom*. The Institute thought that it was vital to stimulate and organize alternative research and opinion in order to break what they considered to be the virtual stranglehold of 'Keynesian' doctrines on the media and the political agenda. In time, the IEA's publications also became news events in their own right, and its seminars provided a home for those journalists who were sympathetic to their cause. Graham Hutton, for example, who had worked on the *Economist* before the war, saw the IEA as a 'haven for refugees' from the new economic othodoxy. Hutton was but one of a number of economic journalists who were active in the founding of the IEA: others included Sir Oscar Hobson, Paul Bareau, Harold Wincott and George Schwartz. In America, Hazlitt, the *Newsweek* columnist, was an enthusiastic propagandist of the IEA's output and philosophy. Over the years the IEA was to prove very effective in providing an intellectual shelter for dissident free-market journalists which was, to a large extent, not needed in America because of the less than complete victory of Keynesian economics. Later on, in the 1970s, the IEA was to provide a major platform for the free-market counter-revolution. Indeed, as Hutton notes: 'One significant feature of British economic and financial journalism after the war is the growing number of once socialist writers who changed nearer the standpoint of Hayek, Robbins, or others in the IEA.'[26] Significantly, as the involvement of Hobson and Wincott *et al.* in the IEA illustrates, City journalists were amongst the first to express reservations about the new economics. Meanwhile in the United States, as the IEA was being established in response to *The Road to Serfdom*, there was also a resurgence of the right which was, apparently, to prompt Galbraith to write *The Affluent Society*, which came out in 1958. In America the impact of Hayek's *Road to Serfdom* had, so Galbraith notes:

> spread rapidly outside the academic world. It was warmly embraced by the editors of *Fortune, The Wall Street Journal*, other business journals and by editorial writers for whom it was an admirable way of placating socially backward publishers in an unexpectedly sophisticated way...[27]

Yet despite Galbraith's remarks, perhaps what was most notable about the state of the US financial press was not that there were some 'Hayekian rumblings' in the *Wall Street Journal* and *Fortune*, but that the press adjusted fairly painlessly and uncritically to the coming of the 'new industrial state', as Galbraith was to term it in his later book of that name. Publications like *Fortune* in America and the *Economist* and the *Financial Times* were, given the need to attract revenues, well placed to observe the changing nature of corporate capitalism. Galbraith, for instance, makes the observation in his memoirs that he owed a lot to his experience as a journalist on *Fortune* for his own personal intellectual development:

> The early *Fortune*, more than any other journal, saw the modern large corporation as a primary economic and social force. My years there as

a writer and editor provided a diversity and intimacy of exposure to its structure, operating goals and economic and social and political influence that could not have been had in any other way. From those years came a lasting immunity to the mythology of the neoclassical textbook economics. To them I owe in part the notion of the technostructure as the decisive managerial and innovative instrument of the large enterprise and much else that became part of my Harvard teaching and of *The New Industrial State*.[28]

Although in the 1950s and 1960s, under the editorship of John Davenport, *Fortune* was to become an exponent of *laissez-faire* ideas, it was, for the most part, uncritical of the kind of corporate capitalism from which it derived handsome advertising income. As John Kobler argues:

> *Fortune*'s politico-economic policies during Luce's later years ranged a narrow spectrum centering on moderate conservatism. There were no iconoclasts among its editors . . . The magazine could still sting, but the full force of its strike was usually reserved for those who had let the System down. With the System itself, however, *Fortune* no longer quarrelled. It mirrored rather than goaded business. It was like a court painter. Junior executives on the way up found it an invaluable textbook. 'In the old days', an industrial public relations veteran remarked, 'you prayed that *Fortune* wouldn't write about your client. Now you pray it will.'[29]

The most significant aspect of this accommodation of the financial press to the postwar situation was the extent to which financial coverage (that is, coverage of the workings of the financial markets and the stock exchange) evolved little beyond what it had been in the 1930s. In America there was a tendency for financial coverage to be less analytical and not as well researched as that given to the 'economic' issues like unemployment, devaluation and fiscal policy. As Sobel notes:

> There was no revival of interest in finance during or after the World War II. Most newspapers did not have financial reporters on their staffs, and relied upon the wire services for whatever news came out of lower Manhattan. The financial pages of the larger big-city newspapers became known as a dead end, and was avoided by ambitious journalists, who yearned for foreign assignments and political reportage.[30]

In Britain, too, there was also a divorce between financial comment and advice, and the discussion of macroeconomic affairs, politics and events. Newspaper coverage of financial matters was preoccupied with catering to the needs of a growing number of investors rather than reporting critically and analytically on how the financial system functioned and malfunctioned. Government and the unions were fair game, but the City pages were curiously quiet about analysing the workings of the stock exchange and uncovering scandals and fraud. As Kenneth Fleet recounts, when he was appointed City editor of the *Sunday Telegraph* the proprietor (Mr Michael Berry, later Lord Hartwell) told him: 'Your job is to make our readers richer'.[31] As in America, then, despite the increased space devoted to financial reports which took place in the late 1950s and early 1960s, it remained the case that until the 1970s financial journalism still addressed itself to the *investing public* – although it was admittedly a wider group than it had been before the war. Furthermore, the misdoings of the system in which readers had invested their money was as badly covered as ever. Blue-collar (trade union) behaviour was duly condemned and reported but, as Simon Jenkins notes of the *Financial Times*, the paper declined to probe too deeply into white-collar crimes and failings and

> averted its gaze from investigative journalism, not least when events in its own backyard might have merited it. The Newton 'puritanism' left other newspapers to delve into the rackets of the 1970s property boom, the secondary bank scandals and . . . City insider-dealing fraud.[32]

The poor coverage of corporate crime by the press was not unique to the *Financial Times* or the British press. A number of studies of the coverage of white-collar crime in America have revealed that papers were averse to employing the language of criminality to describe the actions of business men and corporations. Sandra Evans and Richard Lundman, for instance, concluded in 1983 that, given the evidence, it was accurate to assert that 'newspapers protect corporate reputations by failing to provide frequent, prominent, and criminally orientated coverage of common corporate crimes'.[33]

This ideological or class *bias* in the economic coverage of the press and a sensitivity to the subtle pressures of advertising revenues affected, as Hirsch and Gordon maintain, the range of economic ideas, the quality of critical reporting and furthermore reinforced the division of economic news from financial and business coverage. It was a division between, on the one hand, a predominantly macroeconomic perspective which over-emphasized current political obsessions, and on the other, the overwhelmingly market-orientated financial reporting which was aimed at making money for their readers and which steered clear of controversy and, until comparatively recently, avoided the need for hard investigative reporting or exposition and critical analysis of financial and equity markets.

The ultimate consequence of this division between the coverage of issues like fiscal policy, growth, unemployment, inflation, the balance of payments and so on, on one side, and monetary policy, the financial markets, stock markets, options trading, scandal and so on, on the other, was that the media, by structuring news in a manner which *complemented* the political macro-mania, rather than challenging it, very effectively reinforced the mystique surrounding the City and Wall Street. It is significant that this disjointed portrayal of the 'economy' in the press fitted in rather nicely with the somewhat distorted story of Keynesian theory being advanced at the political level. As Will Hutton observes:

> By bastardising Keynes into the simple advocacy of high government spending, both the right and the left secured important objectives . . . It suited neither to interpret Keynesianism as it actually was: a demand for the state to change the behaviour of financiers and businessmen by prosecuting an active fiscal policy in tandem with an assult on the portfolio preferences of the financial institutions . . . For the Right the City was sacrosanct; for the Left the City was a sanctum that could only be stormed at the risk of colossal loss of confidence.[34]

The division of 'financial' news and 'economic' news – the one concerned with tips and the other with the total economy – only served to affirm the demarcations which, as Hutton says, had been made at a political level. Furthermore, this tendency of the financial media to concentrate on macroeconomic news and fiscal policy underlined the notion that economic problems were rooted in the failure of government policy to correct or compensate for the deficiencies of the market.

The pre-occupation with the macroeconomy and the evaluation of governmental economic performance in largely managerialist terms led to the demand for a new type of economic journalist. As

Peter Jay explained when he was (the first) 'economics editor' of *The Times*, the job called for someone:

> who would specialise by subject rather than by source of information or type of article. This sort of person would, it was hoped, bring some specialist knowledge with him to the reporting, interpreting and comment on an unbroken chain of unconnected events. . .[35]

In America there were fewer examples of this new type of journalist–Leonard Silk in *Business Week* and the *New York Times* is perhaps the only one who readily comes to mind–for the fact is, as Jay points out, that in the American media there are hard and fast divisions between leader writers, feature writers and columnists which, for historical reasons, do not exist in Britain. Another factor which made for the growth of a kind of school of political economy in British journalism was that the British economy was fundamentally more politicized than in America. At the same time, the sense of relative economic decline which gripped Britain in the 1960s was also a more fruitful soil for the growth of a reforming and campaigning style of journalism. Like Galbraith's time at *Fortune*, the economic journalists of the 1950s and 1960s were in the best possible position from which to survey British economic problems and contemplate their possible solutions, and from which to advance a type of political economy that was, for the most part, ignored by academic economists and political scientists.

Thus it was that one of the most remarkable features of economic opinion in Britain during the 1950s and 1960s was the emergence of a number of economic journalists who were responsible for articulating an influential brand of 'Keynesian' economics. In America – as we shall discuss in the next chapter – academic economists were themselves more ready to popularize their ideas and, in the tradition of Keynes, take an active part in public debate. It is noticeable, however, that Keynes's enthusiasm for 'throwing ideas to the wind' and self-publicity was not to be taken up by his fellow countrymen: few British economists engaged in the kind of regular journalism associated with the names of Samuelson, Friedman and Galbraith. There were a few British economists who were more closely involved than the rest: notably Frank Paish's close association with the *Statist*: Paish's father, Sir George Paish, had been a member of the editorial board of the journal until 1916. Another economist with press connections was

Lionel Robbins of the London School of Economics who was appointed (in 1961) Chairman of the *Financial Times* (1961–70) and Director and Deputy Chairman of the *Economist* (1960–73). Robbins was no newcomer to economic journalism. In his youth he had written leaders for the *Outlook* and during the interwar years he was good friends with Oscar Hobson, Walter Layton and Geoffrey Crowther, and many of the following generation of financial journalists were drawn from the LSE including Waldo Forge, Roland Bird, W. T. C. King and Manning Dacey. He also had a great historical perspective on the profession, dating from his definitive study *Robert Torrens and the Evolution of Classical Economics*, the book by which he wished to be judged as a scholar. As Chairman of the *Financial Times* Robbins had great respect for editorial independence and resisted any temptation to interfere with the paper's essentially Keynesian line on economic policy. In his memoirs Robbins makes it clear, however, that his own opinions – he had been a founding member of the Mont Pelerin Society – were somewhat removed from the ruling editorial position:

> The historian of the future, in the remote possibility of his being interested in the detail of thought about economic and financial policy, would be very ill advised to seek it in the running commentary of the leading articles in the *Financial Times* or in the choice of features of special interest.[36]

There were many economists given to making forays into public controversy, like Sir Roy Harrod, Thomas Balogh, John Jewkes and Alec Cairncross, to name but a few, but such contributions were largely sporadic and could not be said to have constituted a sustained dialogue on the lines of Samuelson and Friedman in the US. Perhaps it was because no one asked them!

At the root of this failure of a sustained debate on economic policy and options informed by academic economists to develop was the fact that, as Hutchison observed:

> After 1960 in Britain a whole 'grand design' for economic policy was canvassed . . . which was based upon a systematic refusal or rejection of conflicts or incompatibilities among objectives; or on the notion that insofar as such conflicts or incompatibilities had previously existed, they could comparatively speedily be removed by institutional change.[37]

This preoccupation with institutional reform had many consequences. However, from the standpoint of this present study, what was most significant was that the institutional thrust of policy discussions created an opportunity for non-academic commentators to influence the policy agenda in that area which had been so neglected by professional economists: the relationship between economics and politics. Given the manner in which so much of the discussion about growth, trade and inflation and so on, was informed by essentially political values and judgements the interface between politics and economics was precisely the area where – as the IEA was aware – ideas had to be explored. And yet it was this very domain of 'political economics' which was so neglected by academic economists ever in pursuit of greater mathematical exactitude and professional status. In the United States, on the other hand, this territory was not so abandoned. Inevitably, therefore, the source of British political economy in the 1960s sprung from without academia, namely, the *Financial Times* and the *Economist*. Newton at the *Financial Times* was eager to avoid having the paper come down on one side or the other and gave his journalists considerable latitude in terms of freedom to explore ideas. The result was a curious mix of editorial restraint and free-ranging pieces of political economy by some of the most gifted economic journalists of the day: most notably Andrew Shonfield, Michael Shanks and Samuel Brittan, as well as others like Nigel Lawson who went on to other things, including City editor of the *Sunday Telegraph* editor of the *Spectator* and Chancellor of the Exchequer. The Newton generation had a number of characteristics: a scholarly grasp of economics; an interest in ideas; and a desire to influence policy. They wrote with a different constituency in mind and moved in different circles to that of the conventional financial journalist. Indeed, they hardly considered themselves 'journalists' at all!

Although during the late 1950s financial journalism had moved on to the front page, in many respects it was still in the old City ghetto. The stories about Charles Clore and Arnold Weinstock and other entrepreneurs of the 1960s, and the growth of interest in the stock market and unit trusts undoubtedly led to a more lively, if not yet more critical, City coverage, but in essence it was still geared to share-tipping. City editors took time to cultivate business men, whereas the new economic journalists were far more interested in high table than lunch at the Savoy: they were far more interested in ideas than the stock exchange index and financial gossip. They were also far more critical of the role of the financial system itself than were their colleagues on the City desk and came to regard themselves less as reporters than observers of the economics scene – a role which necessarily included the world of ideas as well as practice. Indicative of this aspiration to stand 'twixt the realms of theory and practice was the fact that they were given to writing books: Andrew Shonfield's *Modern Capitalism* and Sam Brittan's *Steering the Economy* being the two foremost examples of a kind of politically informed economic writing which had, for all intents and purposes, died out in the nineteenth century.

There were a number of reasons why the time was ripe for the emergence of a new kind of economic commentary distinct from the interests of the financial pages. In the first place, particularly during the Macmillan–Wilson years, government and civil servants became more important. There was much discussion about the need for institutional reforms and the desirability of learning from the experiments in economic planning which had taken place in other European countries. Secondly, there was now an audience for economic commentary and explanation which had simply not existed before the war. As the President of the Royal Economics Society observed in 1974, in just a decade or so:

> The number of economists employed by universities has probably trebled; the number teaching the subject in schools has risen faster; those employed by business have multiplied sixfold or more; the number of economists employed by the government has increased . . . some ten to twenty-fold. . .[38]

Furthermore, the emergence of economic commentators and writers coincided with what Hutchison terms the 'economics miracle'; namely, the tremendous increase in the number of graduate economists practising the subject *outside* higher education, as in the booming field of business and management education, all eager for news and analysis which went beyond the traditional financial pages and dealt with those economic problems which beset Britain in the 1960s. Significantly, the consensus which surrounded these problems, like low growth, inflation and trade, were also those areas where economic theory had little to say in comparison with the institutionalist opinion accepted by the political mainstream. Journalists were thus in a powerful position from which to advance the argument that British economic problems stemed from the failure of the nation's institutional structures. To every problem there was an appropriate institutional solution; inflation: incomes boards; trade: the EEC; growth: planning authorities. Thus, as Hagen and White argue:

> Choice among the various economic goals was not contemplated. Rather, new institutions were sought by which the inconsistencies among the goals could be eliminated so that all might be attained.[39]

The first of the new generation of postwar economic journalists to advance the institutionalist view was Andrew Shonfield who was appointed by Gordon Newton to the staff of the *Financial Times* in 1947. He remained with the paper until 1957 and later served as the economics editor of the *Observer* until 1961. At Oxford he was a left winger, and after the war, during which he served as a gunner and intelligence officer, he continued to be close to a number of leading members of the Labour Party like Denis Healey, Anthony Crosland and Shirley Williams. He also wrote for a while on *Tribune*, a Labour party weekly paper. His articles in the *Financial Times* and the *Observer* and his frequent appearances on television and radio established him as one of the best-known economic commentators in Britain during the 1950s and 1960s, whilst his *Modern Capitalism: the changing balance of public and private power*, published in 1965, also gave him a wider academic reputation. He was, in many senses, the British counterpart of Galbraith in that the *Financial Times* provided him with the opportunity to observe at close hand the emerging capitalist order in Europe, as *Fortune* had done for Galbraith in the US: *Modern Capitalism* was – and remains – one of the seminal accounts of the development of the Western political–economic system. What made him a unique figure on the British scene was that, as with Galbraith, his journalism and other writings focused on, as he put it, 'politics, looked at from an economic viewpoint', and *vice versa*, economics with an emphasis on the political context of policy-making. At the *Financial Times* he was, from 1949, the foreign editor, and this experience, as well as that of his wartime career, gave his work an international and distinctively European perspective. He was someone who, above all else, was interested in the trade in ideas and in what he termed the 'international society' rather than national politics. Shonfield tended to write in more of a comparative mode rather than simply looking at British economic problems and political institutions from a purely national viewpoint. With the freedom to develop his ideas under Gordon Newton, Shonfield articulated an influential brand of political economy which made a vital contribution to the prevailing economic discourse. He was therefore less a journalist than a genuinely political economist whose articles helped to define and give coherence to the political agenda, and was a major intellectual influence on the general economic line taken by the *Financial Times*. Shonfield gave up daily journalism in 1957 in order to write a book on the British economy which allowed him to develop more fully the ideas and arguments which he had begun to express in the *Financial Times*. The result of this sabbatical (*British Economic Policy Since the War*) was an attempt to place Britain's problems in the context of the kind of work being conducted by 'forward looking intellectuals on the other side of the channel' and well reflected the fact that Shonfield was far more attuned to the European intellectual scene than he was to British economic opinion. *British Economic Policy* advocated (in terms which later on in the 1960s were to become more widely held) the view that Britain had much to learn from those countries, like France, that had achieved higher economic growth through more positive state intervention and planning. Shonfield saw little alternative to the policy of adopting a more interventionist economic strategy and a highly active role for the state. As he comments in the conclusion to the book:

> It goes without saying that a government which embarked on [a] plan of expansion would have to be prepared to intervene directly, by orders, by threats, by incentives and by exhortation...[40]

Shonfield's 'Penguin Special' soon marked him out, in the eyes of the newly formed Institute of Economic Affairs, as the leading purveyor of 'fashionable fallacies' and 'lofty macroeconomic generalisations'[41]. In 1958 he became the economics editor of one the oldest British newspapers, the Sunday *Observer*. Being a weekly paper, it gave Shonfield the time and space to write more expansively than was possible in a daily paper. The *Observer* also allowed him to reach a more diverse readership than the *Financial*

Times, whilst his broadcasting career, which also developed in this period, also meant that his arguments about planning and the case for British entry into the Common Market reached a larger audience than could have been reached purely through books and the printed word.

The theme which dominated Shonfield's journalism and broadcasting, and which was developed at greater length in his books, was the conditions for economic growth. He was in advance of the opinion which held that Britain's growth rate was poor relative to her industrial competitors because of an institutional malaise. The problem was, he believed, that of the inability of the financial markets and of successive governments to invest in Britain. The solution, he suggested, was to mobilize 'political will and skill', and improve the effectiveness of the institutional apparatus which guided British economic life. At a time when British newspapers were obsessed with publishing growth rate tables Shonfield was a great enthusiast for those governmental techniques which had proved successful in other countries: French planning and its civil service; Italian public enterprise; Swedish industrial relations. In his articles and leaders in the *Financial Times* Shonfield was a formidable spokesman for updating British economic institutions and European unity, and together with William Rees-Mogg made the *Financial Times* the sounding board for debating Britain's economic future. Indeed, in this regard, as Trevor Smith notes in his definitive study of the theory and practice of British planning, Shonfield played an important role in 'consolidating opinion in favour of persevering with the modernisation of Britain generally and in the field of government intervention in particular'.[42]

Shonfield's writing, especially his *Modern Capitalism*, gave clear expression to the great body of opinion which emerged in the early 1960s in favour of economic planning and of improving the techniques and efficiency of government. For Shonfield the future depended on how well we used expertise and how effectively we organized 'positive government'. Given the scale of the changes which confronted Britain and other capitalist societies there was, he believed, no option but to harness technocratic and administrative power to manage the economy so that all could benefit. As far as Shonfield was concerned, the real question was how to make such a process accountable. In raising these issues and in arguing for a radical readjustment of British attitudes and institutions,

Shonfield must be accounted one of the most important figures in postwar British economic journalism as well as someone who occupies a major place in the history of British postwar social thought. In common with Wilson and Bagehot, he saw his journalism as part of a process of educating and moulding opinion, rather than as simply reportage. Indeed, in many ways he was far more of a teacher or a preacher than a newspaper man: he moved into the academic arena in the 1960s although he continued to write for the press. As William Clark put it: 'Andrew Shonfield saw that as government involvement in the economy increased it was essential that there should be an economically literate electorate, otherwise the people would get the government they deserved'.[43]

By 1961 he began to feel that his attempt to arrive at a more comprehensive understanding of the postwar economic order required more time than was available as a journalist and he left full-time journalism to become director of studies at the Royal Institute of International Affairs: he later became its director in 1977. He was also appointed chairman of the Social Science Research Council where he remained from 1961 to 1968, and was thus involved in the funding of research at a crucial time in the expansion of the social sciences in the UK. In 1978 he was knighted and became professor of economics at the European University in Florence. His old paper, the *Financial Times*, gave a fulsome and generous obituary on his death in 1981:

> In his lectures at Cambridge in the late 1940s Dennis Robertson compared Keynes to a searchlight that penetrated the darkness around us, lighting up the areas that nobody had hitherto understood. While he made no similar contribution to economic theory, Sir Andrew Shonfield had this quality of a searchlight, illuminating some of those rugged tracts of contemporary economics and politics. . .[44]

The comparison with Keynes is not so very inappropriate since it was Shonfield who, more than of any other single British commentator, with the exception, perhaps, of his friend Anthony Crosland, was responsible for popularizing a variety of Keynesian political economy which held sway during the greater part of two decades. Sadly, he was not to live long enough to reinterpret the arguments of *Modern Capitalism* in the light of changing economic circumstances of the 1970s and 1980s. He died before he could complete *Modern Capitalism (2): The Use of Public Power*.[45] Even so, there can be little doubt that Shonfield's influence on the style and intellectual seriousness of British economic journalism will be an enduring testament.

Another graduate of Gordon Newton's *Financial Times* was Michael Shanks, a labour and industrial correspondent who joined the paper from the *Economist* in 1953. He later moved on to the *Sunday Times* and *The Times*. Unlike Shonfield, Shanks moved into a more political arena by entering the Labour government as industrial policy director in the ill-fated ministry for economic planning, the Department for Economic Affairs (DEA). He later became the economic adviser to Leyland Motor Holdings and played a major role in the merger which led to the setting up of the also ill-fated British Leyland Motor Corporation and was until 1971 its Director of Marketing and Services and Economic Planning. He went on to head British Oxygen and the Directorate-General for Social Affairs in the European Commission. In 1961, whilst the industrial editor on the *Financial Times*, he wrote a 'Penquin Special' which was, as Trevor Smith notes, 'widely acclaimed and ... contributed significantly to shaping the intellectual climate of Britain'.[46] *The Stagnant Society: a warning* developed more fully the arguments that he had been putting forward in articles and leaders over the previous few years. The problem which, Shanks believed, needed to be solved was that of mobilizing support for a fundamental shake-up of the attitudes and institutions which had held Britain back. Shanks campaigned for reforms in the trade union system and the abandonment of an out-of-date class system, membership of the European Economic Community and the adoption of those techniques and reforms which had proved so efficacious in other countries. Without such changes Britain was doomed to stagnate, and would fail to keep up with the growth rates of other countries. It was not, therefore, an economic problem – or even a 'political' problem – which faced Britain so much as something fundamentally organizational in character:

> We know theoretically how to achieve a continuously expanding society. What we have not been able to do so far is persuade people at large to accept the necessary techniques. The problem is not one of economic management but one of social engineering.[47]

What was significant about the kind of arguments of economic journalists like Shonfield and Shanks was that they represented British economic decline as being located in the failure of organization or planning. Successful modern capitalism required a form of planning which would complement, rather than destroy, capitalism: knowledge was the key. The problem which confronted contemporary western economies was that of arriving at an administrative structure – via the state in France, or the Bundesbank in Germany – which could direct and co-ordinate the planning activities of the public and private sectors and promote more appropriate labour market arrangements. This enthusiasm for the *institutional* dimension of economic policy was shared by other prominent journalists, most notably Norman Macrae in the *Economist* and Samuel Brittan in the *Financial Times*. Macrae was, along with Barbara Ward, an exception to the long-established principle of anonymity in the *Economist*. His *Sunshades in October*, published in 1963, was a typically lively statement of some of the criticisms he had voiced about British economic failure in his weekly articles and longer surveys. Barbara Ward went on to write many books on development and international affairs and became Schweizer Professor of International Economic Development at Columbia (1968–73).

Samuel Brittan, who like Shonfield and Shanks, also started his career on the *Financial Times*, succeeded Shonfield as economics editor of the *Observer* (1961–4) and along with Shanks he joined the DEA in 1964. He left the Department in 1966 and rejoined the *Financial Times*. Shanks and Brittan emerged from Whitehall as much wiser men. In their columns prior to entering government they had been hopeful about the possibility and desirability of reforming the policy-making structures and attitudes of government. They were considerably less sanguine after their experience of the DEA and the National Plan. Nevertheless, Shanks remained convinced that, though the Plan was a 'wasted exercise', the real issue that remained was still not 'whether' to plan, but 'how'. What was required, he argued in 1977, was political leadership, 'coherent thought' and a preparedness to tackle the Treasury and develop a tripartite approach:

We have to recognise that there is no new panacea waiting to be applied, no magic formula which will resolve all our problems, no new hitherto unthought-of path to be taken. The most promising solution to our difficulties is through starting to practise what we have been preaching. We should plan.[48]

Sam Brittan, whose view was that the failure of the Plan had effectively eliminated planning from the British political agenda for good, was not of the same mind as Shanks, and was thus open to new ideas which came from America this time and not from Europe. He reflected that the

real policy error in 1964 was in the institutional sphere. I believed that the setting up of the N.E.D.C 'indicative planning' machinery, and the nominal endorsement of the 4 percent growth target could have exercised valuable back door pressures on official policy. On the contrary, the whole 'planning' movement was a bad tactical mistake which actively delayed the basic reappraisal of the exchange rate and other priorities desired by its adherents. The moral I would emphasise is that it is better for critics and reformers to argue for their beliefs directly and avoid getting caught up in fashionable causes of doubtful validity.[49]

Nevertheless, as we discuss in Chapter 6, Mr Brittan could resist everything except the temptation of getting caught up in fashionable causes, and his name was subsequently to be for ever associated with the importation of 'monetarism' into British politics in the 1970s.

In the 1960s, however, he was, like Shonfield and Shanks, a self-confessed 'enthusiast for increasing the growth rate by sustained and policy-inspired growth of demand'. But by the late 1960s, unlike his colleagues, he began to change his mind in two particular respects: the validity of the institutionalist argument and the wisdom of seeking to sustain 'full employment' at any cost, and came to grasp:

the impossibility of spending ourselves into the target levels of unemployment by demand management of any kind and the likelihood that the attempt to do so would set off ever-increasing inflation.[50]

Over the following decades Brittan was, as Kynaston's history of the *Financial Times* records, to 'establish himself as the pre-eminent economic journalist of his generation'.[51] His articles in the *Financial Times*, as well as numerous books and monographs and contributions to academic journals from the late 1960s on, show that he was already taking on board the kind of ideas being advanced by Milton Friedman and others well in advance of political, administrative or academic opinion in Britain. He was, therefore, as he comments, fully 'immunised' against the interventionist surge under Mr Heath and Mr Wilson in the 1970s.

Given the climate of the times, however, what Brittan describes as the chimera of 'supposing that any institutional device can be an adequate substitute for wise policy decisions' was politically attractive because of its pragmatic, non-ideological quality. For journalists interested in being involved in shaping opinion and influencing policy, the argument that Britain should get its administrative and political house in order was a naturally seductive and very potent proposition. Yet as Barry Gordon argues with respect to the impact of Ricardian ideas in the nineteenth century, economic journalists in the 1960s did not so much determine issues as offer to their readers a 'rational basis for a voice in economic policy'.[52] It was their writings which expressed the basic tenets of British economic consensus in the 1960s: the need for growth to match our European neighbours; membership of the Community: the belief in planning and a (very Keynesian) faith in expertise; and the notion that the key to change was the institutional reform in British central government. As Fred Hirsch once put it: 'Stupidity, not cupidity, was the besetting sin of those at the helm: to govern, it was not necessary to choose, only to think, to count and to manage'.[53] It was economic journalists who articulated this attitude more eloquently, and perhaps more importantly, more *regularly* than any other group. That such ideas were being voiced in the leading organs of the financial press could only have served to enhance its political acceptability. This is not to lessen the importance of the other sources of the managed-economy paradigm – planners in the Conservative party, Crosland, the Federation of British Industry, Political and Economic Planning, and so on. However, what was most significant about the contribution of economic journalists was that they had a capacity to aggregate and disseminate ideas by applying them to events: they caught the mood. The economic question, as they represented it to their readers, was fundamentally enmeshed with the deficiencies of the machinery and attitudes existing in government and society at large.

Whereas the macroeconomics advanced by academics was, to a

large extent, inherent in Keynesian theory, the undeniable institutional, if not the explicitly technocratic, emphasis of British economic policy from the 1950s to the early 1970s was an idea which found its principal exponents outside academia. Indeed, the manner in which this Keynesian-derived notion of economic management attained such pre-eminence is an example *par excellence* of the fact that, as David Henderson observed in the 1985 Reith lectures, economists did not succeed in the postwar period in reducing the influence of the non-professional as completely as other scientists did in their subject areas.[54] The reason why economic journalists had such an impact on the making of the 'Keynesian era' was that they, more than any others, defined the essential political or institutional component to the Keynesian model of economic management: hence, it will be to Shonfield and Shanks that historians of the period will turn to locate the fullest embodiment of the prevailing economic opinion of the 'swinging sixties'. Given Keynes's own extensive journalism, it was fitting that this issue of the politics of his economic ideas should have been most fully developed by journalists rather than 'academic scribblers'. It is to these other children of the revolution to whom we now turn.

NOTES

1. Samuelson argues, for example:

   is it really true? Keynes did not specify what academic scribblers he had in mind, and I am not sure how easy it would have been for him to do so . . . The leaders of this world may seem to be led around through the nose by their economic advisers. But who is pulling and who is pushing . . . ? The prince often gets what he wants to hear ('Economists and the History of Ideas', *American Economic Review*, vol. 52, (1962) p. 18).

   Yet, as Jim Tomlinson maintains, when it comes to explaining how governments came to accept the idea of full employment, economists tend to:

   return to the very rationalism they had otherwise criticised. Full employment was, they argue, taken on board by governments because of the influence of Keynesian theory. In other words neither the neo-classical nor the Marxist approach accepts the adequacy of Keynesian ideas, but both agree with Keynes on how policy develops ('Where do Economic Objectives Come From? The case of full employment', *Economy and Society*, vol. 12, no. 1 (1983) p. 62).

2. J. M. Keynes *The General Theory of Employment, Interest and Money*, (Macmillan, Cambridge, 1973), pp. 32–3.
3. F. Hirsch, *Social Limits to Growth* (Routledge and Kegan Paul, London, 1977) p. 27.
4. H. Hazlitt, *The Failure of the New Economics: an analysis of Keynesian fallacies* (Van Nostrand, New York, 1960) p. 1. See also H. Hazlitt (ed.), *The Critics of Keynesian Economics* (Van Nostrand, New York, 1959). Hazlitt had worked on the *Wall Street Journal* (1914–16), *New York Post* (1916–18) financial editor of the *New York Evening Mail* (1921–3), became business columnist on *Newsweek* (1946–66). His articles were nationally syndicated, 1966–9. *The Failure of the New Economics* was reprinted in 1973.
5. *New Republic*, 29 April 1936.
6. *New York Times*, 16 May 1965.
7. See David Hubback, *No Ordinary Press Baron: a life of Walter Layton* (Weidenfeld and Nicolson, London, 1985) pp. 93–4.
8. *The Economist*, 7 April 1956, p. 22.
9. Ibid. 17 April 1965.
10. See N. Davenport, *Memoirs of a City Radical* (Weidenfeld and Nicolson, London, 1974). p. 202.
11. Lloyd Wendt, *The Wall Street Journal* (Rand McNally, New York, 1982) p. 361.
12. Ibid., p. 420.
13. A. M. Schlesinger, *The Coming of the New Deal* (Heinemann, London 1960) pp. 544–6. See also Raymond Clapper, 'Why Reporters like Roosevelt', *Review of Reviews*, June 1934.
14. *The Economist*, 26 December 1987.
15. Peter Hennesey, *What the Papers Never Said* (Portcullis Press, Politics Association, London, 1985) pp. 96–7.
16. Hedley Donovan, *Roosevelt to Reagan: a reporter's encounters with nine presidents* (Harper and Row, New York, 1987) p. 60.
17. K. Fleet, *The Influence of the Financial Press* (Annual Livery Lecture, London, 1983).
18. Cited in David Kynaston, *The Financial Times: a centenary history* (Viking, London, 1988) p. 139.
19. *Financial Times*, 1 October 1945.
20. *Wall Street Journal*, 2 January 1951.
21. *Time*, 31 December, 1965.
22. 'What economists know', in P. A. Samuelson, *Collected Scientific Papers* (MIT Press, Cambridge, Mass., 1972) vol. 2, p. 1619.
23. *Financial Times*, 12 November 1969.
24. Kenneth Krammer, *Economic Commentary: reflections and critiques from the pages of Business Week* (Business Week, New York, 1966).
25. Fred Hirsch and David Gordon, *Newspaper Money: Fleet Street and the search for the affluent reader* (Hutchinson, London, 1975).
26. In A. Seldon (ed.) *The Emerging Consensus: essays on the interplay between ideas and circumstances in the first 25 years of the IEA* (IEA, London, 1981) p. 14.
27. J. K. Galbraith, *The Affluent Society* (Houghton Mifflin, Boston, 1958) p. xii.
28. J. K. Galbraith. *A Life in Our Times: memoirs* (Houghton Mifflin, Boston, 1981) p. 268.
29. John Kobler, *Luce, his Time, Life and Fortune* (Macdonald, London, 1968) pp. 87–8.
30. R. Sobel. *Inside Wall Street: continuity and change in the financial district* (Norton, New York, 1977) pp. 250–1.

31. Fleet, op.cit.
32. *Sunday Times*, 21 February 1988.
33. Sandra S. Evans and Richard J. Lundman, 'Newspaper Coverage of Corporate Crime', in M. David Ermann and Richard J. Lundman (eds), *Corporate and Governmental Deviance: problems of organisational behaviour in contemporary Society* (Oxford University Press, New York, 1987). See also A. Dershowitz, 'Newspaper Publicity and the Electrical Conspiracy', *Yale Law Journal*, vol. 71 (1961) and for a more historical perspective see E. H. Sutherland, *White-Collar Crime* (Holt, Rinehart and Winston, New York, 1949).
34. Will Hutton, *The Revolution that Never Was: an assessment of Keynesian economics* (Longman, London, 1986) p. 118.
35. The *Listener*, 24 August 1972.
36. Lord Robbins, *Autobiography of an Economist* (Macmillan, St Martins Press, London, 1971) pp. 290–1.
37. T. W. Hutchison, *Economics and Economic Policy in Britain, 1946–1966: some aspects of their interrelations* (Allen and Unwin, London, 1968) p. 265.
38. Cited in ibid., p. 66.
39. Cited in ibid., p. 265.
40. Andrew Shonfield, *British Economic Policy since the War* (Penguin, Harmondsworth, 1958) p. 278.
41. R. Harris and A. Seldon, *Not Just from Benevolence* Institute of Economic Affairs, London 1977. pp. 60–1.
42. Trevor Smith, *The Politics of the Corporate Economy* (Martin Robertson, Oxford, 1979) p. 144.
43. In *The Observer*, 25 January 1981.
44. *Financial Times*, 24 January 1981.
45. The book was edited for publication by his wife, Suzanna.
46. Smith, op. cit., p. 85.
47. M. Shanks, *The Stagnant Society* (Penguin, Harmondsworth, 1961) p. 45.
48. M. Shanks, *Planning and Politics: the British Experience, 1960–76* (Political and Economic Planning, and Allen and Unwin, London, 1977) p. 106.
49. Samuel Brittan, *Steering the Economy: the role of the Treasury* (Penguin, Harmondsworth, 1970) pp. 15–16.
50. Samuel Brittan, *The Economic Consequences of Democracy* (Temple Smith, London, 1977) p. xii.
51. Knyaston, op. cit., p. 329.
52. Barry Gordon, *Political Economy in Parliament, 1819–1832* (Macmillan, London, 1976) p. 17.
53. Hirsch, op. cit., *The Social Limits to Growth*, p. 127.
54. David Henderson, *Innocence and Design: the influence of economic ideas on policy* (Basil Blackwell, Oxford, 1986).

4. Three economists and the Fourth Estate

The American economic journalism scene in the 1950s and 1960s was somewhat different to that in Britain due to one factor as much as any other: geography. New York was the centre of financial reporting – Wall Street news – whereas Washington, especially after the New Deal and the war, was where national economic policy was made. This meant that the Washington beat came to be regarded as essentially a job for *political* reporters, while economic or financial expertise was centred in New York. Although the divisions between the City desk and economic commentary were present in London, financial journalism, given the dominant role of the capital in the political and economic life of the nation, expanded more naturally to take account of the interplay between business and government. As the *Sunday Times* observed in 1961:

> In the old days City editors wrote about the City and about almost nothing else. Now City journalism has come to take the whole of finance, economics, and industry for its subject. The modern City journalist is just as likely to be found visiting a steel works in South Wales as a banker's parlour in Lombard Street. He is as likely to attend a press conference at the Treasury as at the bank of England.[1]

The geographical scale of the country, combined with the greater degree of political centralization and intervention in the economy, meant that British journalists were *physically* closer to both the economic policy-making process and the financial quarter than were their American colleagues. They had the kind of access to politicians, civil servants and business men which meant that it was possible for them to be more fully engaged with both the economic and business community as well as with the academic world than was possible for journalists based in Washington or New York. Brittan and Shanks, for example, went into the DEA; Shonfield

113

headed the Royal Institute for International Affairs and the
Social Science Research Council and was a professor of economics
in Florence; Peter Jay had been a Treasury civil servant, he
married the daughter of a leading Labour politician and was the
son of another. It is also important to bear in mind that the US and
British financial press confronted contrasting economic scenarios,
the most obvious difference being that of the relative positions of
their respective economies in the world. The campaigning zeal
which informed British economic journalism was very much the
by-product of a sense of national economic stagnation and relative
decline and the failure of 'stop–go' economic management. Also,
given the large measure of political consensus surrounding 'Keynesian' policy techniques in the 1950s and 1960s, the aspects of
economic policy which were open to controversy were, as we have
seen, inevitably those associated with reforming the *institutional
apparatus* of British economic management. Journalists like
Shonfield were thus in a key vantage point from which to observe
and ultimately influence prevailing opinion and mood. It was not
so surprising, therefore, that in Britain it was journalists, more
than academic economists, who were responsible for infusing
contemporary opinion and sentiments with a coherence that they
might otherwise have lacked. Whether it was because America
was now the centre of the economics profession or because of the
reticence or narrowness of British economists, there were no real
equivalents of intellectual celebrities such as Samuelson, Galbraith
and Friedman in Britain. Keynes had thought – or hoped – that in
the future economists would be rather like dentists. The truth was
that, as Keynes's own career indicated, the destiny which awaited
homo economicus was that of evolving into a new species of media
personality: the professor as popular expert and prophet. This
brought with it a good deal of ambivalence about the relationship
between economics and journalism which dates back to before the
days of Henry George. When, for example, Barbara Ward was
appointed to the Schweitzer Chair at Columbia, academics were
reported to be somewhat worried by the fact that, although a
'distinguished journalist', she was not really an academic doing
original work.[2] As Alex Rubner comments:

.   the Columbia professors did not catch her writing in salacious *Playboy*,
    nor was she proved to have earned her living by penning articles in

plebian tabloids. Implicitly, however, she was found guilty ... of having been a contributor to journals like *The London Economist*, most readers of which do not have a Ph.D. The Columbia humbug epitomises their split personalities: they wish to be honored as cloistered scientists whilst simultaneously they solicit assignments from mass circulation dailies.[3]

Economists themselves, whilst regarding journalists with some suspicion, were not slow in adapting their ideas so that they could be understood by the layman. As Robert Solow suggests, simplification and rhetoric proved a great temptation when:

> The reporter for *Time* or *CBS News* will listen to a complicated paragraph which specifies assumptions with care and admits the statistical evidence has some weaknesses, and will reduce it to one unqualified, wrong sentence. That being so, there is a powerful temptation for the economist to skip the complicated paragraph and replace it with one declarative sentence. It may not do justice to the issue, but at least it will be one's own.[4]

The long tradition of economic journalism in Britain meant that, in some ways, the relationship of economics to the press was less strained. British economic journalists – like Barbara Ward – were somewhat more respected by the academic community. The leading practitioners in Britain were, as Robbins noted, regarded as fully capable of 'holding their own with professional economists from the universities'.[5] They were also seen to have the advantage of being more in touch with practical affairs than the increasingly abstract and specialized academic economists. Perhaps because of the existence of a tradition of economic journalism dating from the nineteenth century, British academics were less inclined to 'fling their ideas to the wind' than their American colleagues. Consequently, the important books of postwar British political economy were written by journalists and politicians rather than by academic economists. There was also less of a demand for their words of wisdom: the *big names* were now in America. In America, however, there were no counterparts to the likes of Shonfield, Shanks and Brittan. Saying this is not to lessen the quality of the economic commentary provided by writers like Silk and Hazlitt, but simply to make an observation about the influence of the British journalists and the fact that they supplied the economic ideas which informed public opinion which in America was provided by professors.

In addition to these differences in terms of the demand and supply for economic mediation, there was also the fact that Washington had not experienced as full a dose of the Keynesian enlightenment as had London. As James Tobin points out, the 'new economics' came to the centre of political power in America rather later than elsewhere:

> The economics brought to Washington by the Kennedy Council of Economic Advisors and other academic economists close to the new President was not new to economic literature and classrooms. It was not new to the practice of governments in Scandinavia, Holland and Britain. Much of it was not new to official doctrine. . . But it was new to Washington nonetheless.[6]

Notwithstanding the Employment Act (1946), it was not until the Kennedy administration that economists really came to town. The 'new economics', as the financial writers and commentators began to term it (Tobin suggests that its earliest use in the press was in 1962 in *Newsweek*, yet Hazlitt was using the term somewhat earlier than this) brought with it a more definite emphasis on the belief that business cycles were not inevitable and that government policy should aim at steady growth and full employment. Along with this 'new economics' in Washington came a renewed public interest in what the experts had to say: and it was a very good time to be an expert. The economy was powering ahead and economists, partly credited for all this growth and prosperity, became public figures and politically partisan. And, as in Britain, along with this increased demand for expert support, assessments, forecasts, predictions and explanations, came a demand for 'intermediation' and interpretation. It was to be expected that, as Sir Alec Cairncross has pointed out:

> If policy is dominated by economics and framed by economists, the public has a natural curiosity in what is going on. There is a need for economists who can translate what their fellow economists are saying into a language intelligible to the layman and communicate their contentions through the press, on radio, on television, and in other ways.
>
> It is not a long step from intermediation to missionary activities.[7]

What the British economic journalists and American economists had in common was, apart from their 'missionary' zeal, a formidable ability to communicate ideas to the general public. The difference was that in America the professors wrote newspaper articles and appeared on television; in Britain it was the journalists who wrote books, attended seminars and became professors and fellows of Nuffield.

As a group, American economists were far more prepared to write journalism – and become more overtly political – than their British counterparts. Nobel Laureates like Lawrence Klein and James Tobin were, for example, regular columnists (Klein in the *Los Angeles Times, Newsweek, Business Week* and *Nouvel Observateur*; Tobin in the *New Republic, Challenge* and the *New York Times*. Galbraith, Samuelson and Friedman, all of whom had close ties with the Democratic or Republican parties, enunciated a political economy which in Britain had fallen to journalists to articulate. And their international standing as 'personalities' and economists well reflected that the leadership of economics had passed across the Atlantic. In addition to which, as Samuelson has noted: 'The sheer number of American economists gave them unfair advantage over economists abroad'.[8] Naturally, this postwar boom in economists followed a surge in public interest in what economists had to say about politics and policy – especially after the 'new' economics had become established. The economists themselves were, in turn, not shy in coming forward. And their prominent position in public discussion of economic policy issues was also indicative of changing attitudes towards mixing politics and economics, which Keynes's own stress on persuasion had done so much to bring about. Before the war economists had, with a few notable exceptions such as Keynes himself, maintained a high degree of Marshallian detachment from daily controversy over policy and events. After the war the social status of economic knowledge stood higher than ever before – perhaps higher than it was to be ever again. Thus it came to pass that, as Sobel recounts:

> By the mid-1950s ... as economic issues and debate became more important and familiar – and as some leading economists came to accept their political roles and learned how to communicate with an informed public – several practitioners achieved influence in their own rights and spoke from independent pulpits.[9]

A number of publications provided platforms and responded to the demand for coverage of economic ideas and news. In the forefront of this new journalism was, as we discussed earlier, *Business Week* and the *New York Times*. However, in the mid-1960s it was *Newsweek* which made the most significant innovation in American economic journalism. The magazine already had a longstanding reputation for economic analysis in its signed economic commentary, most notably, in the anti-Keynesian pieces of Henry Hazlitt. In September 1966 the magazine introduced Friedman and Samuelson as tri-weekly columnists to replace Hazlitt who was leaving for the *Los Angeles Times*. (The magazine had earlier – in 1964 – contracted Henry Wallich, a former presidential advisor.) It proved to be a unique experiment in stimulating an exchange of economic views between two of the world's leading economists and provided them with a national and international platform from which to debate issues of the day in a less formal way. The columns were one of the most graphic manifestations of the manner in which economists were endeavouring to extend their influence beyond the professional world into the realm where opinion is formulated. It was an instance of both supply creating its own demand – there were more economists in America than anywhere else – and of the demands of the media and society at large for professional advice and predictions. There were preachers with the urge to preach, and there were congregations waiting for the word.

Galbraith, Samuelson and Friedman stand at different points on the evolutionary scale of the modern economist. Of the three, Samuelson was the least interested in mixing up his economics and non-formal writings, and took the view that his scientific work and his journalism were two different things entirely. Friedman, on the other hand, had no hesitation about using his popular writings to persuade and convert public opinion to his economic theories. Galbraith's attitude to the public role of the economist – if not to economic policy itself – was nearer to Friedman than to Samuelson, yet markedly different to both in respect of making no real distinction between his academic and journalistic activities. In this, as in other aspects of his career, Galbraith has been closest to Keynes, with whom he has often been compared.

The comparison between Keynes and Galbraith is not entirely inappropriate. He has certainly had a career which bears some likeness to Keynes in terms of its diversity. In brief, as the details of Galbraith's life and times are well known: a Canadian by birth, he studied agricultural economics at Toronto, then took a PhD at the University of California, and was awarded a Research Fellowship to Cambridge. He has taught at the universities of California, Princeton and Harvard. During the war he headed the price control activities of the Office of Price Administration and was later director of the US strategic bombing survey and of the Office of Security Policy. For a while he was a journalist on *Fortune*, before returning to academic life. He has been a prominent Democrat, and was tempted to pursue a political career. From 1961 to 1963 he was appointed US Ambassador to India. Galbraith has been the friend of writers, poets and presidents, a TV personality and, without doubt, the most well known 'liberal' and economist of our times. As John Gambs notes in his study of Galbraith:

> To those who read books and dollar magazines, John Kenneth Galbraith stands out as a brilliant name . . . He gets more space in the *New York Times Index* than Zsa Zsa Gabor.[10]

Unlike Miss (*sic*) Gabor, in addition to being talked about and photographed, he has also written rather a lot! Being literate, controversial and non-technical – a rare thing in postwar economics – his ideas effected a rapid translation into popular economic discourse and, as was the case with Keynes, Galbraith 'the man' has also been an important aspect of the speed with which his views were taken up by the news media, and not just in the US and Britain. In 1971, for example, following the success of the *New Industrial State*, *Paris Match* led one edition (4 December) with a picture of Galbraith surrounded by photographs of Adam Smith and Malthus, representing his economic predecessors; Jackie Onassis, as a reminder of his close association with John F. Kennedy; and McLuhan and Marcuse as representing other great contemporary social theorists. Earlier (2 February 1971) *Le Nouvel Observateur* had devoted the greater part of a whole issue to discussing Galbraith's economic ideas. Few economists, before or since Keynes, have enjoyed such popular international acclaim and notoriety. The publication of *The Affluent Society* in the 1950s launched him as major media personality as well as confirming his status as the originator of some of the better known *bon mots* of contemporary economics and one of the leading advocates of prices and incomes policies. His main achievement as an economist has undoubtedly been that, more than any other single economic writer, Galbraith shaped much of the discourse which informed the discussion about the nature of modern capitalism in the 1960s and 1970s. At the same time, it is well to remember that the ideas and terminology themselves were well suited to the issues which preoccupied the attention of these decades – especially consumer sovereignty and the power of big corporations. So successful has been the spread of Galbraithian ideas and concepts that, as Breit and Ransom observe, by the 1970s 'Galbraith had himself become part of the conventional wisdom' he so often ridiculed.[11]

Galbraith gained early journalistic experience as a young columnist dealing with agricultural prices on his hometown newspaper in St Thomas, Ontario, which provided him with much needed spending money. Later on, he became editor of his college newspaper and, as we discussed in the previous chapter, his experience on *Fortune* after the war was both a more remunerative and undoubtedly a more formative journalistic episode. Business journalism gave him both a taste for the wider audience and an intuitive feel for the new economic forces which were shaping modern capitalism. Above all, perhaps, it gave him a perspective on how the modern economic system functioned that, he believes, could not have been obtained at a professor's desk. Journalism, however, could not provide him with the kind of influence that, as a civil servant in the 1940s, he was used to and desired. Galbraith was an agenda man. As he explains in his memoirs:

> There was a strong feeling that *Fortune* was kept around business offices and better homes as a prestige item and not read. Surveys always showed otherwise, but the neglect was considerable. I rarely encountered anyone who had read anything I had written ... It occurred to me, as it would again, that one could spend a lifetime writing well for a miniscule audience, and this had much to do with my departure. A writer gradually accumulates reputation and associated capital from his writing, but at *Fortune*, as at *Time*, this didn't happen ...[12]

Nevertheless, *Fortune* – with the insight it provides into corporate affairs – has remained an important source of material for a number of his books. Whether because of his experience as a journalist or no, Galbraith has remained a prolific commentator throughout his life, especially in the *New York Times* as well as in other magazines and newspapers both in America and Britain. *The Liberal Hour* (1960), *The Economics of Peace and Laughter* (1971) and, more recently, *A View from the Stands* (1987) contain but a selection of some of his vast and varied journalistic and literary output. In addition to his books on economics and journalism he has written novels (*The McLandress Dimension* and *The Triumph*); an account of his life and times as an Ambassador (*Ambassador's Journal*); a book on Indian painting; an autobiography of his early years (*The Scotch*); and a number of 'broadsides' including *How to Get Out of Vietnam, How to Control the Military, A Lucid Proposal for the Nation*. The sheer extent of his output and range of activities has meant that he could not avoid – not that he has ever tried – being a focus of media attention. In consideration of this, some economists have described him more as an economics *writer* than a serious *academic* economist; and it is often suggested that his message is very much the outcome of the medium which he has chosen to employ. Given that he has addressed his attention to influencing public opinion rather than the winning over of his fellow professional economists it is, as G. C. Allen has remarked:

> too much to expect that he should always temper sweeping and emphatic assertions with the kind of qualifications that would be appropriate to an academic discussion.[13]

Allen's (all too typical) accusation is one which betrays not a little jealousy that Galbraith's writings are read with pleasure and that his books sell in great numbers. Even so, he was elected President of the American Economics Association in 1972 and has taken his share of academic honours. He is still, however, one of the few 'famous' American economists not to have been awarded a Nobel prize.

Galbraith's interest in shaping economic opinion rather than the acclaim of his peers came early on in his career with the publication in 1952 of his book *American Capitalism: the concept of countervailing power*. In the preface he argues that the book was aimed explicitly at the layman, rather than the professional community. *American Capitalism* is an important expression of his desire to capture the imagination of the general public rather than the approval of his academic colleagues. It was an immediate bestseller. So much so, that he was quite unprepared for the rather muted reception that awaited his more academic study, *A Theory of Price Control*. It taught him, as he once claimed in the *New York Times*, an important lesson in persuasion:

> I made up my mind that I would never again place myself at the mercy of the technical economists who had enormous power to ignore what I had written. I set out to involve a larger community. I would involve economists by having the larger public say to them, 'Where do you stand on Galbraith's idea of price control?' They would *have* to confront what I said.[14]

The reception of his study of price control was a turning point in the development of his approach to economics. Thereafter he would take the high road to public acclaim, whilst leaving his colleagues to take the lower to more limited professional influence.

The tactic was, of course, very Keynesian: theorizing by persuading. Galbraith, more than any other modern economist, has largely bypassed the more circuitous academic route to the public mind by making his ideas, language and personality newsworthy. Taken to its logical conclusion this should have led him to seek political office. Not that he failed to give this some consideration. With the belief that 'academic scribblers' can have far more of an impact than a mere politician, Galbraith was reluctant to engage in a political career. However, as an economist Galbraith has been as concerned about public opinion and attitudes as any politician. Indeed, as Friedman has argued: 'Instead of regarding him as a scientist seeking explanations, I think we shall get more understanding if we look at him as a missionary seeking converts'.[15] In this desire to persuade and convert, Galbraith clearly has much in common with Keynes, but unlike Keynes he has rarely, leastways since the early part of his career, felt the urge to engage in a more private professional debate. Galbraith has been a very public economic theorist. In *American Capitalism* he also employed another Keynesian technique: that of inventing new words and discourse; 'countervailing power', for instance, entered into the language. And the success of Galbraithian wit and wisdom in the domain of the media has meant that academic attention has come because of the public acclaim and notoriety, not the other way around, as was the case for Samuelson and Friedman. Through his books and articles, of which relatively few of the latter were published in academic journals, Galbraith made *himself* into an issue and a focus of media and public interest. He has always been good copy. In 1955, for example, his book on the 1929 crash which had developed out of an article for *Harpers*, caused a great stir. The 'financial press hovered on guard' for his evidence (given, prior to publication of *The Great Crash*) before the Senate Committee on Banking and Currency. When the book eventually came out it was on the *New York Times* bestseller list for a week. By this time, he had achieved the status of becoming one of the few economists to become a household name: television chat shows and other programmes followed. In 1968 he was to be found in the pages of *Playboy*.

Professor Galbraith has never been one to be bothered by the limelight of such popular attention. Indeed, his memoirs record with pleasure the reception of his books in the press rather than by reviews in learned academic journals. Of his *The Affluent Society*, he records, for instance:

> The *Chicago Tribune* . . . was poetic: 'Lo, what a man of wit has arisen to do biopsy on what Carlye called the "dismal science" of economics'. Philip Graham, publisher of the *Washington Post* devoted a full page to praise. A little later Malcolm Muggeridge said, 'I put it in the same category as Tawney's *The Acquisitive Society* and Keynes's *Economic Consequences of the Peace.* . . . Only a strong character can resist such praise. I made no effort . . . In Rio, visiting the Embassy, my eyes lit on the familiar bulk of the *New York Times*. *The Affluent Society* was second on the best seller list. This achievement is not universally a mark of intellectual excellence, but I was able to persuade myself that there might be exceptions.[16]

The Affluent Society was, like *American Capitalism*, a book which was designed as an assault on the public imagination rather an attempt to storm any academic paradigms. The book focused on what he terms the 'conventional wisdom': those ideas and myths which sustain an economic system that tolerates extremes of wealth and poverty. The dilemma was captured in another vivid phrase which was a gift to producers and newspaper men: 'private affluence and public squalor'. Ideas, he maintained, were powerful

allies of conservatism, and he saw the book – as his other writings –
as a way of undermining the social and political legitimacy of the
status quo. Changing American society, he explains in *The
Affluent Society*, depended upon the impact of circumstances on
the dominant ideologies and theories, rather than, as Keynes
tended to believe, the gradual encroachment of ideas and the
influence of great men. The power of ideas to change the world is,
Galbraith believes, the result of an interaction of ideas with
events. And, as this battle of ideas took place in the public
domain, the 'conventional wisdom' had to be tackled in a language
which could be readily understood and communicated. Because of
this, Galbraith's economics has been composed with an eye on the
prevailing illusions which shape public opinion, rather than being
conceived as exercises in theoretical controversy. His place in the
economics community since *The Affluent Society*, if not before,
has been that of professional outsider; he has been regarded as
more of an economic publicist than the very model of a modern
economist. The rampant success of *The Affluent Society*, one of
the most popular books by an economist in the post war era next
to some mega-texts, only served to confirm the suspicions of the
professional community. Had it not been so well written, had
numerous footnotes and only been mentioned when two or three
academics were gathered together, Galbraith may have been
hailed as having made a major contribution. But that was not his
way. Perhaps the most accurate description of his position in the
profession is that of Galbraith being someone who was 'out of the
mainstream of economic thought but in the mainstream of economic events'.[17] And he has maintained this role of critic-at-large
and general commentator at a time when the name of the game in
economics has been specialization and narrow expertise. Inevitably, therefore, his work has been far better received in newspaper
reviews than in academic journals. Not that this has bothered him
too much: apart from the early stages of his academic career,
Galbraith has never been dependent on professional acclaim, or a
teacher's salary!

The hallmark and charm of Galbraith's economics has been that
of its wit and style. He has not been an economist given to writing
in professional jargon and mathematical formulae. His technique
has been, like Veblen and Keynes, the ability to coin memorable
phrases which have the knack of getting into general currency. In

an age when mathematics has been the dominant language of economics, his approach has been to write in polished and entertaining prose. Indeed, no other economist since Keynes can claim to have established such a fine literary reputation – he is the only economist (to the author's knowledge) who has been made a fellow of the National Institute of Arts and Letters. Alas, literary reputation has not endeared him to his fellow economists as much as it has to the general public. Furthermore, as he has not sought to construct elaborate theories with little obscure nooks and crannies which generate comment and analysis, there has been little confusion surrounding the substance of what he has said: even if his fellow economists have criticized him for a lack of technical precision in his arguments, vagueness and unoriginality. There is surprisingly little professional analytical comment attached to his work; rather, critique's of his argument as a whole, particularly in terms of the fact that his ideas are founded upon over-simplification and over-generalization. Nevertheless, as Samuelson has argued, the professional criticisms have had little impact on his popular reputation, or on his place in the history of economic ideas:

> To compare [*The Affluent Society*] with *The Theory of the Leisure Class* would be in some of our common rooms to damn it; in some, to praise it. Gibbon tells us how he found his *Decline and Fall* on every boudoir table soon after its publication ... I am afraid people in the boudoir, today or twenty years from now, will not seek the benefit of professional reactions ... But whatever the verdict about the operational meaning of its propositions, we can no more recall or wipe out half a line of it than we can – by professional exegesis – expunge Henry George's *Progress and Poverty* from the historical record.[18]

As a rejoinder to this comparison of *The Affluent Society* with *Progress and Poverty*, Galbraith has pointedly observed that in his time, and even for decades after his death, George was in fact the most widely read of all American economists. His ideas, he argues, actually entered into the 'social subconscious' of American economic opinions and attitudes. All of which gives the lie to the idea that, in Galbraith's words: 'no journalist can ever be taken quite seriously as an economist'.[19] And, as far as his professional colleagues are concerned, *vice versa*. No doubt because of the contempt with which George is held by economists, Galbraith found it necessary to give him far more space (and other 'non-formal' economists) in his *History of Economics* than is usually the case in volumes on the history of economic theory. To do so would, he maintained, be to ignore a 'great sweeping current in the flood of economic ideas'.[20] It is important to understand, therefore, that his own desire to communicate economics through 'non-formal' language reflects both his belief in the essentially public purpose of economics itself, as well as his attitude towards influencing the agenda and the 'conventional wisdom'. As he once commented in a *Newsweek* interview: 'No economist ever had the slightest influence who wrote only for economists'.[21]

In addition to being a writer, Galbraith has also been an enthusiastic broadcaster – especially on British television and radio. In 1966 his *New Industrial State* was given as a series of (Reith) lectures. The lectures were published in *The Listener*, and when the book was published in 1967 it became another best seller – a million copies in a year! Ten years later he was commissioned by the BBC to write and present a television series – *The Age of Uncertainty* – which charted the development of economic theory and ideas. It was broadcast in 1976 and there then followed French, German and Japanese versions. For his critics, Galbraith's success on television and radio was very depressing. Arthur Seldon, for example, held it up as clear instance of the inability of the press and other media to distinguish between ephemeral and profound economic ideas, whilst Galbraith's facility to express his ideas in a compact and attractive fashion were seen as designed to:

> commend themselves to the communications media which look for entertainment to flavour enlightenment. Professor Galbraith may be one of the best known economists to non-economists, but he has made very little impact on economics or on his fellow economists. That has not deterred the BBC from awarding him pride of place in the opportunities they have given to American economists, or indeed to British economists, to explain to the general public what economists are saying that can elucidate the economic world to them.[22]

And as far as Sir Keith Joseph was concerned, the 'long and costly TV series' was not merited since:

> His views are idiosyncratic and partisan. He does not support them with any evidence. No other economist, as far as I know, has supported

them. Yet he is the guide which the BBC has invited to conduct viewers on a ramble through economic and general history. The choice tells us more about the BBC than it does economics.[23]

Yet such comments are also as revealing about Galbraith's critics. What bothers both politicians and economists is (as was equally true with regard to Henry George) the fact that although his ideas are dismissed as being inadequate, unoriginal and misinformed, they have entered into the public imagination. Satire seems to have proved more potent a persuader than science.

His economics for everyman well illustrates the fact that he has been more of an exogenous, rather than an endogenous, economist. That is to say, unlike Friedman or Samuelson his writings have been stimulated by the real world and events rather than by theoretical or policy debate within the professional community. *The Great Crash*, for example, grew out of a magazine article; *The Affluent Society* and *The New Industrial State* were prompted by his desire to hold back the recovery of free-market attitudes in the late 1950s. The impetus for his work has come largely from the political agenda, although Keynes, Chamberlain and Veblen have all had an influence on his economic ideas as well as his style of presentation. In particular, he has shared Keynes's intellectual confidence and persuasive abilities, and Veblen's facility for argument, illustration and the use of language. Like them he also possesses a marvellous talent to amuse.

As an *ideas* man, rather than a man of *theory*, Galbraith has been more interested in influence than academic Brownie points. this has meant that there is very little of Galbraith's work that is not accessible to the ordinary intelligent reader: perhaps that is why it irritates so many economists. Friedman, for example, who has himself done a fair share of preaching to the layman, dismisses Galbraith because he has 'written for the public at large', and his arguments are easier to understand and 'more satisfying to the ordinary man' than to the professional economist. Unlike his own theories, Galbraith's ideas have not led to the formation of an academic following or school: it is 'very hard to name academic people who have contributed to the Galbraithian view'.[24]

The irony is that, even though, according to his many critics, Galbraith has *nothing* to say and *cannot substantiate* his theories, he has been on the receiving end of so much criticism from both politicians and economists. That this is so is largely due to the fact that his ideas have influenced – or contaminated, depending whether or not you are a fan – popular economic discourse. They have had to take Galbraith seriously, even if they are outraged by his lack of professionalism and academic formalism. As David Reisman observes:

> By engaging in a wide readership . . . Galbraith was not merely seeking to provoke the general public to question their assumptions . . . but to force unpopular truths on the economics profession by means of the back door precisely because he regarded the front door as securely locked and bolted.[25]

Galbraith is one of a kind. His reputation as one of the more original social philosophers and commentators of our time has been achieved in the face of private disdain among economists and public acclaim. Whereas most others of his contemporaries have been concerned with theoretical development and academic prestige, Galbraith has, like Keynes, been primarily concerned with the problem of outside opinion and insider influence. His focus has not been economic theory as such, so much as the formation of the economic opinions and culture – the ruling economic ideas – which sustains and reinforces the economic, social and political order. Galbraith has viewed economic discourse as largely responsible for obscuring the realities of power and the actualities of modern capitalism. In various ways he has always been an economist fascinated by illusion and preoccupied with the relationship of ideas to the state of public belief. Galbraith has thus been involved in exploding publicly held myths rather than academic theories: the myth of the market; the myth of affluence: the myth of free competition; and the myth of consumer sovereignty. His goal has been to make the 'conventional wisdom' less secure and less acceptable. His mission was to disrupt the ritual and ceremony of prevailing economic discourse. Ultimately, as he has observed, it is events which do for received knowledge. Galbraith's contribution to events was to offer not so much a theoretical challenge as an alternative framework of public discourse. The strategy worked: 'countervailing power', 'the new industrial state', 'conventional wisdom', 'the technostructure', 'the dependence effect', 'the affluent society' and so on, have all entered into the language and culture. A good phrase, as H. L. Mencken once noted, is better than a Great Truth.

If Galbraith has been what Samuelson has called the 'non-economist's economist',[26] then it is Samuelson himself who has been the economist's economist *par excellence*. Contrary to Galbraith's dictum that no economist has ever had any impact by writing just for economists, Samuelson's influence on economic thought and discourse has, without doubt, been the most extensive of any economist in the postwar era: even if he has written, in comparison with J. K. Galbraith, little for the general public. Paul Samuelson has always made the distinction very clearly between his popular journalism and commentary and his serious scientific work. Although he has been responsible for spreading the 'Keynesian revolution' amongst the postwar generation of students of economics, as Marshall was for spreading the 'marginalist revolution' in the nineteenth century, Samuelson cannot be described as a missionary in the sense in which Galbraith and Friedman have tried to make converts. Yet, unlike Marshall, Samuelson has been far more engaged with the public discussion of economic policy – notwithstanding the fact that he has been as fervent an advocate of the use of mathematics in economics as Marshall was of the use of plain English! Through his textbook and his huge number of other publications, Samuelson has shown himself to be a consummate communicator of economic ideas to the beginner and the layman. It is surprising, for instance, to find that amongst the five volumes of his scientific papers there are a good number of journalistic articles. Yet his instructions to the editors of his collected papers leave no doubt as to how he rates them: 'When in doubt, include – of course excluding all non-scientific writing, such as periodic financial journalism for the London *Financial Times*, the *Nihon Keizai Shimbun*, and the *Washington Post*.' Even so, the collected papers do contain a number of pieces of journalism which, as Martin Bronfenbrenner has noted: 'have been, and remain, influential in "neo-New Deal", "compassionate liberal" and "anti-monetarist" directions'.[27] At the same time, he is not entirely dismissive of the academic value of his journalism since a number of pieces appear in his *Readings in Economics*, the text which supplements the *Foundations*. Undoubtedly, however, his main influence on journalism, as on much else, has been through his great textbook which mentally equipped a whole generation of commentators, politicians and civil servants. With over ten million copies of his *Foundations* sold, he never had to be as much of a publicist as either Galbraith or Milton Friedman. He has been the leading interpreter and disseminator of Keynesian economics, to the extent that the common international language of economics owed as much to the *Foundations* as to the *General Theory*. As Samuelson once boasted: 'let those who will make the nation's laws if I can write its textbooks'.[28] Yet, despite this sentiment, he has also been a theorist with a great practical perspective, and for someone who has campaigned for the use of more mathematical technique in economics, he has proved to be one of the more literate of modern economists – the style of the textbook has often been considered by some to be a little flippant. He has defined his interest as an economist as topics that are 'suitable merely for captive audiences in search of a degree – and even then only after dark'. Yet as an economist he has been willing to think aloud over contemporary issues through a sizeable collection of journalistic articles both in American and British publications (and in other countries), but especially in the pages of *Newsweek* which have served as a kind of ongoing dialogue with all those readers who learnt their economics from his textbook. Like Galbraith, he has been a very political economist and committed Democrat, but unlike Galbraith and Friedman, his journalistic output has tended to be more concerned to inform, educate and explain rather than persuade his readers to come over to a particular set of economic values or conclusions. Samuelson has not been an ideas man, and he has not had any particular theory or political economy to sell. Even at his most outspoken, Samuelson has always managed to sustain a balanced *professional* opinion and leave his readers to make up their minds, as in an article for the *Sunday Telegraph* on monetarism which concludes:

> When Professor Friedman formulates his system in generality ... it coincides with the post-Keynesianism of the Tobin-Modigliani type. When he speaks less guardedly, the consensus is rudely shattered ... Britain does seem in need of greater recognition that monetary and credit policies count, and count for much. But why should it be necessary to go overboard and import crude monetarism? Gresham's law does operate in the realm of ideology: 'Strong ideology drives out weak – among the gullible that is.' But why fall into such company?[29]

He has held steadfastly to a position between the strident demands from Galbraith for controls and redistribution and the equally forceful calls for a return to the market from Friedman. This was all very well in the 1960s, but as inflation and unemployment developed in the 1970s, sitting on the fence was not the place to be. It was a time for conviction and clear voices; it was a time for barricades. Yet as Sobel comments:

> Samuelson could recommend no clear solution to the problem of how inflation could be held down without recession or a major alteration in the nature of American capitalism. Those hoping to find one in his columns, testimony, or scholarly papers were disappointed. Still considered the best exemplar of modern neo-Keynesian economics, Samuelson could do little more than present the alternatives, analyse them, offer critiques, and then end by saying the matter cannot be resolved by economic analysis alone. Keynes sounded the battle cry in the 1930s. Galbraith and Friedman do the same today. But there is none from Samuelson.[30]

That this was so is due to the fact that he has always adhered to the kind of strict distinction between positive and normative economics as set out by Lionel Robbins and has kept the is/ought aspects of his commentaries in well-defined compartments.[31] As Silk notes, he has declined the role of a 'rabbi or prophet'.[32] Although he frequently voiced his support for or against particular policies and politicians, Samuelson has not expressed a political economy or general political philosophy. In practice, notwithstanding his political connections, Samuelson has been more of a teacher than a preacher. Whereas Friedman's *Newsweek* pieces were designed to win minds and arguments, Samuelson avoided taking sides and played the honest broker. His *Newsweek* columns displayed an admirable professional detachment that echoes the views of Pigou and Marshall with regard to the need for economists to be detached from political controversy and arguing in the streets. During a period when the whole economic consensus was in the process of breaking up, Samuelson rather curiously restricted himself to giving investment advice, comment on forecasts and explanation – all the while emphasizing that economic theory and economists do not have all the answers. At times, this stress on ethical values as opposed to politics or theories takes the reader quite by surprise, as when discussing the issue of payments for blood:

> We have in our everyday language the not very nice words 'blood money'. Today we should add the pejorative phrase 'money blood'. In

terms of quality . . . the blood you get for a buck is simply not as good
as that you get for love. This should not surprise anyone. Wise people
have always known that the love you get for love is better than the love
you get for money.[33]

For someone who could write with such a powerful moral sense,
his journalism was pretty dull stuff in comparison with the
certainty of Friedman and the iconoclasm of Galbraith. For the
most part, Samuelson seems to have regarded his journalism as an
opportunity to express views and ideas which, he thought, had no
place whatsoever in his scientific papers. He rarely responded to
the challenge of Galbraithian or Friedmanite arguments with the
passion and commitment that they themselves displayed, as when
he dismissed the arguments for a radical change in economic policy
in 1970 with the view that 'this is not the time for taking chances or
for *laissez-faire*. It is a time for prudent action'.[34] Samuelson has
not been an economist to stick his neck out too far and endeavour
to convince the reader that he is right. He has not sought
followers, nor the ear of princes. The fame he has desired is that of
the respect of his peers.

> No celebrity as a *Newsweek* columnist, no millions of clever-begotten
> speculative gains, no power as the Svengali or Rasputin to the prince
> and the president could count a pennyweight in my balance of worth
> against the prospect of recognition for having contributed to the
> empire of science.[35]

In his famous Presidential Address to the American Economics
Association he mused on the risks which are run when an
economist dares to address the public:

> While we should not minimise the importance of vulgarisation – I mean
> communication – we must not blink the fact that this is an area where
> Gresham's law operates in its most remorseless fashion: vulgar vulgar-
> isation drives out the subtle, just as strong ideology outsells weak . . .
> No one gets a Nobel prize for an essay on the relationship of quantum
> mechanics to free will and God; but one who has already received such
> a prize will get a better hearing for his random or systematic thoughts
> on the topic. Nor, these days, do you get appointed to chairs of
> economics by virtue of your social eloquence; indeed, until academic
> tenure has come, you are best advised not to write for *Harpers* or the
> *Manchester Guardian* (to say nothing of the *National Review* or the
> *New Republic*) lest you be indicted for superficiality. Good writing can
> be suspect.[36]

Where does this leave his attitude to his own journalism? He was, after all, in Richard Nixon's bad books as a journalist rather than as an economist! Early on, as we have seen, Galbraith came to the conclusion that he would bypass professional opinion of his work after the reception of his book on prices. In Samuelson's case, the opposite decision seems to have been taken. In 1944 he wrote a series of articles for the *New Republic* which forecast the return of a severe economic depression after the war. The prediction was way out, and thereafter Samuelson appears to have kept his big thoughts and predictions to himself rather than communicate them to the general public. Samuelson has not been a macro thinker or a political philosopher. His intention has been less to influence public opinion than to inform it. Unlike Galbraith and Friedman, Samuelson has not manifested any ambitions to have a specific political role. (He thus turned down the opportunity to head Kennedy's Council of Economic Advisors, in preference to pressurizing from outside via his columns and articles.) Contrary to Galbraith, Samuelson has argued that in the long run the economist should work for the 'only coin worth having', the acclaim of fellow professionals and not the 'limelight and applause' of non-economists. As he stresses, however:

> This is not a plea for 'art for art sake' . . . It is not a plea for leaving the real world problems of political economy to non-economists . . . Rather it is a plea for calling the shots as they appear to be . . . even when this means losing popularity with the great audience of men running against the 'spirit of the times'.[37]

The 'limelight and applause' for Samuelson has been essentially marginal to his life as an economist: the same cannot be said for Galbraith or Friedman. Having achieved fame so early on, in his twenties, he needed neither the money nor the applause. That he became so newsworthy was ultimately a testament to the standing of economics and his own professional pre-eminence, for he was no publicist. Samuelson's public influence has emanated wholly from his professional reputation rather than from his opinions or ideas. Having written the textbook he had no need to write the editorials. Nevertheless, as George Feiwel has commented:

> As a political economist, Samuelson feels that he has to be on the firing line, not only to influence the course of events, or to mold public

opinion as in his *Newsweek* columns, but also to shoulder the burden of anxiety. 'When my descendants gather about my knee and say, 'granpa, what did you do to add to the gross national product?' My reply will have to be, 'I worried.[38]

Of the three economists who have attracted most public attention since the war Milton Friedman is the only one who could really be termed a propagandist. Whereas Samuelson's journalism expressed his personal worries about unemployment, inflation, the balance of payments, growth, and so on, Friedman advanced solutions which were derived, so he believed, from scientific and empirical evidence. Given the dominance of Keynesian economics, both in government and at the universities, Friedman actually had an argument to win and converts to make. Galbraith and Samuelson were, in effect, spokesmen for the conventional wisdom. Whereas Galbraith and Samuelson employed their journalism for essentially reformist purposes, Friedman, as one of the founding members of the Mont Pelerin Society, deployed his popular writings for more revolutionary ends: the re-establishment of conservative political economy. Friedman believed in the power of ideas to change the world. Thus the major difference between Friedman and Samuelson and Galbraith was that Friedman's popular economics has been devoted to attacking the very liberal consensus which Galbraith's satire and Samuelson's science helped to create and sustain.

Although Friedman's name is synonymous with anti-Keynesianism, in one crucial respect, therefore, he is very Keynesian indeed: his belief in the importance of ideas and of changing the climate of opinion. Friedman has argued that changes in the role of government in the economy have invariably been preceded by changes in public opinion: 'What a change of public opinion created another change in public opinion can modify'.[39] Indeed, Friedman's faith in the power of ideas, in contrast to Galbraith's emphasis on the importance of events and circumstances, marks him out as being, in this regard at least, more Keynesian than many a Keynesian. It is this intellectual climate of opinion which, Friedman believes, 'determines the unthinking preconceptions of most people and their leaders', and conditions their reflex to courses of action.[40] Friedman's involvement with the Mont Pelerin Society in the 1940s shows that he had come to his political conclusions early on. The monetarism of *A Monetary History of the United States* was a much later development: Friedman was first and foremost an exponent of economic liberalism. He came to prominence as a spokesman for free-market economic liberalism in 1962 with the publication of lectures given in the 1950s – *Capitalism and Freedom*. His support for Barry Goldwater and the publicity which surrounded his various statements on the American economy, as with his evidence before the Congressional Committee on Employment, Growth and Price levels in 1959, brought him into the public arena. He was, as he expressed it before Congress, a professor always willing to profess. As he has explained:

> I have been active in public policy. I have tried to influence public policy. I have spoken and written about issues of policy. In doing so, however, I have not been acting in my scientific capacity but in my capacity as a citizen, an informed one, I hope.[41]

From the middle 1960s onwards, the majority of his output was not aimed at the professional community at all so much as the general non-specialist public. Friedman was not, like Samuelson, to write a hugely successful textbook nor, unlike Galbraith, was he given to writing with the bestseller list in mind. His real impact was felt through his ability to translate the ideas of the classical economists and Austrian economics into relevant examples of the relationship between economic liberty and political freedom. In great part the differences between Friedman and his *Newsweek* adversary, Samuelson, stem, however, not from their political or ideological positions as from their differences in economic methodology. In his celebrated *Essays on Positive Economics* he set out his understanding of positive and normative economics.

> Positive economics is in principle independent of any particular ethical position or normative judgments. As Keynes says it deals with 'what is', not with 'what ought to be'. Its task is to provide a system of generalizations that can be used to make correct predictions about the consequences of any change in circumstances. Its performance is to be judged by the precision, scope and conformity with experience of the predictions it yields. In short, positive economics is, or can be, an 'objective' science, in precisely the same sense as any of the physical sciences.[42]

This unequivocal conceptualization made for a highly forceful style of argument and rhetoric. His notion of scientific, empirically rooted economics inspired a belief that his scientific investigations provided a foundation upon which he could construct a body of political opinion and predictions. (Students of political thought will be all too familiar with other examples of theorists who, safe in the knowledge that they have science on their side, could then proceed to extrapolate views and opinions and confidently dismiss the arguments and objections of their opponents as simply misguided and the products of willful misunderstanding.) Keynes's conviction that he was right stemmed from his own sense of intuition and intelligence: he was Keynes. Friedman possessed an equal measure of faith in his arguments for the opposite reasons. Intuition had nothing to do with it: Friedman rested his case on science. Friedman's political economics derived their force from the rock-solid belief that he was empirically and positively correct. He therefore had none of Samuelson's qualms about mixing his political statements with his economic analysis, or making it clear that his arguments were grounded in decades of scientific investigation.

When approached by *Newsweek* to contribute a regular piece he accepted with some hesitation, 'and largely because of pressure from my wife and son'. Rose Friedman collaborated with him on his books aimed at the general reader rather than the economics profession: *Capitalism and Freedom* (1962), *Free to Choose* (1979) and *The Tyranny of the Status Quo* (1984). The last two were linked to television series of the same name.

His initial reluctance overcome, Friedman was to become a persistent advocate of what the media summed up as 'monetarism', and of the importance of bringing market forces into play. The *Newsweek* columns provided him with a highly effective channel through which he was able to 'express technical economics in a language accessible to all'. In one of his early *Newsweek* pieces he observes about inflation that, for example:

> Housewives have a justifiable complaint. But they should complain to Washington where inflation is produced, not to the supermarket where inflation is delivered. Prices have been going up because the quantity of money increased too much from 1961 to the spring of this year [1966]. And the quantity of money increased as much as it did because the monetary authorities planned it that way, or to be less generous, let it happen.[43]

Addressing a *Playboy* audience in February 1973, he makes his point in these terms:

> Technically, inflation isn't terribly difficult to stop. The real problem is the favourable effects of inflation come early, the bad effects late. In a way, it's like drink. The first few months or years of inflation, like the first few drinks, seem just fine. Everyone has more money to spend and prices aren't rising as fast as the money that's available. The hangover comes when the prices start to catch up. . .[44]

Always emphasizing that his normative prescriptions derive from positive scientific research he has frequently played on the relationship between popular opinion, scientific knowledge and the deficiencies of the political process. Commenting on Carter's anti-inflation plan in 1980, for example, he argued for monetary and fixed restraint and a curb on regulations and controls in these terms:

> We badly need a coordinated attack on both inflation and declining productivity.
> The obstacle to launching such an attack is not a lack of knowledge of what to do. The obstacle is a lack of political will and leadership to do what has to be done . . . In my opinion, the American public is far ahead of Washington. It will recognize cosmetics and political opportunism for what they are. It is ready to be told the truth.[45]

Such contributions to the magazine and other assorted journalism fill three volumes: *An Economist's Protest* (1972), *There's No Such Thing as a Free Lunch* (1975) and *Bright Promises, Dismal Performance* (1983). These, with his television programmes, surely qualify Friedman as, if not a writer of the same class as Galbraith, then certainly a formidable propagandist: an Aaron to Hayek's Moses! He had a formidable line in attacking the old wisdom:

> We have heard much these past few years about using the government to protect the consumer. A far more urgent problem is to protect the consumer from government.[46]

> I know hardly any do-gooder legislation . . . whether it be minimum-wage laws or rent control or urban renewal or public housing or fair-employment legislation – which on examination of its full consequences, does not do more harm than good . . . It is about time that liberals asked themselves whether the fault may be in the system they favour . . . rather than in the way the system is operated. It is about time that they appealed to their heads as well as their hearts.[47]

As inflation persisted in the Carter years and the impact of floating exchange rates from 1971–2 began to be felt, Friedman was to take on the Keynesians and come off the winner. And, as events and the tide of opinion seemed to be going Friedman's way, he adeptly employed, as Keynes had done, both academic and public opinion to get his message across. He also used the argument that Keynes had advanced in the 1920s and 1930s, that 'public opinion' was ahead of politicians, to add weight to his arguments for controlling the money supply and letting the people go. In so doing, Friedman thus proved to be more influential in shifting the political agenda than any economist since Keynes. As Galbraith has observed:

> In the latter part of the [1970s] strong monetarist action was initiated. The Keynesian revolution was folded in. In the history of economics the age of John Maynard Keynes gave way to the age of Milton Friedman.[48]

Despite his great success in the sphere of political argument, Friedman has maintained that ultimately he wishes to be judged by his fellow professionals and his scientific work rather than by his impact on public opinion. History may yet record otherwise. In political terms it was Friedman who was largely responsible for undermining the dominant position of Keynesian economics and rhetoric. His emphasis on sound money and the importance of choice and individual freedom was a radical and convincing assertion of ideas which had been consigned to history by Keynes and those who followed him. It is significant that, whereas Keynes (and Samuelson) largely ignored the political dimension of economic ideas, Friedman's most important contribution to the success of the 'counter-Keynesian revolution' has been his forthright renewal and reconstruction of classical liberal political values. By showing how free-market solutions could actually be applied to contemporary economic and social problems Friedman hit at what most modern liberals thought were the strongest parts of the Keynesian edifice: its superior moral foundations and its political superstructure.

Of the three economists we have discussed, it is Friedman who has been the most important journalist. Whereas Galbraith's newspaper articles and broadcasting were in a sense inseparable from his work as an academic, and Samuelson's journalism afforded him the opportunity to express values and ideas that he would not permit to be put forward in his scientific investigations, Friedman's journalism enabled him to extend his economic researches on to a more normative and practical plane. Indeed, it is difficult to imagine how the ideas of Hayek and the Mont Pelerin Society could have become so much part of the fabric of politics in the 1970s and 1980s if not for the fact that Friedman was so involved in what Keynes termed the 'daily task of persuasion'. Since the 1930s the 'market' and *laissez-faire* had not been notions to stir the blood: the moral and political arguments seemed to be on the side of those, like Galbraith and Samuelson, who advocated various forms of controls and regulations. Friedman was, without question, the man who, at the popular level, reinstated the notion that capitalism *qua* a free-market system was ethically better as well as economically more effective a problem solver than statism in all its forms, and that the principles of the free market could best provide for the least well-off, just as they could better guarantee individual liberty. His role in reinstating the political and moral case for the free market in his *Newsweek* articles and his television broadcasts and other non-technical publications may very well come to have as prominent a place in future assessments of Milton Friedman as that of his positive economics. Ironically, however, his very success in projecting 'Friedmanism' have, perhaps, ill-served the actual influence of 'monetarism'. The inexorable process of simplification that has accompanied the rise of monetarism in the media and its political translation has meant that, as Walter Eltis has observed: 'many economists are naturally critical of the simplified versions of Friedmanite economics which has propagated in the media, while his most important journal articles are 15 or more years old'.[49] It was inevitable that Friedman was later to deny that he ever was a monetarist, if by that was meant what was being practised by the Federal Reserve and reported in the press. For an economist to become so closely involved in politics and persuasion carries a heavy price tag: the risk that the purity of academic abstraction will be sullied by contact with the real world. There is, after all, no such thing as a free lunch.

The prominence of Professors Friedman, Galbraith and Samuelson obscures, however, the fact that their popular discourse and desire to communicate economics to the general public was not the chief characteristic of economics in this period. Quite the opposite is true: alongside the rise of personality economics was the continuing story of the privatization of economic discourse and what many felt to be a crisis of abstraction. Notwithstanding the preparedness of the big names to articulate their views and lend their support to politicians, the problem was that the agenda of policy makers and the public and that of the economics profession was becoming ever more divergent. The 'internal' preoccupations and discourse of the economics profession and the 'external' problems and arguments of the 'real world' were, by the 1970s, becoming increasingly divorced from one another. As Tobin has argued, the occasions when the 'endogenous' and 'exogenous' aspects of the economic agenda coincide are rare events indeed.[50] Periods when the research agenda and the political agenda are being informed by the same problems, as in the early nineteenth century and the 1930s, are infrequent conjunctions in history. to some extent it may be said that the fame of Friedman, Samuelson and Galbraith overshadowed the process whereby a younger generation of economists were, as Leonard Silk notes, becoming 'more and more remote from the real world problems that overlap economics and other disciplines'.[51] Words were fast being replaced by symbols as the language of economics. As Wassily Leontief complained in *Science* magazine, professional economics journals had become, by the end of the 1970s, filled with mathematical formulae which led the reader 'from sets of more or less plausible but entirely arbitrary assumptions to precisely stated but irrelevant conclusions'.[52] The line between professional and amateur had never been so boldly laid down. Thus the economic journalism of the famous was very untypical of the growing communications gap between the layman and the professional, but highly representative of the relationship of economic expertise and society. Disenchantment with this professionalism was to follow. This was not a phenomenon peculiar to economics, for as we shall discuss in the next chapter, the 1970s was also to witness a more widespread disillusionment with professional expertise and a turn towards alternative practitioners and less scientifically respected remedies. As in the days of Henry George, the issue of taxation was one about which there was considerable difference of opinion between professional economists and the political propagandists.

It was not just, as Friedman believed, the hegemony of

Keynesianism that was coming to an end in the uncertain and changing circumstances of the 1970s: the relationship of economic knowledge to the new and more ideologically informed politics of the decade was also undergoing a transformation.

As the following chapter shows, the economic crisis of the 1970s ultimately led to the big names losing their monopoly on economic discourse and their hold on the economic agenda. In America, in particular, the economic policy agenda came to be influenced by academic outsiders rather than the professionals. The old prophets were out of joint with the times: Samuelson admitted that he had no answers; Galbraith, that controls on prices and incomes were necessary; and Friedman, that painful belt-tightening was now vital if stagnation and inflation were to be beaten. Personality economics seemed just another variant of the dismal science. Politicians, ever eager for solutions that were more attractive to the voter, began to look elsewhere and to their own reservoirs of 'common-sense' economics. The professors were suffering from what media men might term a bad case of over-exposure. Familiarity breeds contempt, and in being prepared to popularize their ideas and theories, the household names greatly contributed to the politicization and de-professionalization of their subject. As the activities of Galbraith, Samuelson and Friedman showed, economics was politics, and politics was increasingly all about economics. The temptation to preach rather than, as Keynes hoped, pull teeth, proved wholly irresistible. And, as is sometimes the fate of those who in good faith stand in pulpits, the danger was that when the economy took a turn for the worse, their followers would be led into the ways of 'dogmatic fundamentalism'[53] and not into the truth. As David Stockman, a leading 'supply-side' character who figures in the following chapter, more eloquently expressed it:

> whenever there are great strains or changes in the economic system, it tends to generate crackpot theories, which then find their way into the legislative channels.[54]

NOTES

1. *Sunday Times: a pictorial history of one of the world's great newspapers, 1961* (*Sunday Times*, London, 1961).
2. *New York Times*, 17/18 December 1967.

3. Alex Rubner, *The Price of a Free Lunch: the perverse relationship between economists and politicians* (Wildwood House, London, 1979) pp. 15–16.
4. Robert Solow, 'Does Economics Make Progress?', *Bulletin of the American Academy of Arts and Sciences*, vol. 36 (1981) p. 17.
5. *Financial Times*, 12 November 1969.
6. J. Tobin, *The New Economics One Decade Older* (Princeton University Press, Princeton, New Jersey, 1974) p. 2.
7. In F. Cairncross (ed.), *Changing Patterns of Economic Policy: essays in honour of the 70th birthday of Sir Alec Cairncross* (Methuen, London, 1981).
8. Samuelson in W. Breit and R. Spencer (eds), *The Lives of the Laureates* (MIT Press, Cambridge, Mass., 1986) p. 34.
9. R. Sobel, *The Wordly Economists* (Free Press, New York, 1980) p. 6.
10. John S. Gambs, *John Kenneth Galbraith* (St Martins Press, New York, 1975) p. 5.
11. William Breit and Roger L. Ransom, *Academic Scribblers* (Dryden Press, Chicago, 1982) p. 189.
12. J. K. Galbraith, *A Life in Our Times* (Houghton Mifflin, Boston, 1981) p. 5.
13. G. C. Allen, *Economic Fact and Fantasy: a rejoinder to Galbraith's Reith Lectures* (Institute of Economic Affairs, London 1967) p. 5.
14. *New York Times Book Review*, 25 June 1967, p. 3.
15. M. Friedman, *From Galbraith to Economic Freedom* (Institute of Economic Affairs, London, 1977) p. 30.
16. Galbraith, op. cit., p. 354.
17. Lester Thurow, cited by M. Prowse, *Financial Times*, 15 February 1988, p. 39.
18. Presidential address delivered at the American Economics Association, New York 1961, P. A. Samuelson, *Collected Papers*, vol. 2, op. cit., pp. 1053–4.
19. J. K. Galbraith, *A History of Economics: the past as the present* (Hamish Hamilton, London, 1987) p. 166.
20. Ibid., p. 3.
21. *Newsweek*, 8 August 1960.
22. Friedman, op. cit., p. 8.
23. Foreward to Frank McFadzean, *The Economics of John Kenneth Galbraith: a study in fantasy* (Centre for Policy Studies, London, 1977).
24. Friedman, op. cit., p. 36.
25. David Reisman, *Galbraith and Market Capitalism* (Macmillan, London, 1980) p. 173.
26. *Newsweek*, 3 July 1967.
27. M. Bronfenbrenner, 'On the Superlative in Samuelson', in G. R. Feiwell (ed.), *Samuelson and Neo-classical Economics* (Kluwer Nijhoff, Boston, 1982) p. 346.
28. In Breit and Spencer, op. cit., p. 68.
29. Cited in P. A. Samuelson (ed.), *Readings in Economics*, 7th ed. (McGraw Hill, New York, 1973) pp. 325–6.
30. Sobel, op. cit., p. 116.
31. See L. Robbins, *The Nature and Significance of Economic Science* (Macmillan, London, 1935).
32. Leonard Silk, *The Economists* (Avon Books, New York, 1976) p. 37.
33. *Newsweek*, 17 December 1971.
34. See *Newsweek*, 22 June 1970.
35. In Breit and Spencer, op. cit., p. 72.
36. Samuelson, *Collected Papers*, op. cit.
37. Ibid.
38. In Feiwel (ed.), op. cit., p. 21.

39. Milton Friedman, *The Tyranny of The Status Quo* (Penguin, Harmondsworth, 1980) p. 70.
40. M. Friedman, *Free to Choose* (Penguin, Harmondsworth, 1980) p. 332.
41. Breit and Spencer, op. cit., p. 90.
42. M. Friedman, *Essays in Positive Economics* (Chicago University Press, Chicago, 1953) p. 4.
43. *Newsweek*, 28 November 1966.
44. *Playboy Magazine*, February 1973.
45. *Newsweek*, 24 March 1980.
46. *Newsweek*, 17 August 1970.
47. *Newsweek*, 27 July 1970.
48. J. K. Galbraith, *A History of Economics: the past as the present* op. cit., p. 274.
49. *Financial Times*, 15 February 1988, p. 41.
50. See Silk, op. cit., p. 228.
51. Ibid., p. 229.
52. Cited in Rupert Pennant-Rea and Clive Crook, *The Economist Economics* (Penguin, Harmondsworth, 1986) p. 19. They add:

   Younger economists – particularly academics – hear these criticisms but reject them. Most believe that their subject is developing in fruitful ways. They do not see the new methodologies as a threat to the 'real' economics of theory and observation – only to amateur economists who have failed to keep up.

53. See R. D. Collison Black, 'Dentists and Preachers', in R. D. Collison Black (ed.), *Ideas in Economics* (Macmillan, London, 1986).
54. *Atlantic Monthly*, December 1981.

5. How Keynes left America

The Keynesian revolution arrived in the US, as Galbraith argues in his *New York Times* essay (published by way of being a belated review of the *General Theory*) on 'How Keynes Came to America', largely through professional and intellectual channels:

> the trumpet . . . that was sounded in Cambridge, England, was heard most clearly in Cambridge, Massachusetts. Harvard was the principal avenue by which Keynes's ideas passed to the United States.[1]

In the years which followed, the ideas contained in the *General Theory* found their way to Washington and during the war, as Keynes predicted, the younger economists enthused by his ideas rose to the top. As a revolution that which went under the name of 'Keynesian' was something which more resembled a *coup* by an intellectual and professionalized élite than a movement of political opinion. As Galbraith mantains, Keynesianism entered America largely as the result of the impact of an influential research community and because of the war, rather than as a result of a shift in public or political opinion. Keynes came to America via textbooks and seminars, and ultimately through the occupation of Keynesians in key areas of wartime and postwar administration in Washington. The children of this revolution, schooled in their Samuelson, went on to occupy positions of power and influence in all quarters of American life. They were men who, as the *Economist* noted when reviewing the 12th edition of Samuelson's *Economics*, 'later inflicted the fruits of their learning on everybody else'.[2]

In the best Keynesian sense, the American economic revolution came about through persuasion, generational change and an alteration in élite attitudes rather than through the politics of crude interest.[3] It was thus a revolution without an organization. As Galbraith observes:

> All who participated felt a deep sense of personal responsibility for the ideas; there was a varying but deep urge to persuade. There was a

strong feeling in Washington that the key economic posts should be held by people who understood the Keynesian system and who would work to establish it . . . But no one ever responded to plans or orders, instructions or any force apart from his own convictions.[4]

It was a revolution from above, a revolution from inside, and above all else, a revolution in the *professional* standing of American economists. The Keynesian revolution in America was, in short, a quiet affair. Disagreements between economists were essentially private matters: until the 1970s there were no manifestos in *Newsweek*. However, the counter-revolution which was to mark the end of this phase of largely technical and internal disagreements was altogether more noisy and more organized. Anti-Keynesians in the 1970s and 1980s opted for a more public platform than that of the professional conference and journal. In contrast to the Keynesian revolution, the revolt against the 'new economics' was an expressly political process. To begin with of course, there was the skilled publicism of Milton Friedman which, as we saw in the previous chapter, was framed with an eye to making his monetary theories and political opinions win the public argument. As Tobin points out:

When the New Economics stumbled over Vietnam and fell from public favour monetarism was waiting in the wings and burst upon the scene. The press thrives on drama, conflict and novelty. These made the New Economics newsworthy in the early sixties, and they now favoured the propagation of monetarism. Here was a doctrine that had formidable but heterodox academic credentials, claimed to forecast GNP accurately and simply, fixed blame for the unpleasant oscillations in the economy after 1965, alleged that both monetary and fiscal policy had been based on false economics, and asserted that fine tuning caused or accentuated the instability it was designed to correct.[5]

Coupled with monetarism was another set of ideas which profited from the turn of events and which ultimately came to have as much prominence in the US as monetarism was to have in the UK: the so called 'supply-side' revolution. Although far less academically developed than 'monetarism', supply-side ideas were to have a dramatic impact on American economic opinion in the late 1970s through the way in which it complemented social and political views then current in neo-conservative quarters and by offering a politically attractive solution to the problems of productivity, the supply of labour, regulation, capital formation and the threat to resources. As *Business Week* commented at the time:

> One reason the concept of supply-side economics is gaining wide acceptance is that it is broad enough to encompass a wide spectrum of views – from those who want to increase supply by reducing the role of government in the economy to those who want more economic planning. Even such Keynesians as Walter W. Heller and Arthur M. Okun, chief economists under Kennedy and Johnson respectively, make nods in its direction . . .[6]

The intellectual background to the supply-side movement in the 1970s and 1980s may be dated to the proposal by Colin Clark in the late 1940s that a tax burden of over 25 per cent would promote inflation and reduce output. Later on, in the 1950s, the Harvard Business School made a number of studies into the effects of taxation, work and incentives, but these did not yield significant results to support the case for tax cuts.[7] It was not until work by Martin Felstein and Arthur Laffer in the 1970s, which showed how high marginal tax rates acted as a disincentive, that the ideas of cutting taxes as a remedy for low growth and inflation came to the fore.[8] In practice, the modern day 'supply-siders' had four key objectives: tax cuts to stimulate economic activity; control of the money supply; cuts in government spending, especially in welfare and increased defence spending; and the initiation of a programme of deregulation.

These proposals and the theories which underpinned and legitimated them were – like Henry George's ideas in the late nineteenth century – far more of a home-grown affair than the Keynesian economics imported from England. Supply-side economics was more the outcome of a flow of ideas between New York and Washington than between Cambridge, England, and Cambridge, Mass. 'Reaganomics' – a term which was apparently coined by a copyeditor on the *New York Times* – was also more the result of a policy process than a by-product of a theoretical community influencing practical men in authority. Indeed, the big difference between the two 'revolutions' was that the Keynesian revolution was very much an inside 'Eastern' intellectual product: supply-siders however were, to a man, *outsiders* whose mode of operation had little in common with an earlier generation of revolutionaries. As Herbert Stein observed, they were people who felt that they were not getting on professionally and wanted to make a political 'splash'.[9] Supply-side economics (a term first used by Stein and later taken up and popularized by the journalist Jude Wanniski), or the idea of cutting taxes to promote enterprise and hard work, was a body of ideas whose point of entry to the political agenda came via the leading American financial newspaper, the *Wall Street Journal*, as Keynesian ideas had earlier entered through one of America's leading universities, Harvard.

The Keynesian revolution in America was led by economic professionals. In the vanguard of the 'supply-side' counter-revolution, however, in keeping with the growing disillusionment with experts in general at this time, were amateurs – journalists and politicians. Jude Wanniski's book, *The Way the World Works*, which did so much to give coherence to the Laffer curve, appeared coincidentally in the same year – 1978 – as Ivan Illich's essay on the decline of professional expertise, *The Right to Useful Employment*. Illich argued, in terms which have an immediate relevance to the then status of economics and economists, that the age of professional dominance was coming to an end in the face of an economic and cultural crisis. Trust in professors would, he predicted, become a thing of the past: the Age of Dominant Professions was over. Professional power, he concluded, was being threatened 'by increasing evidence of the counterproductivity of its output'.[10] In Illich's sense, Messers Galbraith, Samuelson and Friedman were, as their journalism and public status well exemplified, instances of an aspect of public affairs that had passed from the layperson to a professionally credited élite. In the 1970s there was clearly a reclamation of a domain long held to be expert territory. As Samuelson remarked with respect to his own career, like many others of his generation it was buoyed along by the great wave of Kondratieff economic and educational expansion which had begun with the New Deal and the war and continued in the postwar boom. Sooner or later it had to come to an end:

Trees do not grow to the sky. Every Kondratieff wave has its inflection point. The 1932–1965 expansion in economists' prestige and self esteem has been followed by some leaner years. We have become more humble and, as Churchill said, we have much to be humble about. Economists have not been able to agree on a good cure for stagflation. That disillusions non-economists . . .[11]

This disillusionment with economists, professionalism and 'action intellectuals', especially in neo-conservative circles, had many consequences. As the hegemony of professional expertise collapsed, the economic amateur, that breed which had apparently died out with Henry George in the nineteenth century, was, like the invisible hand itself, on the way back. The reasons for this are rather obvious and need not be laboured: in the 'stagflation' which beset the 1970s, economists no longer looked so smart. The amateur economist had much to offer in an atmosphere of crisis, when the experts' predictions were not as accurate as they had been in the past. (The same turn to amateurs frequently occurs in Britain when the public tires of bad weather and bad forecasts). The time was therefore right for 'commonsense' economics articulated in a way that the man-in-the-(Wall)-street could understand. The badge of amateur could be worn with pride. Warren Brookes, for example, who was responsible for promoting tax cutting in Massachusetts in his columns for the *Boston Herald American*, and which were often grist to the supply-side mill in Wall Street, notes, for instance, that his book *The Economy in Mind* was not the work of anything as dubious as a professional economist. He was pleased to say that he was a *journalist*:

> Given the present esteem for economists, this may prove to be a modest asset.
> As Martin Feldstein admits . . . 'The economics profession has discovered a new humility as the economy's performance has worsened.'
> The dreadful failures, both in the United States and in Great Britain, of the more extreme redistributionist notions of Keynesian economics have proved a bitter vindication for its critics.[12]

The failure of the old gurus, and the fact that economics itself had become an activity clothed in every more complex theory and language meant that it was an open season for 'do-it-yourself' economics. In the 1930s, an economic revolution could have happened only in Harvard seminars. In the 1970s it is true to say that it could only have happened outside the classroom. As Jude Wanniski comments, it also had

> to be in New York City, the centre of a financial storm. The view from Washington, too, is parochial, conducive only to hysteria in a crisis; the political capital imports ideas created elsewhere.
> The vantage point had to be at a newspaper, one without a political

commitment to economic dogma, and one with an international not regional bias. It could only be the *Wall Street Journal* and it could only be the editorial page of the *Journal*, an enclave of generalists surrounded by the finest specialists in economic and financial writing that the journalistic profession can assemble.[13]

This shift away from an academic perspective was, of course, symptomatic of the fact that the monopoly over economic wisdom enjoyed by the economics profession, and which the celebrity (and newsworthiness) of the likes of Galbraith, Samuelson and Friedman had typified in the 1960s, was well and truly over. At the same time, there was a strong undertone of anti-intellectual, or at least anti-academic, sentiment within the emergent 'new right' which delighted in pointing out the errors of (Eastern) liberal professions and their refusal to engage with the new realities.

The economic agenda which emerged in the 1970s was, therefore, very different to that which had emerged in previous decades in one crucial respect. Whereas in the past it had been the big-name academic economists who provided much of the intellectual context of the policy agenda and of economics *qua* news, in the 1970s and culminating with the election of President Reagan, that context was to be shaped to a much greater extent than for many a year by those who were located somewhat at the margins of academic respectability and who were outside the circle of East Coast liberal intellectualism. It was therefore most appropriate that the man who was to take the counter-revolution in economic ideas to the White House should himself be a former journalist and actor.

The *Wall Street Journal* had an absolutely vital role to play in disseminating and legitimating the ideas which became associated with Ronald Reagan and without its support it is difficult to see how the supply-side argument could possibly have achieved such a leading position in the economic policy debates which took place from the mid-1970s onward. It is a role which, in some senses, is comparable to that of the *Economist* in the nineteenth century and the *Nation and Athenaeum* and the *New Statesman* in the 1930s in Britain. The *Journal*, more than any other publication, provided a platform for dissent and a medium through which an emerging policy could be advanced and legitimized. In addition to the *Journal*, *Public Interest* was also an important supply-side vehicle and a number of the seminal articles of supply-side theory were published in this journal. The founding editor of *Public Interest*, and leading member of the 'new right', Irving Kristol, was himself on the *Journal*'s board of contributors, and his columns were a regular feature on the paper's opinion page.[14] Besides *The Public Interest* there were, by the mid-1970s, a host of other publications in which the anti-Keynesian/conservative case received favourable coverage. Despite neo-conservative criticism with regard to the liberal bias of the press, television and journals of opinion, the fact was that in this period their own position in the media was becoming ever stronger.[15] Anti-Keynesian, pro-market economics triumphed at the political level, not least because it found a public voice and policy solutions which translated well into forms of conservative economic rhetoric. Against such rhetoric liberal economists had little defence. Galbraith's remedy of controls was not in tune with the times and Samuelson was reluctant to advance 'solutions'. Supply-siders had the answers: they were also answers which made good politics. As George Gilder explained in *Wealth and Poverty*:

> Government cannot significantly affect real aggregate demand through policies of taxing and spending . . . All this shifting of wealth is a zero sum-game and the net effect on incomes is usually zero, or even negative . . . The only way tax policy can reliably influence real incomes is by changing the incentives of suppliers. By altering the pattern of rewards to favour work over consumption, the sources of production over the sumps of wealth, taxable over untaxable activity, government can directly and powerfully foster the expansion of demand and income. This is the supply side mandate.[16]

The supply-side policy revolution successfully undermined the *political* viability and saleability of Keynesianism in the face of problems for which it seemed to have better solutions. Not the least of its better theoretic qualities was, as with early Keynesianism, its apparent simplicity and its political attractiveness. When it came to winning over opinion with simple common-sense solutions – stop printing money (monetarism) and cut taxes (supply side) – it was a non-contest. The propagandizing zeal of Friedmanite economic positivism and the supply-siders was in stark contrast to the reluctance of leading Keynesians to engage in making converts and public argument. It was a point which was nicely observed by Malcolm Crawford in the *Sunday Times* in 1981 when commenting on James Tobin's Nobel prize. Professional economists, he argued, considered him to be a most effective critic of monetarism but someone who never engaged in a public debate. Most people, suggested Marcus Miller, 'felt that Tobin won all the intellectual arguments, but Friedman wins all his debates in public'.[17] The supply-siders took the same route: they took the argument on to a public, non-professional platform, rather than attempting to convince the academic community. Their strategy was to build an economic theory by winning over opinion.

The 'supply-side revolution', which culminated with the election of Ronald Reagan to the White House, was less a triumph of an academic paradigm, like the 'Keynesian revolution', than the mark of the victory of an economic vision and vocabulary. And, as Helco and Penner observe, the political attractiveness of this supply-side faith was not difficult to understand:

> It seemed to allow the Reagan candidacy to escape the dismal prospect offered by the traditional Republican economics and by monetarism, a prospect of austerity and distributional conflict in the name of long term solvency. Tax-induced 'growthmanship' meant that there could be economic success without pain, as monetary policy held back inflation and faster growth in the private sector relieved of high taxes benefited everyone. As far as treating an ailing economy was concerned, supply-side theory was the equivalent of laughing gas when compared to the monetarists' and orthodox conservatives' devotion to chemotherapy. It is not difficult to convince people that the world would be a better place if taxes were cut.[18]

The problem was that the rhetoric was in desperate need of a coherent body of theoretical justification. The supply-side was, as the *New York Times* commented, an idea waiting for a textbook and a broad-based theory which *Business Week* aptly described as 'looking for a Keynes'[19] In the meantime, the ideas were articulated in two areas: politics and the media. Supply-side 'theory' as such, evolved out of an interaction between the two. As Paul Craig Roberts pointed out:

> Unlike the Keynesian policy that it was displacing, the supply-side economics came out of the policy process itself and not out of the universities. The previous fiscal revolution that swept Washington was preceded by years of preparation. However, the luxury of long preparation was denied to supply-side economics. Its time had come before many professors had learned what it was. Fortunately, a new

policy was ready, but the only people who were thoroughly familiar with supply-side economics were those who had participated in the congressional debates or were readers of the editorial page of the *Wall Street Journal*. It was important that people learn about the new policy, especially journalists who would be reporting on it . . . The missing textbook that the *New York Times* was asking for needed to be provided.[20]

'Supply-siders' at this stage – in the mid-1970s – were involved in defining (making up) their ideas as events unfolded rather than through academic debate and theoretical controversy. The 'supply-side' revolution was, therefore, essentially a change in opinion in search of economic and intellectual consistency and a large measure of political influence, rather than a theory in the process of generating a theoretical community. It was here that the role of the *Wall Street Journal* was so important in providing the supply-siders with a medium through which to spread the message.

The idea of tax cuts to stimulate the 'supply side' of the economy was first argued out in Congress between 1975 and 1978 through the Kemp-Roth Bill, which called for a 30 per cent cut in income tax. As Roberts notes:

> Supply side economics won its spurs in the congressional policy process . . . Between the summer of 1975 . . . and the fall of 1978, some important analytical and political battles were fought, with the supply-side case prevailing against the Congressional Budget Office and the econometric establishment.
>   The Republicans were ahead of the economics profession both in seeing the deficit as a problem and in being suspicious of the argument that the nation could spend its way to prosperity . . .[21]

The arguments of Republicans in Congress led by Jack Kemp – a former quarterback on the Buffalo Bills – campaigning for a balanced budget and tax cuts attracted little support from the economics profession. Friedman, for example, was keen on the tax cuts, but only as a way of curbing government spending, rather than out of the belief that lower tax rates would lead to increased incentives to work harder and lower deficits. Friedman thus criticized Kemp-Roth for holding out the possibility of a free lunch for everyone:

> If Kemp-Roth were enacted without a simultaneous reduction in government spending, the deficit would, at least initially go up – and so would . . . hidden taxes.[22]

Liberals such as Galbraith and Heilbroner not surprisingly dismissed the whole notion contemptuously in articles in the *New York Times* and elsewhere. Galbraith, like Friedman, also pointed to the difficulties – although with a little more style and wit:

> There are some contradictions in life and experience that can quite possibly be reconciled. The Israelites did manage to walk on dry land across the Red Sea. To combine a vigorous expansion of the economy with a policy of deliberately induced contraction, recession and unemployment will be more difficult. [23]

Significantly, the critics were not as forthcoming about advancing their own new solutions. Of course, to those who believed, the cynicism of Galbraith *et al.* served to confirm, as Gilder put it, the 'irrelevance of liberal economics' [24] as practised by academics and commentators like Leonard Silk in the *New York Times* and Hobart Rowen in the *Washington Post*. The dilemma which faced Kemp *et al.* in Congress was of making their arguments into an effective intellectual idea: it needed a respectable theoretical paradigm and it needed a book. In Congress the task of providing the economics fell to Kemp's advisor, Paul Craig Roberts. It was Roberts who was largely responsible for putting together the economic arguments in defence of tax cuts in the crucial policy debates of 1977–8. And it is important to stress that this policy process was something which was largely independent of the thesis being advanced in the pages of the *Wall Street Journal*. Roberts himself is at pains to emphasise in his book, *The Supply-Side Revolution*, that the Congressional debates really predated the supposed conversion of Kemp to the infamous 'Laffer curve'. As to the 'book', this was provided with the help of Jude Wanniski, formerly of the *Wall Street Journal*: *An American Renaissance*, published in 1979. There was, Kemp argued, no telling what the American people – the most free, 'most educated, talented, energetic, and healthy people' in the world – could achieve if government understood the relationship between taxes and incentives. The problem was big government and high taxes; the solution which would pave the way to a new America was the Laffer curve. [25]

The appeal of the curve was that it (rather too neatly) defined a relationship between tax rates and tax receipts. If, so it demonstrated, tax rates were nil, then the government would receive no revenue; if the tax rate were 100 per cent then government would also be in receipt of no tax income since no one would have the incentive to work. From this Laffer suggested that there was an intermediate rate at which tax receipts would be at their maximum. If the tax rate were below this optimum rate then cutting taxes would reduce government receipts, and if it were above it then a cut in income taxes would actually increase the government's income. And, wonder of wonders, the philosopher's stone had been found: tax cuts could pay for themselves. Taxes would fall and the coffers swell. In the spring 1981 number of the *Cato Journal*, for example, Laffer expressed his confidence that Reagan's proposed tax cuts would do the trick:

> It is reasonable to conclude that each of the proposed reductions in tax rates would, in terms of overall tax revenues, be self-financing in less than two years. Thereafter, each installment would provide a positive contribution to overall tax receipts. By the third year of the tax reduction program, it is likely that the net revenue gains from the plan's first installment would offset completely the revenue reductions attributable to the final 10 percent tax rate cut.[26]

Roberts argues that the tensions between the supply-side arguments of the Washington politicians and those of the publicists on Wall Street who could not agree as to exactly what tax cuts would do to the budget (even though they were agreed that they would increase the incentive to work harder) were highly damaging to the implementation of the idea as a practical policy. From Roberts's point of view, supply-side theory was a premature baby. It was induced from its political womb and distorted by those who wanted to force the ideas into a specific theoretical framework which stressed that tax cuts would pay for themselves: the Laffer curve. And,

> By making the Laffer curve the issue, Wanniski and Laffer covered the supply side movement with hyperbole. It brought publicity to the movement, but criticism as well. Their exaggeration reflected their enthusiasm, which was catching . . . The problem with the Laffer curve was that it obscured the issue.[27]

Yet for better or worse, as far as the public were concerned, the Laffer curve *was* supply-side economics: 'No news magazine . . . feature[d] the supply-siders without a diagram of the curve, a word

with the author, and a shot of Dr Laffer's macaw bird.'[28] The
supply-side argument made rapid progress in Washington in spite,
if not because, of its obscurity or lack of consistency and theoretical coherence, and because it had some powerful sections of the
financial and other media on its side. The Laffer curve was a good
story: an economic theory that could be easily grasped by journalists, politicians and actors.

The 'supply-side' became an issue due to the way the economy
was going, or not going: inflation, the fall in the dollar, unemployment, the energy crisis and the weakness of the Carter presidency.
Jack Kemp and the Republican supply-siders got the idea of tax
cuts on to the Washington political stage, but by 1978 they were in
dire need of a theory to rationalize their political instincts into
some theoretical model. Kemp was a politician in search of a
message: Laffer was an economist searching for a politician.
Wanniski and the *Journal* were the media through which the two
made contact with one another. Thereafter, as Lekachman notes:

> Kemp's political reputation began to change... For Kemp and
> probably for the United States, the meeting had momentous con-
> sequences. Congress is notoriously stuffed with conservatives ...
> invariably predisposed to save the Republic from the fate of the
> Roman Empire by cutting taxes and limiting social spending. To
> distinguish oneself against competition requires both extraordinary
> enthusiasm and a favorite nostrum.[29]

It is also true to say that America was just as 'stuffed' with
economists searching for a favourite politician to carry their
thoughts to the centre of power: Laffer got lucky. And by the time
of Reagan's conversion to the Laffer curve, via California's
Proposition 13, supply-side rhetoric had built up a sizeable constituency of support. Wanniski and Laffer thus gave some much-
needed semblance of intellectual integrity to the ideas being
floated in Washington and in various tax-cutting states.

At around the same time as the issues of tax cuts and balanced
budgets were being championed by Kemp in Congress and being
advanced in a number of states, Art Laffer and Jude Wanniski
came to the forefront of the debate in promoting the former's
'Laffer curve' and its supplementary political economy which was
largely developed by Wanniski. Rather as Galbraith had decided
to bypass the academic paths in favour of the fast lane carriageway

of public opinion, Laffer also came to the view that the academic game was not one he wanted to play. Laffer's reasons were, however, somewhat different to Galbraith's. Quite simply, Laffer was an economist who had failed to make it in the academic world and thus had no other option but to shake the dust of academia off his sandals and preach in another country. Events came to a head when the University of Chicago claimed that he had misled them over the completion of a PhD. The affair convinced him once and for all that he would always be without honour amongst the academics, and that if he wished to make friends and influence people, then it had to be through persuading sections of economic opinion to coming around to his way of thinking. As he subsequently expressed it:

> It was horrible. I knew there was no way on God's earth that I could make it in the profession. So, I went other routes – the press, the political process, consulting.[30]

The strategy was spectacularly successful. Despite, or because of, the absence of a tried and tested academic theory, Laffer managed to gain the support of the key people in the tax-cutting 'new right' lobby in a very short time indeed. Within a few years Laffer's ideas had, as Heilbroner observed: 'taken Washington by storm'.[31] He thus became, as Max Moser comments, the 'creator and catalyst of the taxpayers revolt'[32], and the acknowledged intellectual leader of the movement by providing a theoretical framework to add scientific weight to the political demands for tax reform.

Laffer was an economist denied, so he claims, access to the usual channels and was in search of a medium. Kemp, on the other hand, was a politician with little access to academic theorists and in dire need of a message. It was a matter of kismet that they should meet. While he was at the O.M.B. (Office of Management and the Budget) Laffer met Jude Wanniski and introduced him to the ideas of the Canadian economist, Robert Mundell. In 1974 Mundell had urged a programme of tax cuts, and his ideas were taken up by Wanniski, the *Wall Street Journal* writer. The rest was, as they say, history!

Wanniski himself was an odd choice as an economic Boswell. His first degree was in political science, and his master's was in journalism. As is so endearing a characteristic of the amateur, what he lacked in knowledge he made up for in enthusiasm. He was, as we have said, an early convert to the ideas of Robert Mundell, and his American protégé, Arthur Laffer. In the early 1970s he began to put forward the idea of cutting taxes in the *Wall Street Journal* – 'It's Time to Cut Taxes' (1974) – and in Irving Kristol's *The Public Interest* – 'The Mundell–Laffer Hypothesis: a new view of the world economy' (1975).[33] The ideas advanced in these and other articles quickly became associated with the policies being advocated by Jack Kemp and other Republicans and the Proposition 13 movement in California. Wanniski saw in the ideas of Mundell and Laffer an 'exceedingly simple but powerful analytical tool':

> From the dawn of civilization, the tension in any political economic unit and in the global economy as a whole lies between income growth and income distribution. The Laffer curve merely posits that in any political economy, there are always two tax rates that will produce the same revenues. Political leaders must forever strive to find that rate which maximizes income growth while permitting a distribution of income consistent with welfare.[34]

In his book, *The Way the World Works* (1978), Wanniski set out with the modest claim that he aimed to 'set forth a new view of the global political economy' in the belief that 'the world's political leaders will find it of compelling usefulness'. Employing the free-market fiscal theories of Laffer and Mundell, Wanniski sets about constructing a model of a 'global electorate' motivated by self-preservation and self-interest. Capitalism is held to be the natural order of things and production is maximized in those conditions where there are optimum incentives for the individual to work and make a profit. The crucial relationship between government and the electorate is, therefore, the level of taxation which the Laffer curve showed largely to determine the incentive to produce. Taxation, he maintains, thus lies at the heart of the possibility of good government and an efficient economy. The Laffer curve is introduced as a device to show the relationship between tax rates and revenues, and Wanniski maintains that it is a powerful political guide to the point at which the electorate desires to be taxed. At a stroke Wanniski shows how Laffer both provides for a new political theory and a way by which tax cuts could actually increase the income of the government! Other economic models

– Keynesian, Marxist and monetarist – are considered and are dismissed as failing to take account of the basic reality which the Laffer curve delineates. The economics of Keynes and Friedman derive, Wanniski claims, from the errors of their common parentage, Marshall. Wanniski argues that a realistic political economy has to be based on Walras's general equilibrium analysis. Having established this, Wanniski proceeds to construct a theory of history, an argument for the return to the gold standard, and offers solutions to the third world and the energy crisis!

What is significant about this *general theory* of supply-side political economy was that it was made *analytically* and *intellectually* operative by a *journalist* and the media rather than by its actual inventors in the privacy of academic research. Indeed, as one critic has observed:

> If it is curious that the supply-side economists have spent no time theorizing while the supply-side journalists have been breaking their backs with the heavy chore of model-building, it is equally odd that so little feedback has been traded publicly between disagreeing compatriots. Should not the economists seek to lend their precious expertise to their hard-working friends embarked on a mission of such great import?[35]

Outside Wanniski's *Journal* articles and his *The Way the World Works*, the ideas attained scant intellectual support or interest from fellow economists. But the Laffer curve had events (particularly the cutting of local taxes movement) and Washington politics on its side, and in the *Wall Street Journal* a highly effective propaganda medium. But the real credit for getting the show on the road must go to Wanniski who effectively took an idea which had, at this point in time (1978), been little more than graffiti on a table napkin (so it is rumoured) and promoted it to the position of being a major form of policy discourse: he literally made Laffer news. As a 'scientific' theory it did not really begin to evolve technically until *after* it had won its way to the White House. The Latter curve was taken up because it offered a slice of social philosophy which even Mr Reagan could apparently understand: its success in the media bore witness to how it could be sold politically. At one level it offered an ill-defined vision, at another a metaphor for conservative rhetoric which complemented the political arguments being advanced for tax cuts and balanced budgets. Thus until the 1980s the thesis was, as Don Fullerton argued, largely discussed in the spheres of journalism and politics, rather than in the academic literature.[36] Significantly, the earliest and most complete defence of supply-side theory (though not the Laffer curve), Paul Craig Roberts's 'The Breakdown of the Keynesian Model', occurred in Kristol's *Public Interest* in the summer of 1978. At the same time, despite his argument that he was denied the conventional academic route – a point which is not supported by any evidence that he actually submitted his ideas to an academic journal – Arthur Laffer made few attempts to develop his arguments more fully elsewhere. He himself wrote no book, although he warmly endorsed Wanniski's effort as quite simply 'the best book on economics ever written'. (And in the immortal words of Miss Rice-Davies, 'Well, he would say that, wouldn't he!')

Laffer's strategy of going for public opinion and politicians paid off to the extent that, as other supply-siders bitterly complain, Laffer and Wanniski effectively took over as the gurus of the supply-side economic programme. Laffer's access to the media via Wanniski was, to a great extent, responsible for the way in which the 'Laffer curve' came to such a pre-eminent and dominant position over other free-market theories like monetarism. By concentrating his efforts into cultivating the *Wall Street Journal*, rather than trying to score academic points, his version of supply-side theory achieved a political notoriety which it otherwise could not have so quickly attained. The *Journal* sustained an economic dialogue which must be considered unique in the history of American economic thought. Supply-side economics *qua* the Laffer Curve was a discourse which, despite the attempts by Wanniski *et al.* to give it a more substantial intellectual pedigree, was essentially a body of economic opinion, a proposal whose main justifications were presented in the press rather than in professional journals, and which, unlike the political economy of the nineteenth century (which also had its fair share of press spokesmen and publicists), was a theory without a *private* discourse. The opinions aired in public were the theory. Whereas the organs which propagated the ideas of the political economists largely articulated and popularized a theoretical discourse, the *Wall Street Journal* actually invented and interpreted ideas. The paper became the principal platform for Wanniski, Laffer, Roberts and others to develop their ideas, and in so doing publicly made an important and unprecedented contribution to the formation of a new policy discourse, both through its opinion columns and in the reporting of news in a form that could be employed as 'examples' by non-economist 'supply-siders' like George Gilder. (*Wealth and Poverty*, for example, contained some nine references to the *Journal*.)

Wanniski's role in all this was, as we have stressed, crucial, but so too was that of Robert Bartley, his editor. Bartley was initially reluctant to embrace the new gospel, but he did allow Wanniski to have his head on the editorial pages. Bartley was a pragmatic conservative and like Wanniski he was a political science graduate, not an economist, and someone who was very interested in ideas. In 1980 he was awarded a Pulitzer prize for his 'distinguished editorial writing'. Bartley grew up in Minnesota, took his first degree at Iowa State and a master's at Wisconsin. He joined the *Journal* in 1962 and became the editor of the opinion pages in 1972. That same year the *Journal* made its move into an area which had previously been regarded as the natural domain of the *New York Times* and *Newsweek*: economic ideas. The paper thus shifted into the kind of intellectual territory long thought to be the preserve of the (economically liberal) *New York Times*. Wisely, the *Journal*'s board of contributors was composed so as to maintain a philosophical balance: Irving Kristol, Herbert Stein and Paul McCracken, Walter Heller and Arthur Schlesinger. Bartley encouraged a very positive and direct style of debate in the paper and, more than anyone else, was responsible for making the *Journal* into a *journal of opinion* as well as a newspaper for business 'facts' and news. It was in keeping with this principle of encouraging controversy that, in December 1974, Bartley allowed Wanniski to write the piece on the rationale for tax cuts. Soon after Bartley himself became more interested in the ideas. The *Journal* thereafter, with Bartley's energetic support, quickly evolved into the most important medium of the supply-side debate. As Dan Morgan observed in the *Washington Post*, the editorial page became:

> a sort of national bulletin board for political and military commentary by the network of conservative and neo-conservative intellectuals and out-of-power policymakers. But it was on economic matters that Bartley's page played its most active role, the publicizing and

popularizing theories that still seemed extreme to people grounded in orthodox economics.[37]

And so it was that, as we have noted above, Wanniski's articles came to the attention of Kemp, the former professional football player; in turn, Kemp was adopted by Wanniski, the amateur economist, as the political vehicle for supply side ideas. Eventually, in 1978 Wanniski became too closely involved in political activities for the likes of the *Journal* and he resigned to become a private consultant and advisor to Reagan. In turn he was replaced by Paul Craig Roberts, Kemp's economic advisor. Roberts took charge of a political economy column and, as he argues,

> welcomed the opportunity to restate supply-side economics. Wanniski ... had helped to make supply-side economics an issue. But as a journalist he had sensationalized it and left the impression that Jack Kemp was the only person in Washington who wanted to cut taxes. Perhaps that was the right tactic to use in order to bring public attention to a new idea. But now that supply-side economics was noticed it needed a broad base.[38]

In the course of the 1980 election the *Journal* announced its support of Reagan, and during the campaign its pages became essential reading for those interested in what was happening on the economic policy scene. Naturally, many supply-siders contributed to its pages, such as Laffer, Stockman, Ture, Lehrman and Gilder. But what was more significant was that a good few non-supply-siders also contributed to the debate being conducted through the pages of a newspaper which, until this period, never sought a reputation as a journal of ideas, being content simply to be America's premier business paper. It relished its new role: Herbert Stein, Milton Friedman, Walter Heller and Arthur Schlesinger were among some of the distinguished men who contributed to a lively controversy which permitted even those who were anti the 'new, new economics' (as Laffer described it) space to pull the theory apart. Doubts were given full expression, as when Herbert Stein made his position absolutely clear:

> economists cannot say that they know with certainty that the Kemp-Roth tax cut would not raise the revenue. They can, or should only say that the available evidence makes the outcome extremely improbable. It may turn out that there is human life on Mars. But I would not invest

much in MacDonald's franchise on that planet, and I wouldn't bet the nation's economic policy on the assumption that the tax cut will increase the revenue.[39]

By so stimulating debate the *Wall Street Journal* came to occupy a pivotal role in the formation of economic opinion during a period of deep crisis in economics and economic policy – when *new* ideas were thin on the ground. Republicans were firing off economic policies without any real technical back-up of the kind demanded in modern economic debate: Wanniski and the supply-side arguments of the *Journal* filled this gap. Bartley's page focused the political debate on economic policy in a way which few other newspapers had done since Walter Lippman's columns on the New Deal.

As Bartley realized, there was not just a 'breakdown in the Keynesian model' in the 1970s – an end to the intellectual hegemony of Keynesian economic discourse – but also, and perhaps more significantly as the impact of the *Journal* illustrated, there was a more fundamental breakup of the long-held hegemony of the economics profession on economics. Reflecting on the presidential campaign of 1980 the *Journal* could therefore claim, with some justification, that:

> However supply-side ideas work out, they are the only ones on the economic horizon that seem at this moment to offer any ray of hope for our current circumstances. The Keynesian notion has played itself out; witness the flight of many Keynesians into the desperation of wage-price controls . . . It certainly seems to us that a new idea that may offer the possibility of a way out should be applauded rather than ridiculed.[40]

And even its critics like Stein had to concede that, by this time, the supply-side debate had come to play an important role in forcing the pace on the economic front:

> Despite the tone of much of the current argument, the propositions of supply-side economics are not matters of ideology or principle. They are matters of arithmetic. So far one must say that the arithmetic of any of the 'newer' propositions is highly doubtful. Supply-side economics may yet prove to be the irritant which, like the grain of sand in an oyster shell, produces a pearl of new economic wisdom.[41]

Whilst waiting for the pearl to appear there was a window of opportunity when, as Lekachman suggests, 'outsiders'[42] stood a chance of influencing the terms of the debate. The only real professional economist involved in the selling of the supply side was Roberts, who had a PhD. Even so, like Laffer, Roberts did not submit his arguments to any academic journal. Apart from his articles in the *Journal*, his views had been put forward in non-professional publications: *Congressional Record*, *National Review*, *Fortune* and *The Public Interest*.

The most important aspect of the 'supply side' revolution was, then, that it was not a product of an academic debate conducted through the professional journals – as has been the normal course of events for advances in economic theory in the postwar era. The experience of supply-side economics approximates more closely to, on the one hand, the work of Keynes in the years preceeding the *General Theory*, and on the other, the single-tax arguments of Henry George. Supply-side 'theory' was the result of an evolving policy discourse: from the start it was more a media event than an intellectual revelation on the lines of Galbraith on first looking into the *General Theory*. The Laffer curve as revealed by George Gilder was:

> not chiefly a mathematical formula, but a vision of how to cut the Gordian knot of government growth and private sector stagnation . . . The idea was simple and demonstrably true. But liberal economists derided it and conservative ones were cooly sceptical . . . For whatever reason America's normally most sophisticated and interesting economists were incapable of comprehending an economic reality . . . that was manifest to a football player trained in physical education, Congressman Jack Kemp: a *Wall Street Journal* editorial writer with little economic training, Jude Wanniski; and an economist, Arthur Laffer, who was widely seen as 'unsound' by his more prestigious colleagues.[43]

Gilder himself, of course, was amongst those who were responsible for actually popularizing the Laffer curve (if not actually defining it more precisely than most) by the exposition of the theory in his hugely successful book, *Wealth and Poverty* (often described as the bible of the Reagan administration), which endorsed the *Journal*'s line and greatly assisted its intellectual standing amongst conservative circles by placing the opinion page in a wider philosophical context than could be attained in a business newspaper.

None the less, it is important to point out that Gilder's book (*Wealth and Poverty*) was itself the outcome of contributions to

Harpers, Forbes, The American Spectator and *Policy Review*, and the influence of Wanniski's columns in the *Journal* and Brookes's articles in the *Boston Herald American* is clear. The book was subsequently serialized in numerous publications, including the *Los Angeles Herald Examiner, Nation's Business, New York Times Syndicate* and the *Reader's Digest*, as well as ten printings in the first five months of publication. Gilder's articles gave the supply-side argument a formidable national stage and an intellectual mystique which it could not otherwise have achieved. The supply-siders were not shy in showing their admiration for Mr Gilder's endeavours. In Jack Kemp's view, it was the 'first book in years that compellingly makes the case for the moral as well as the practical case for capitalism'. David Stockman was equally, if not more, effusive when commending the work as 'Promethean in its intellectual power and insight'. Such comments (from the dust-cover) attest, as Lekachman observes, the existence by 1981 of a 'smooth' supply-side network:

> Political and literary coteries have from the dawn of literacy played the game of scratching each others backs . . . The newcomers should be congratulated for catching on so quickly.[44]

In so knitting together the various aspects and themes of conservative thought with the economic ideas of Wanniski and Laffer, Gilder's contribution to propagating the supply-side message was considerable. It was, however, the *Journal* in providing a common network and channel of communications for a community of publicists and politicians and would-be-theoreticians that had the premier part in selling the supply-side to politicians and the media. The economic line taken on Bartley's pages itself reached a potential audience of 2 million through satellite technology and printing in twelve cities. This gave the paper an opportunity to popularize and interpret the supply-side argument to a national audience as well as get the ideas across to a more select policy and business community in New York and Washington. (It has to be said, however, that one survey showed that the opinion pages were not too popular with the *Journal's* readers: 70 per cent read the business news, as compared with only 29.4 per cent for the editorials.[45]) The *Journal's* advocacy of supply-side economics reassured its readership that the revolution was in the hands of those who understood the real business world. In pushing a vigorous free-market line, which oftentimes had upset big business, the paper managed to perform a neat balancing act; as Ben Bagdikian in the *Washington Journalism Review* argues:

> Executives and stockholders really do want to know the unpleasant truth about corporate life when it affects their career or incomes. At the same time, however, most of them are true believers in the rhetoric of free enterprise . . . By reporting critical stories about realities in particular industries in news columns, but singing the grand old hymns of unfettered *laissez-faire* on the editorial pages, the *Journal* has it both ways.[46]

By getting the message across to corporate capitalism as well as political America, the paper was a catalyst in altering the terms of conservative debate in the years preceding the Reagan presidency. This is not to underestimate the importance of the Republican 'supply-siders' in Washington led by Kemp, but it was the *Journal* which was responsible for actually articulating and aggregating the new policy discourse into an identifiable policy language. In the long term, this process of popular dissemination carried with it the danger of gross over-simplification. As Robert Bartley once commented with regard to Wanniski, he sometimes gave the impression that 'a tax cut can stop an SS–18 in midflight'.[47] However, such dangers are inherent in the business of selling new ideas. In George Stigler's words:

> Wares must be shouted – the human mind is not a divining rod that quivers over the truth. The techniques of persuasion also in the realm of ideas are generally repetition, inflated claims, and disproportionate emphases, and they have preceded and accompanied the adoption on a large scale of every new idea or theory.[48]

In the attempt to extradite the influence of Keynes from America, the political victory went to those who could, as Keynes himself had said, speak with the 'greatest appearance of clear, undoubting conviction and could best use the accents of infallibility'.[49] The supply-siders were much less successful in convincing the academic community than they were in attracting the interest of the media and politicians. All the hype in the world could not make *The Way the World Works* or *Wealth and Poverty* into the kind of powerful theoretical toolbox which could sustain and *contain* argument and serve to rationalize decision making – which is one of the essential political functions of theoretical frameworks. In the end this was a crucial failing of the supply-side strategy. In practice, supply-siders were deeply divided about what exactly their theory actually meant. With no agreed holy writ to guide them, the conflict over policy implementation inevitably surfaced in public disagreements on the very platforms which had served as a launch pad for their ideas. Here there is an interesting comparison to be made between the supply-siders and the political economists in the nineteenth century. The Ricardians, as we saw in Chapter 1, tended to argue in a more private manner, and as far as the public were concerned they spoke with a single voice – as Keynes saw it, 'controversy disappeared'. The big mistake of the supply-siders – who saw themselves as true heirs of the political economists – was that they conducted their intellectual and policy disagreements in loud voices via newspapers and press leaks in the attempt to out-flank their colleagues. Coupled with this inability of the supply-side community to generate a private conversation was the fact that, for the media, supply-side economics meant one thing: tax cuts = increased revenue. Despite the very best efforts of those who did not take this view to disabuse journalists of this opinion, the 'Laffer curve' was firmly lodged in the public imagination. As is the way the media world works, supply-side economics became reduced to the Wanniski version and the Stockman story. Having shown such ability to shape the agenda in the 1970s, the supply-siders thus found it impossible to control it in the White House. The failure of the supply-side revolutionaries to construct a theory and generate a professional debate ultimately meant that the supply-side rebellion was without a heavyweight economic guru who could do battle for them both outside and inside the policy-making process: the boy David was not enough. In the 1970s 'making it up as they went along' brought with it all the advantages of ambiguity: the theory could be all things to all men. In power, however, 'making it up as they went along' carried as many disadvantages. Not the least of these was that in being so disunited about tax cuts and deficits they also failed to score points in the political battle in the media, which were ever eager to cover a good fight and gleefully report on the demise of 'Reaganomics'. with the exception of the *Journal* and *Forbes*, the press was, by and large, hostile to supply-side ideas and naturally stood ever-ready to exploit the differences of opinion in the White House. Wanniski, for example, even before the supply-side show hit Washington, gave Leonard Silk of the *New York Times*, an anti-supply-sider if ever there was one, a copy of a memorandum from Stockman and Kemp to the President Elect warning of an 'economic Dunkirk', so as to 'maximize pressure on Reagan to plunge ahead with his program'.[50] Other supply-siders subsequently aided and abetted the media campaign by their propensity to leak stories to the press, most noticeably in the celebrated interview of David Stockman with William Greider in the *Atlantic Monthly* in December 1981, in a (misguided) attempt, as Stockman saw it, to 'penetrate the citadel of establishment opinion makers'.[51] The *Atlantic* fiasco, wherein Stockman detailed the splits in the Reagan administration over tax cuts and the budget, brought the fatal flaw of the supply-side experiment into sharp focus. The interview showed that 'metaphor and reality had been at odds from the beginning'.[52]

> The fact was, due to the efforts of myself and my supply-side compatriots, Ronald Reagan had been made to stumble into the wrong camp . . . In December 1980, Governor Reagan's campaign managers had sent him to school for a few days to get brushed up on the National issues. There, Jack Kemp, Art Laffer, and Jude Wanniski thoroughly hosed him down with supply side doctrines. They told him about the 'Laffer Curve'. It set off a symphony in his ears. He knew instantly that it was true and would never doubt it a moment thereafter.[53]

Stockman himself argues that the problem was that the Laffer curve was an 'academic paradigm', and therefore its 'translation into the real world . . . was complicated and slippery'.[54] But, in truth, the Laffer curve was not so much a paradigm as a form of discourse which served, for a time, to give a technical, quasi-scientific legitimacy and gloss to other 'new' and 'old' right policies. As Stockman argued in the *Atlantic*, supply-side economics was just a disguise for old-fashioned trickle-down theory: give money away to the rich in the hope that the poor might get some on the way. It made a good story. However, as the 'non-Lafferites' maintained, it was certainly not the whole story; but by this time it was far too late for theoretical clarification. The press thrived off supply-side simplification as did their political opponents. In practice, the something-for-nothing rhetoric, which so well served the cause in the 1970s, came to dominate the perception of supply-side theory totally. As it had lived off the media in the early days, it was fitting that the press should have been in at the kill. The rise and fall of supply-side economics was, as Mark Shields of the *Washington Post* neatly expressed it, an open and shut case of death by 'Leak, Leak, Sink, Sink'.[55]

Whether Lord Keynes actually did leave America after Mr Reagan arrived at the White House is a moot point: the soaring deficits attracted some wry Keynesian praise. As Leonard Silk commented:

> The fiscal and monetary blunders of the Hoover era opened the door to the Keynesian revolution in economics. While using supply-side rhetoric Reagan's top economic policy advisors had joined that revolution.[56]

Keynes himself would have undoubtedly understood the process whereby anti-Keynesian ideas made their way to Washington by capturing a dominant position in the arena of economic opinion. The supply-siders achieved the kind of rapid success that Keynes had so much desired in the 1930s. Where they fell down was that, unlike the 'Ricardian' or 'Keynesian' revolution, 'voodoo economics', as George Bush termed it, never managed to go beyond the stage of devising a policy rhetoric which was most effective as a media metaphor but totally inadequate as an operational theory. Mr Reagan's economic revolutionaries lacked a handbook: the best the supply-side ever came up with was the *Journal*'s opinion page, Wanniski and George Gilder. In the end, however, the press was as much involved in the undoing of supply-side as earlier it had been in the forefront of putting its ideas into general currency. In power, the supply-siders soon came to blows in public and ended up washing the kind of soiled clothes which ought to have been washed well before they ever got to the White House. By enabling the supply-siders to bypass the academic roads which had for so long monopolized all routes to Washington and public opinion, the *Journal* accelerated the political development of the ideas, but ultimately this speeded-up rate of political growth did the emergent 'new' theory no great favours: the failure of Reaganomics ironically revived the fortunes of Keynesianism![57]

In conclusion, the 'supply-side' episode has an important place in American intellectual history since it was, perhaps, the first example of the media popularizing and translating economic ideas and discourse for a (relatively) mass audience as well as amongst the policy-making community. The most obvious precedent is that of an earlier tax campaign led by a forerunner of supply-side politics, Henry George. Although the latter's ideas also upset the professionals and attracted much press interest, they did not actually make it to Washington. The supply-side 'revolution' heralded a recovery of 'non-professional' economics during a period when there was considerable uncertainty surrounding what to do about the economy and the future of democracy in conditions of economic stagnation. As we shall see, these themes were also to be found in the political debate which was taking place across the Atlantic.

NOTES

1. *New York Times*, 16 May 1965.
2. *Economist*, 14–20 March 1987.
3. For a critique of the view that the fiscal revolution in America was entirely the outcome of intellectual processes, see Herbert Stein, *The Fiscal Revolution in America* (Chicago University Press, Chicago, 1969).
4. Galbraith, *New York Times*, 16 May 1965.
5. James Tobin, *The New Economics One Decade Older* (Princeton University Press, Princeton, New Jersey, 1974) p. 5.
6. *Business Week*, 17 September 1979.
7. For an account of the development of supply-side ideas see Robert E. Keleher and William P. Orzechowski 'Supply-side Fiscal Policy: an historical analysis', in R. H. Fink (ed.), *Supply-side Economics: a critical appraisal* (University Publications of America, Maryland, 1982). Laffer himself identified the historical antecedents of his theory as the Moslem philosopher Ibn Khaldun; (see 'Taxation and the Reason for High and Low Tax Revenues', *Wall Street Journal*, 30 September 1978), Adam Smith, J. B. Say, Henry George in *Progress and Poverty*. See A. B. Laffer, 'Government Expectations and Revenue Deficiencies', *Cato Journal*, no. 1, Spring 1981.
8. See, for example, M. Felstein and L. Summers, 'Inflation, Tax Rules, and the Long Term Interest Rate', *Brookings Papers on Economic Activity*, vol. 1 (1978) M. Felstein, 'Incidence of a Capital Income Tax in a Growing Economy with Variable Savings Rates', *Review of Economic Studies*, vol. 41 (1974) D. Meiselman and A. B. Laffer (eds), *The Phenomenon of World-wide Inflation* (American Enterprise Institute, Washington DC, 1975); A. B. Laffer and Jan Seymour (eds), *The Economics of the Tax Revolt* (Harcourt Brace Jovanovitch, New York, 1979).
9. *Wall Street Journal*, 8 October 1981.
10. Ivan Illich, *The Right to Useful Employment: and its professional enemies* (Marion Boyars, London, 1978) p. 86.
11. W. Breit and R. Spencer (eds), *The Lives of the Laureates* (MIT Press, Cambridge, Mass., 1986) p. 64.

12. Warren Brookes, *The Economy in Mind* (Universe Books, New York, 1982) p. 11.
13. Jude Wanniski, *The Way the World Works*, rev. edn (Simon and Schuster, New York, 1983) p. xxxiii.
14. Some of Irving Kristol's *Wall Street Journal* articles are contained in *Two Cheers for Capitalism* (Basic Books, New York, 1978).
15. See P. Steinfels, *The Neo-Conservatives: the men who are changing America's Politics* (Touchstone Books, New York, 1979) pp. 8–10; and Alan Crawford, *Thunder on the Right: the 'new right' and the politics of resentment* (Pantheon Books, New York, 1980) passim.
16. George Gilder, *Wealth and Poverty* (Bantam Books, New York 1982) p. 63.
17. See the present author's 'Politics Without Promises: the crisis of overload and governability', *Parliamentary Affairs*, vol. 35, no. 4 (1982) p. 427.
18. H. Helco and R. Penner, 'Fiscal and Political Strategy in the Reagan Administration', in Fred I. Greenstein (ed.), *The Reagan Presidency: an early assessment* (Johns Hopkins Press, Baltimore, Md, 1983) p. 27.
19. *Business Week*, 17 September 1979. The magazines's own policy was that of a social contract between business and labour in order to achieve growth and reindustrialisation. See 30 June 1980.
20. Paul Craig Roberts, *The Supply Side Revolution: an insider's account of policymaking in Washington* (Harvard University Press, Cambridge, Mass. 1984) p. 101.
21. Ibid, p. 23.
22. In *Newsweek*, 7 August 1978.
23. *New York Times*, 13 August 1981; see also J. K. Galbraith, 'The Market and Mr Reagan', *New Republic*, 23 September 1981; and R. Heilbroner, 'The Demand for the Supply-side', *New York Review of Books*, 11 June 1981.
24. See Gilder, op. cit., p. 203.
25. See Jack Kemp, *An American Renaissance* (Basic Books, New York, 1979).
26. A. Laffer, 'Government Exactions and Revenue Deficiencies', *Cato Journal*, vol. 1 (Spring 1981) p. 21.
27. Roberts, op. cit., pp. 28–9.
28. T. W. Hazlett 'The Supply-Side's Weak Side: an Austrian's critique', in Fink (ed.), op. cit., p. 105.
29. Robert Lekachman, *Greed is Not Enough: Reaganomics* (Pantheon Books, New York, 1982) p. 47.
30. *Wall Street Journal*, 8 October 1981.
31. Hielbronner, op. cit.
32. In R. H. Fink (ed.) op. cit., p. 204.
33. See also J. Wanniski, 'Taxes, Revenues and the Laffer Curve', *Public Interest* (Winter 1978).
34. Wanniski, *The Way the World Works*, op. cit., p. xxxii.
35. T. W. Hazlett, in Fink (ed.) 'The Supply-side's Weak Side', op. cit., p. 94.
36. Don Fullerton, 'Can Tax Revenues go Up when Tax Rates go Down?' (Department of the Treasury, Office of Tax Analysis, Washington, DC. Paper 41, September 1980).
37. *Washington Post*, 15 February 1981.
38. Roberts, op. cit., p. 91.
39. *Wall Street Journal*, 18 July 1978.
40. Ibid., 4 April, 1980.
41. Ibid., 19 March 1980.
42. Lekachman, op. cit., p. 45.
43. Gilder, op. cit., pp. 214–15.

44. Lekachman, op. cit.
45. J. M. Rosenberg, *Inside the Wall Street Journal* (Macmillan, New York, 1982) p. 204.
46. Cited in Rosenberg, op.cit., p. 206–7.
47. *Wall Street Journal*, 29 November 1979.
48. G. Stigler, *Essays in the History of Economics* (Chicago, 1965).
49. J. M. Keynes, 'My Early Life', in *Essays in Persuasion*, The Collected Writings of J. M. Keynes, vol. 9, (Macmillan, London 1971–   ) p. 85.
50. Leonard Silk, *Economics in the Real World: how political decisions affect the economy* (Simon and Schuster, New York, 1984) p. 173.
51. David A. Stockman, *The Triumph of Politics* (The Bodley Head, London, 1986) p. 85.
52. Ibid., p. 8.
53. Ibid., p. 10.
54. Ibid., p. 11.
55. *Washington Post*, 14 January 1983.
56. Silk, op. cit., p. 198.
57. See, for example, E. Ray Canterbery, *The Making of Economics* (Wadsworth, Belmont, California, 1987) pp. 249–71.

6. How Friedman came to Britain

In Britain, as in America, the 1970s was a period which witnessed the emergence of a campaign in a number of newspapers against the receding tide of Keynesian managerialism and in favour of more free-market economic policies. And, as was also the case in America, the progress of anti-Keynesian ideas and arguments owed more in the first instance to the force of inflation and economic crisis and to the fact that non-professional, or leastways non-academic, economists took to publicizing the ideas than it did to the impact of academic scholarship. Confronted with the catch 22 of 'stagflation' (a term apparently introduced to Britain by the *Economist*)[1] the old 'Keynesian' political formulae for managing the economy prompted a crisis in economics and in the economics profession. The trade-off between inflation and unemployment and the difficulties of world trade and floating exchange rates from 1971 to 1972 all served to reinforce the argument that the old solutions of demand management, prices and incomes policies and so on, were no longer sustainable. Monetarism, on the other hand, was new and it offered a clear solution to inflation. Professor Friedman's brand of 'monetarism' had captured some important points in the British economic community from the late 1960s and these served as bridgeheads in the assault on Keynesian economics in the 1970s. Harry Johnson, Brian Griffith and Alan Walters at the London School of Economics were, for example, influential exponents of monetarist theory, as were the departments of economics at Liverpool, Manchester and the London Business School. However, perhaps the most vital territory occupied by the forces of economic liberalism was not academia but the financial press. The acceptance, some would say uncritical acceptance,[2] of the free-market position by leading commentators was unquestionably a major factor in the legitimizing and propagating of the new economics. Journalists like Samuel Brittan and Peter Jay were thinking radically about ideas being aired across the Atlantic whilst the greater part of the economics profession and politicians were desperately trying to fit Keynesian theory around the prevailing economic realities of rising inflation and unprecedented levels of postwar unemployment by arguing for price and wages controls and various technical adjustments to demand management policy. What Keynesian academics were totally unprepared for was winning the argument at the level of *political* debate. Friedman and the various groups and individuals who were in the vanguard of 'liberal' political economy were, however, more than prepared to take the argument to the citizen by focusing on the policy failures of the past and emphasizing the relationship between political liberty, governmental effectiveness and economic freedom.

Professor Friedman's success in Britain owed much to the way in which, as in America, he skilfully deployed instances of economic failure to discredit Keynesianism and promote the idea of controlling the money supply as the *only* alternative to state interventionism, as well as market his own version of events and his radical brand of economic liberalism. He was a prolific writer of articles and letters and made frequent visits to London to publicize his theories and offer his opinions on the state of the British economy. Friedman's British campaign culminated in a television series, *Free to Choose*, in the spring of 1980, shortly after Mrs Thatcher's election victory. It was an enterprise which served to confirm the fact that, as Peter Jay put it (on the cover of the book), by this time 'Friedmanism' had indeed become the 'central issue in British domestic political debate'.

The idea for the series came from Robert Chitester of WQLN, Pennsylvania, in 1977. Harcourt Brace Jovanovitch helped to finance the videotaping and also distributed the tapes in the US. A number of lectures and question-and-answer sessions were taped in the US and later in 1978–9 filming was completed by Video Arts of London. In Britain the ten films were condensed into six programmes, together with a discussion between Friedman and a number of British academics, businessmen and politicians. The aim of the broadcasts and the 'book of the film' was to give substance and 'concrete examples' for the principles which he had set out earlier in his *Capitalism and Freedom*, and took its arguments further by incorporating many of the new political ideas emanating from the 'public choice' school. Unlike Galbraith's earlier (1977) series, *The Age of Uncertainty*, which was intended more as a piece of economic education than Galbraithian propaganda, Friedman's programmes were frankly designed to convert and persuade. The book was, unlike Galbraith's own television spin-off, aimed at winning over people to a definite political viewpoint rather than explaining the development of economic thought:

> Television is dramatic. It appeals to the emotions. It captures your attention. Yet we remain of the opinion that the printed page is a more effective instrument for both education and persuasion ... Anyone who is persuaded in one evening (or even ten one-hour evenings) is not really persuaded ... You must turn the issues over in your mind at leisure, consider the arguments, let them simmer, and after a long time turn your preferences into convictions.[3]

The series began with a general statement of political and economic liberty, the ideas of Smith and Mill, and a review of economic liberalism in nineteenth-century Britain and America. From the outset, Friedman emphasized the power of markets: in Hayekian terms, *only* markets could transmit all the information which drives economic activity. The free functioning of the price system guaranteed, he stressed, both economic efficiency and political freedom. When an economic system is controlled or regulated by governments or monopolies then things begin to go awry. The programmes then proceeded to give examples of this process: the monetary system; the welfare state; the pursuit of equality; schools; consumer protection and state regulation; the power of labour unions; and inflation. The series concluded on an optimistic note with the claim that, as witnessed by the election of Mrs Thatcher and by the Proposition 13 movement in the US, the tide of opinion which the programmes had sought to explain and promote was at last on the turn.

The programmes and their accompanying publicity and comment was the high point of Friedmanism's influence on the British political agenda. And the (bestselling) book received perhaps the most extensive reviewing in the British press of any modern work in economics. Even the liberal *Guardian* had to admit that: 'Whereas in the past it might have been possible to ignore a Friedman work on the grounds that it had no significance, this is no longer possible.'

Professor Friedman's media attack on the 'Keynesian' consensus which had dominated the British political scene since the 1940s had been greatly assisted by the fact that, in addition to the base camps at the London School of Economics and think-tanks like the Institute of Economic Affairs, the Adam Smith Institute and the Centre for Policy Studies (headed by a journalist, Alfred Sherman), he had made two important converts to the cause in the form of two of the country's leading and highly respected economic journalists. Peter Jay and Samuel Brittan had begun to introduce their readers to Friedman's ideas in the late 1960s and early 1970s and were really ahead of many academic economists – and political scientists – in realizing that the collapse of Keynesian-based politics would have many consequences for the shape of the economic agenda. That, as in the 1960s, it was to be journalists who were to be in the forefront of reviving political economy in the 1970s is a great testament both to their own powers of communication and observation, and a comment on the narrower perceptions and intellectual preoccupations of economists and other social scientists.

The influence of Brittan and Jay derived from the way in which they acted as a channel between the world of economic ideas and political and economic events and public opinion. Of course, the problem for the 'Keynesians' was that the tide of events and opinions was running so much against them that the public defence of their case was bound to be less effective and less attractive than untried 'Friedmanism' with its simple message of controlling the money supply and enhancing the freedom of the individual. The role of British economic journalists in disseminating monetarism was, however, somewhat different to that played by the *Wall Street Journal*, in selling the supply-side. Although both responses were reactions to political and intellectual vacuums, the main difference between them was that monetarism had a worked-out theory and a respectable academic pedigree: the function of Brittan and Jay in Britain was that of disseminators rather than, as was the case for Wanniski and Roberts *et al.*, active formulators.

The similarity to the 'supply-side' episode in the US and the rise of monetarist journalism in Britain was that, in both instances, the press clearly had a role in stimulating and mediating economic controversy to a readership involved at a political or intellectual level in the politics of economic policy and more generally assisted in the formulation of a political economy which restated the case for the market and the price system as being economically effective and politically desirable. Samuel Brittan had, as we saw earlier in Chapter 4, come out of the Labour government more doubtful about planning than when he had entered it. His departure from Mr Wilson's government and his disillusionment with demand management and planning in the mid-1960s coincided with the growing influence of Milton Friedman in America. As he explains:

> It was in the late 1960s that I grasped the impossibility of spending ourselves into the target levels of unemployment by demand management of any kind and the likelihood that the attempt to do so would set off an ever-increasing inflation. This was the message of Professor Milton Friedman's 1967 Presidential address to the American Economic Association, which caught my imagination as earlier arguments about monetary versus fiscal policy did not . . . I can fairly claim to have been ahead of most of the U.K. in this field – academic as well as political and official . . .[4]

Brittan's commentaries during the Heath years show that, as he notes, he was largely immune to the interventionism and dash for growth in the period prior to the onset of 'stagflation'. His conversion to Friedman's arguments about the need to reinstate market forces meant that the Professor's ideas could attain an audience far larger than seminars held at the I.E.A. Brittan's articles in the *Financial Times* and elsewhere in the mid-1970s made the point that the markets were the only viable alternative to the failed demand management politics of the past. In 1973, for example, his *Capitalism and the Permissive Society* developed this theme in a radical assessment and analysis of the corporatist culture which had come to dominate British politics and society. He showed how union power ill-served their membership and the nation as a whole, exposed some of the problems of political control of state industry, and maintained that democracy was becoming dangerously deadlocked by the workings of vested interests. The following year the miners' strike dramatically brought into focus Brittan's argument. He was convinced that much of the conventional economic and political wisdom, both here and in America, provided inadequate explanations and he began to further elaborate his ideas on the relationship between economic and political liberty after:

> casual observations as an economic journalist, which made me feel that there was something seriously deficient in the British academic economic

tradition as well as in the Eastern seaboard US texts favoured in this country. Above all I was profoundly dissatisfied both with the conventional lapses from 'perfection' in the workings of markets, and with the text book case from free enterprise, which described the optimum allocation of resources with known static tastes and techniques.[5]

Brittan, despite the way his critics tend to portray him as one of the chief instigators of the 'monetarist' revolution and the precursor of Thatcherism,[6] was never a simplistic monetarist and could certainly not be described as a Thatcherite. Indeed, he has not infrequently been highly critical of Mrs Thatcher's authoritarian approach to economic and other policies – something which has annoyed her more enthusiastic supporters in the Conservative party. He has endeavoured to tread a difficult middle course between the excesses of the new right and the out-dated interventionism of the old Keynesians and between the conservatism of Hayek and the flights of fantasy to be found in some neo-conservative political economy and philosophy. His pragmatism has been highly English but never inward looking as has been true of so many of his academic contemporaries. Indeed, his writings were amongst the first to draw together and to popularize the ideas of Friedman and Hayek and the Virginia school. Over the years Brittan has striven to define a liberalism compatible with British political culture and institutions whilst at the same time pointing towards the relevance and importance of moving towards a more social market economy. Again, some of his critics find this too much of an intellectual compromise. Brittan contends however that:

> It is possible to be in favour of redistribution without either being an egalitarian or believing that there is such a thing as a 'just reward' for particular occupations which a body of wisemen can ascertain ... A social market economist should make common cause with the New Right in an onslaught on state monopoly, union monopoly, and practices and institutions which price people out of work. But unlike the New Right, he should be concerned with the distribution of capital ownership and with transfers through tax and social security system ...[7]

From the late 1960s his articles began to spell out the view that the old economic problems had to be approached with a new radicalism: government does not always know best and oftentimes markets know better; lower unemployment carries the price of higher inflation; the problem of union power had to be faced; exchange rates had to be flexible; and the money supply had to be subject to tighter control. His fear was that the British economy was being managed by yesterday's ideas, and the problem which he set himself was to formulate a more relevant political economy. He became convinced that Britain was ruled by the 'Wenceslas myth' – the notion that government can and should provide benefits even when such benefits do not make economic sense. It was now time, he began to argue in the mid-1970s, for a change in some fundamental areas of economic policy:

> We have come to our present pass through the pursuit of 'full employment' by the wrong means. We have seized on policies with temporary and fleeting effects, resulting from the slowness of human beings to adapt to changing opportunities and elevated them into fundamental truths of economics.[8]

Brittan's writing has been primarily concerned with the clarification of economic issues and controversy and has been informed by the belief that even given the powers of organized interests, ultimately it is *ideas* in economic affairs, as in other human activities, which really shape history:

> Like language, law, money and many other human phenomena, opinion is more the result of evolution than of conscious attempts to influence it. But evolved opinion throws up contradictions and unsolved problems to which political economy is entitled to make a contribution. For make no mistake, it is neither force, nor self interest, but opinion that counts in the end.[9]

In making his own contribution to changing opinion, Brittan was advantaged by the fact that, as a non-academic, his own research agenda could be shaped by the freedom to think aloud in the *Financial Times* and respond to events and ideas, rather than by professional or peer-group pressures. This was especially important at a time when economics was becoming ever more technical and forbidding to the outsider. Brittan had the luxury of taking a broader *political* view of economics – something which was out of favour in the contemporary economics profession. What was needed, he believed, was not simply 'a revolution in economic theory, but a revolution in constitutional and political ideas which will save us from the snare of unlimited democracy'.[10] Brittan's intellectual development has, therefore, been concerned with this relationship between economic ideas and political problems and has frequently sought to link the need for constitutional and political reform with changes in macro- and microeconomic policy. Like Bagehot in the nineteenth century, Brittan has attempted not simply to disseminate certain economic ideas, but also to articulate a grander *political* theory. Whereas Bagehot commentated on the success of the British constitution and economic system, Brittan has been an equally perceptive chronicler of its failings in the twentieth century. By the middle 1970s Brittan began to reach the conclusion that the underlying problems which beset the UK, in common with other industrialized societies, was that of the interaction between politics and markets, especially the way in which the political process had become dominated by the power of interest groups. A number of books and articles were forthcoming on this theme. *Government and the Market Economy* (1971) and *Participation Without Politics* (1975), for instance, made the case for harnessing market forces to deal with those problems, like welfare, which had become overly politicized through government intervention. Other works emphasized the relationship between economics and democracy, most notably in his influential essay, 'The Economic Contradictions of Democracy' (1974),[11] which argued that British democracy was in danger of being undermined by a political system which had fuelled the growth of excessive expectations.

Brittan's writings have therefore possessed a comprehensiveness that finds few parallels in the academic world. His reputation has owed much to the fact that, as was also the case with Bagehot, his ideas have evolved through a close involvement both with the daily course of events as well as the flow of ideas and opinions. As a journalist he has been more attuned to new developments in both economic theory and political thought than many of his academic contemporaries and has demonstrated a ready ability actually to apply these ideas to the practical issues of the day. This too was one of Bagehot's great gifts. Brittan has thus established for himself a unique position in modern British social thought as the 'foremost exponent of a popular (but extremely sophisticated) classical liberalism'.[12]

His career as a journalist on the *Financial Times*, his academic reputation (he has been a Research Fellow at Nuffield College (1973–4 and 1974–82) and a Visiting Professor at the Chicago Law School (1978)), together with his political contacts (his brother is a former Conservative Cabinet minister and Nigel Lawson is a friend and former colleague), have enabled him to occupy a key role in studying both the intellectual traffic between the US and the UK as well as the British political scene and the climate of international financial opinion. In the 1970s Brittan was, therefore, in a most advantageous location from which both to observe and influence economic opinion. Later, in the 1980s, Mr Brittan's support for the European Monetary System and the idea of stablizing inflation around 5 per cent had considerable influence on the debate surrounding the Thatcher government's economic policy, if not on the actual economic strategy pursued by Chancellor Lawson.

Peter Jay, like Brittan, had a reputation for being a (very) clever man interested in ideas. Like Brittan, he had close connections with the Labour government. His father was Douglas Jay (see Chapter 2) and his father-in-law James Callaghan. On leaving the Navy he entered the Treasury and rose to the level of Principal. In 1967 he left the civil service and became the first economics editor of *The Times*. When the paper expanded its business pages in 1969 Jay became associate editor of the Business News section. During this time (1972–7) he was also a television presenter on ITV's *Weekend World* and *The Jay Interview*. He thus became what Alan Ryan once described as the 'self-appointed educator of the influential classes'.[13] He was later appointed, not without some controversy, by his father- in-law to the post of British ambassador in Washington, and subsequently returned to London to head the *Economist Intelligence Unit*. Later in the 1980s he was a prominent figure in TV AM (mark I), a breakfast television channel, from which he resigned in 1983 following the channel's failure to pull in a large enough audience. Unlike Samuel Brittan, however, Jay was not to sustain his involvement with the economic scene and the debate in the 1980s, save by the publication of selected essays, lectures and journalism under the rather grand title of *The Crisis for Western Political Economy*[14] and a book (written with Michael Stewart) which attempted to forecast the shape of things to come, *Apocalypse 2000*.[15] Jay's conversion to the ideas of Friedman, or leastways to taking them seriously, occurred around the same time as that of Brittan, namely during Mr Wilson's second term. The fact that his father had been given the sack by Mr Wilson in 1967 also did not endear him to the administration. Monetarism offered, at first, a new framework for the discussion of economic policy and, as things got worse in the Heath and Callaghan governments, Jay began more positively to advocate monetarist solutions. He was also at this time becoming critical of the way in which the British media had failed to explain and present new ideas. In May 1968, as the government came under increasing pressure to alter its monetary policy, Jay began to give some attention to explaining the monetarist case.[16] He was, however, highly critical of simplistic versions of monetarism and arguments against deficit spending, such as those which Enoch Powell was putting forward. However, the fact that it was also an argument being advanced by the Bank of England and the IMF – more 'sophisticated voices' – brought forth more detailed analysis. Jay had his doubts, but nevertheless maintained that:

> even if the more extreme claims of the monetarists are inapplicable to the British economy, this is no sufficient reason to assert that the money supply does not matter at all in economic policy.[17]

In the months which followed in that revolutionary year of 1968, *Business News* pressed for an 'intelligent debate' on the issue of the money supply which had come to a head in October with disagreements between the 'consensus of British economic opinion' and the IMF. Jay came out on the side of the monetarists:

> The fact that Mr Thorneycroft as chancellor in 1957 is remembered for having fallen into the crude error of believing that price inflation could be tempered by printing fewer notes is no reason to ignore the increasingly impressive analytical and predictive results of the Chicago school of monetary economists in the United States.[18]

A few years later, in 1974, Jay was enunciating a more urgent political economy.

> When, in 1980 or so, democracy as we know it has been suspended and people have accepted that the depression is established for a decade or so, the question may be asked, 'Where did we go wrong?'[19]

His analysis of the British disease was that it was the outcome of an 'irreconcilable quadrilateral':

1. Government whose authority rests on renewable popular consent;
2. The commitment to full employment – not just as an ultimate objective, but as a necessary requirement year by year and quarter by quarter;
3. The dependence on stable prices, or at least on stable rates of inflation or some stable basis of economic exchange; and
4. The durability of collective bargaining as the primary means of determining pay in the labour market.

The breakdown of Britain could, he maintained, be avoided if firm action were taken to extricate the economy and polity out of the deadlock of these four features:

> The only way the disaster can be avoided is for the government resolutely to pursue disinflationary (though not contradictionary) policies and for the country to back them in doing so by accepting the means as well as by willing the ends . . . It means Britain balancing the budget . . . and keeping the growth of the money supply in single figures.[20]

The outlook otherwise was grim indeed. Jay's pessimism was also shared by his editor on *The Times*, William Rees-Mogg, who, like Jay, was also involved with the IEA.[21] Rees-Mogg had previously worked on the *Financial Times*, and was for a short while City editor of the *Sunday Times* (1960–1). A historian by training, he became political and economic editor of the paper in 1961 and later deputy editor and editor during the period 1967–81. He made his own commitment to monetarism clear in *The Reigning Error: the crisis of world inflation* (1974) and in an IEA paper entitled *Democracy and the Value of Money: the theory of money from Locke to Keynes* (1977) which argued that Keynes had done much damage to the state of world inflation. The only solution that Rees-Mogg saw in sight was greater monetary discipline on the lines being advocated by Friedman and a return to the gold standard. Such was also the stuff of *Times* editorials. It is important to add that at this time the IEA's brand of monetarism was also supported by the paper's political columnist, Ronald Butt, who also wrote for the *Sunday Times*.

Jay's influence also extended, apparently, to his father-in-law

– the Prime Minister – who in 1976 announced the death of the Keynesian order in a speech to the Labour party conference which was heavily rumoured to have been inspired, if not actually drafted, by Jay himself. It became perhaps the most widely quoted recantation of Keynesianism in British politics, and served the monetarist cause well:

> We used to think that you could just spend your way out of recession, and increase employment by cutting taxes and boosting government spending. I tell you in all candour that that option no longer exists, and in so far as it ever did exist, it worked by injecting inflation into the economy. And each time that happened, the average level of unemployment has risen. High inflation, followed by higher unemployment. That is the history of the last twenty years.

The previous year (1975) Jay had expanded on the reasons for his own change of mind in the Harold Wincott lecture. As he confessed at the outset of the lecture:

> I, alas, never knew Harold Wincott personally; but I was a frequent reader of his memorable columns in the *Financial Times*. I must be honest and admit that I do not actually remember ever reading a column of his with which I agreed; but then I was in those days a youngish man who still believed in the at least theoretical possibility of benign government . . . Now, of course, I am wiser.[22]

With all the natural enthusiasm of a convert, combined with what he later termed a 'mission to explain', Jay lost little opportunity in his own columns, lectures and articles to explain and promote a change of direction in British economic policy and institutions. As far as the latter was concerned he was, for example, a strong advocate of workers' co-operatives as a method of solving many of the problems which the wage relationship had generated in Britain as elsewhere. He also supported the idea of setting up a select parliamentary committee on the economy. Jay saw the rise of economic journalism, in a BBC talk entitled 'On Being an Economic Journalist' as the by-product of a literary lacuna in British intellectual and political life:

> The great heritage of political economy, as developed in this country by Adam Smith, David Hume, David Ricardo, John Stuart Mill, Marshall and Keynes, is essentially a literary tradition oriented to the illumination and solution of real problems. It was perhaps inevitable

that as fewer of the limited store of discoveries remained to be made, the hankering of economists for a more strictly scientific reputation should have steered the subject further and further away from broad general truths and the real world ... economics has offered diminishing returns to policy-makers.[23]

As many Keynesian economists were reluctant to engage in the kind of political discourse which was emanating from the right, so others, including most noticeably Jay himself, 'rushed in' in the 1970s to provide literate analyses of 'broad truths'. The lead given by Brittan and Jay in interpreting the new economics for their readers was unquestionably a vital stage on the way to intellectual and political credibility for ideas which, until they took them up, were for the most part of interest to off-the-curve economists and the off-beat IEA. Jay and Brittan gave 'monetarism' and 'the market' a currency and a level of publicity which it would not otherwise have achieved had discussion remained the property of the IEA, Keith Joseph and the 'new right' wing of the Conservative party. So much so that, as Keegan and Pennant-Rea note:

At times the traditional Keynesians in Whitehall complained bitterly in private about the degree to which the responsible press was in the hands of the monetarists. There was an interplay between the views of these commentators and the financial markets, which seemed to reinforce each other. This public campaign hardly weakened the hands of the burgeoning monetarist school within the Bank of England. And while protesting all the way that they were in any sense 'monetarists', ministers and the official machine reluctantly appeared to absorb a large part of the Friedman/Brittan/Jay message.[24]

The conversion of Brittan and Jay was a sign of the fact that, certainly by the Chancellorship of Mr Denis Healey, the context of economic and financial news commentary in key papers had moved into a more market-orientated direction than had been the case for the greater part of the postwar period. The international situation had much to do with this. Under the pressure of rising inflation, with unemployment at new postwar heights and the end of the Phillips curve, the old intellectual order and its attendant political consensus began to break up; the role of Brittan and Jay in reconstituting a new consensus was but the clearest public manifestation of the search going on to work out a political economy more in tune with the circumstances then prevailing. At another less public level, this process was also taking place in publications with more limited circulation than *The Times* or the *Financial Times*, particularly through bankers' circulars. Alan Walters, for example, later an economic advisor to Mrs Thatcher, wrote for the firm of Joseph Sebag. But perhaps the most influential circular was that written by Gordon Pepper of Greenwell's. Pepper himself had been won over to monetarism in the late 1960s after an encounter with Beryl Sprinkel of Harris Trust and Savings Bank of Chicago. In 1972 he published the first of his *Monthly Bulletins*. They attracted great interest from both financial clients and politicians and established him as the leading monetarist guru in the City. His thoughts were said to influence the Labour government of the time, Conservative politicians as well as the markets:

> Our regular bulletins were moving markets, clients were constantly plaguing me to find out what was in the next one, life had almost become a nightmare. I was seriously contemplating whether being a guru of that standing was compatible with remaining a stockbroker.[25]

Another influential voice was that of Tim Congdon who had worked on *The Times* under Peter Jay and later joined L. Messel and Co., but continued to write for the paper as well as for the *Spectator* and the *Banker* – the latter publication had begun to campaign for monetarist policies in the late 1960s. In addition to these platforms for monetarist views, there was also the London Business School, whose forecasts by Messrs Burns and Ball published in the *Sunday Times* became, by the middle 1970s, increasingly more monetarist in outlook.

The *Sunday Times*, although its editor was hostile to monetarism, was none the less instrumental in launching another key attack on the prevailing consensus through the publication in 1974–5 of a series of articles by Robert Bacon and Walter Eltis. Bacon and Eltis were approached by the managing editor of the paper, Bruce Page, after he had read their NEDO monograph, *The Age of US and UK Machinery*, which had demonstrated that a major problem facing British industry was overmanning and low productivity. Page suggested that they develop this theme of overmanning and underproduction for an article on the growth of the 'non-productive' sector in the British economy: 'Budget Message for Mr Healey: Get More People into Factories'.[26] Such was the interest shown in their arguments that they were encouraged to go on and develop their theories more fully. They were subsequently commissioned to write three articles of 6000 words each for publication in the autumn of 1975. The final product owed much to the editorial advice of Harold Evans, the then editor of the *Sunday Times*, and Ron Hall as well as the economics editor, Malcolm Crawford. The series began with a bold statement of 'how we went wrong',[27] and on the principle that one picture is worth a thousand words, the piece contained two graphics which nicely summed up the thesis. A cartoon showed an industrial worker with a spanner, bowed under the weight of supporting tiers of local government workers, nurses, teachers, policemen, civil servants, the army and so on. Whilst a photograph of passengers on a number 17 bus illustrated the reality of Britain 'going to work'. Of nineteen passengers only two were employed in industrial manufacture, the rest were in the public sector or in 'non marketed' occupations. The article prompted a lively debate and succeeded in putting a good deal of technical discussion into layman's terms. As one correspondent (John Moores of Liverpool) commented the following week:

> I have been interested in economics all my life but for the first time I feel I have a grasp of what is going wrong . . . If any subsequent articles are to be of this high standard I would strongly urge you to work out a popular version because every adult in this country should understand what you are saying.[28]

The final article ('What We Should Do') left no doubts as to what they believed the future held if Britain did not alter course and tackle the fundamental *structural* problems of the economy:

> The economically ungovernable nations of the world are those which combine high public expenditure with low investment . . . In consequence their productive sectors become too small for what is required of them. The result is chronic inflation, structural employment and requests for aid and loans from the rest of the world. This all too often leads to 'strong' governments which either preside over chaos or use their powers to repress the living standards of all but those who keep them in power. Since 1962 Britain has unwittingly been developing such an economy.[29]

In the following five weeks the *Sunday Times* gave over its comment pages to a debate to which over twenty economists, politicians, business men and trade unionists contributed. Indicative of the broad consensus which their ideas facilitated was the response of David Basnett of the General and Municipal Workers Union:

> Many points in Eltis and Bacon's valuable analysis echoes what the TUC and the unions have been saying, with increasing force but as yet with little serious attention from the economic establishment.[30]

Whilst Sir Geoffrey Howe, later to become Mrs Thatcher's first Chancellor, made it clear how much of the argument – about the public (non-productive) sector – had been taken on board by the 'right wing':

> I have no doubt that we need to proceed broadly in the direction of the 'Right' solution, foreshadowed by Bacon and Eltis ... It must be the business of government to create the conditions for profitable, and increasingly efficient, expansion of marketable goods and services. This must imply a very substantial reduction in the size of the non-marketable public sector.[31]

In the years which followed it was the *size of the public sector* which was the aspect of the Bacon and Eltis argument that was to come to the fore, rather than the problem of investment and manufacturing output. In their response to their critics the authors made their position clear in terms that were to be a familiar component of 1980s Conservative rhetoric:

> We have not claimed that control of the size of the man-market sector will solve all Britain's problems. But this sector has a major influence on the economy, and failure to recognise the wide-ranging effects of the rate at which it expands has contributed substantially to Britain's troubles. The economy will be managed more sensibly if its importance is understood.[32]

The impact of the debate fuelled by the articles (and later the book, *Britain's Economic Problem: too few producers*, published in 1976) should not be underestimated. As Chancellor Denis Healey said at the time, the articles proved to have 'been the most stimulating and comprehensive analysis of our economic predicament'[33] to have appeared in a newspaper. There can be little doubt that they did much to alter the terms of the economic debate and, as Peter Jackson notes:

> divide the nation into two parts: the wealth creating manufacturing sector and the wealth consuming parasitical public sector. From the mid-1970s, this physiocratic notion of the need to create wealth was an integral part of the supply side message. It also did much to provide an intellectual foundation for those crude policies that were aimed at rolling back the frontiers of the state. This could not be done in the name of the expanding wealth creating base of the economy.[34]

The Bacon and Eltis case, and the extent to which it became a popular explanation of the British disease, was an important addition to the arguments being advanced by Jay, Brittan and Friedman.

In intellectual terms, however, the strength of the arguments advanced by the 'monetarists', when taken along with the structural arguments of Bacon and Eltis, were that they combined an economic analysis with a new political diagnosis. Jay and Brittan, in particular, aimed at framing a political theory of economic crisis based on the notion that Britain was becoming ungovernable and overloaded. Such arguments added intellectual weight to the more technical arguments about micro- and macroeconomic policy. One may question whether the ambition of Brittan and Jay to formulate a new political economy was actually realized, but there can be no doubt that their ideas made a significant contribution to the relocation of the British economic agenda in the 1960s and 1970s to a more market-orientated context.

Events are ever the engines which power a change in opinion and public policy. Keynes's ideas were successful in the 1940s and the postwar period because they had the answer to the problem of mass unemployment. In the 1980s Friedman's ideas along with 'structural' (Bacon and Eltis type) arguments came to the fore because the concept of monetary policy and big government was more appropriate to the problems of dealing with rampant inflation and the economic stagnation of the 1970s. As Friedman noted in his Wincott lecture:

> the public at large cannot be expected to follow the great masses of statistics. One dramatic episode is far more potent in influencing public opinion than a pile of well-digested, but less dramatic, episodes.[35]

Clearly, as the statement of Peter Jay's father-in-law to the Labour party conference demonstrated in 1976, the old Keynesian consensus *had* finally collapsed in on itself and in so doing left something of a hole in the ideological fabric of British politics. Mr Healey's Chancellorship signified that, for all practical purposes, there was, as Mrs Thatcher was later to express it, 'no alternative' to a more rigorous monetary regime. Monetarism arrived in British economic policy not as a result of a theoretical revelation but as a matter of political expediency. Ironically, when the government was forced to sit down with the IMF to discuss budget cuts, *The Times* and the *Financial Times* took the line that deflation was inappropriate and dangerous at that particular moment. Samuel Brittan, for example, writing in the *Financial Times* (15 November 1976), argued that from the point of view of a 'dissenting monetarist' there was 'no case for any restrictive measures in view of the depressed outlook for activity and the probability that unemployment is already above its sustainable minimum rate'; an observation which itself gives the lie to the view that Mr Brittan was ever an uncritical monetarist.

The *political* campaign for 'monetarism' and the abandonment of the long-accepted rules of postwar British political debate began in earnest in the autumn of 1974. A notable contribution to that debate by F. A. Hayek in the *Daily Telegraph* made his position on the causes of Britain's decline very clear:

> The responsibility for current world-wide inflation, I am sorry to say, rests wholly and squarely with the economists, or at least the great majority of my fellow economists who have embraced the teachings of Lord Keynes.
> What we are experiencing are simply the economic consequences of Lord Keynes.[36]

Prior to the publication of Hayek's article Sir Keith Joseph had launched a major attack on these consequences of Lord Keynes in a major speech in September 1974 which was given full coverage in *The Times* and was also given prominence in other conservative papers. The front page headline summed up the argument: 'Sir Keith blames full employment for inflation'. It was, as Peter Jay commented: 'an extraordinary political testament' from someone who had been a member of Conservative governments for the previous fifteen years. The paper published the full text of the speech. Sir Keith argued that the prerequisite for tackling Britain's deep seated economic problems was 'monetary control'. 'Our inflation', he maintained, 'has been the result of the creation of new money – and the consequent deficit financing – out of proportion to the additional goods and services available. When the money supply grows too quickly inflation results.' The paper's leader argued that Sir Keith's words were nothing more than the 'sharp shock of truth':

> Sir Keith Joseph's speech at Preston is certainly one of the most important political speeches of recent years. It does what is the most important job of a politician out of office: it takes the most threatening problem of the time and offers a serious intellectual analysis of the way in which that problem can be overcome.
>   In our view the main lines of argument are unquestionably right. Inflation is threatening to destroy our society. The threat is political as well as economic. Inflation cannot be cured without stabilization of the money supply ... Sir Keith is also right in regarding the whole of postwar economic policy in Britain as being overinfluenced by the fear of unemployment ... We also believe that Sir Keith is plainly right in his judgement that mismanagement of the money supply, either too much or too little will prevent any other policy producing favourable economic results ...

Although *The Times* dissented from Sir Keith with regard to the need for incomes policies and the importance of the international context, the paper wholeheartedly backed the monetarist position.

> Many people of all political opinions are coming to realise that whatever else is done, [sound money] is the essential condition of bringing inflation to an end, and that inflation must be brought to an end if democracy is to survive.[37]

The report prompted a lengthy debate which extended over several weeks and spilled over into other papers. The letters pages in subsequent weeks resounded with vigorous debate on the merits or otherwise of Sir Keith's *mea culpa*. In an unusual and quite unprecedented intrusion into public controversy, a former governor of the Bank of England (Lord O'Brien) voiced his immediate support for the monetarist cause, with the admission that he too had to plead guilty and take a 'share of the blame' for the state of the British economy!

May I through your columns extend my warm congratulations to Sir Keith Joseph on his speech on the economy reported and commented on in *The Times* . . . I hope the speech will be widely read by men and women of good will who are more concerned for the search for truth than with striking political attitudes . . . in broad terms he has in my view arrived at the right answer.[38]

Many other letters – including one from Sir Oswald Mosely – were forthcoming which commended Sir Keith's courage at voicing his change of mind. One colleague, Reginald Maudling, a former Conservative Chancellor was, however, not so complimentary and a lively correspondence ensued. There were (long) letters from economists, including Phelps-Brown, Wynne Godley and Alan Walters (later to become Mrs Thatcher's celebrated personal guru), who offered a stiff rebuke to the old fashioned Keynesian arguments of Mr Maudling *et al*. Professor Walters argued that getting inflation down would take time:

But politicians eyes are focused myopically on the next election. They want results and immediate euphoria. Mr Maudling's letter dramatically illustrates the politician's short sight. When he was Chancellor in 1963/4, Mr Maudling pursued a policy of rapid expansion of the money supply. He produced instant euphoria – but at the cost of a large current balance of payments deficit and mounting inflationary pressure.[39]

Ten days after the speech the controversy continued in *The Times*. Lord Kahn, for example, wrote a lengthy rebuttal to Sir Keith's view that the only way to 'bring Britain to its senses' was through a dose of Sir Keith's 'horrible medicine'.[40] The paper later offered Sir Keith the opportunity to make a full answer to his critics (inflation: government has to resist temptation just to print more money)[41] which in turn provoked even more correspondence from Michael Foot, the Employment Secretary, Lord Kahn and Wynn Godley, amongst others.

The *Economist*, then edited by Alastair Burnet who was committed to holding the line on the paper's essentially Keynesian stance, was critical of Sir Keith's conversion to monetarism and rather worried by the way in which Professor Friedman was 'taking Britain by storm'.[42] In October Peter Jay came to the defence of Professor Friedman and Sir Keith and concluded that it was now

'Time to break the familiar economic cycle we stagger round each year'. Sir Keith's warning could not be ignored:

> At stake, as is now increasingly recognised, are the whole system of our post-war prosperity and the continued authority of our elected Parliament. The threats come from two opposite directions. If inflation . . . were to accelerate under the influence of a new pay explosion, the fatal transition to runaway inflation would have to be arrested by any policies which a democratic government could make effective. Runaway inflation can only end in the destruction of the whole financial order, the almost total interruption of economic activity and unpredictable damage to the institutions of democracy. At the same time the world economy is moving rapidly into its most severe recession since the second world war . . . Those of us whose ivory towers command a lofty view of the meandering progress of post-war policies towards the brink of hyper-inflation find it harder and harder to avoid the conclusion that gradual disinflation by fiscal and monetary means should be the overriding priority with the social contract and other incomes policy seen as a way of mitigating the amount of unemployment that may result.[43]

Sir Keith's Preston speech and *The Times* hype which accompanied it was a turning point – if not *the* turning point – in the economic agenda in Britain, and may be counted amongst one of the more important economic dialogues in postwar British history. In openly advocating monetarist ideas and in challenging the long-held assumptions about full employment Sir Keith had uttered a truth which until then had dared not speak its name. He was commended for his honesty and bravery in coming out with views which had been, until *The Times* debate, considered to be politically unacceptable. *The Times* debate broke the ice which had for so long preserved the consensus on 'full employment'. Indeed, it is true to say that the controversy which Rees-Mogg and Peter Jay had stirred up in the autumn of 1975 was a landmark in the progress of 'monetarism' as a form of public discourse and as a politically viable alternative to the old Keynesian consensus which the *Economist* found increasingly difficult to defend. Its editor resigned in October 1974 berating the passing of the Keynesian era. The *Economist* under Sir Alastair's successor, Andrew Knight, was, however, less reluctant to move with spirit of *The Times*. As Mr Knight commented on his departure from the paper:

we were certainly slow on this paper to see the significance of Mrs Thatcher, and it has been an enjoyable irony . . . that *The Economist* should be so frequently classed as Thatcherite for the clarity of its liberal, free-market, reforming view.[44]

But what is, perhaps, most interesting was not the slowness of the *Economist* in finally coming round to accepting free market ideas so much as the rapidity with which the rest of the financial and popular press took up with 'monetarism' and the 'big government' argument. It was a process which (as Fontana shows in the case of *laissez-faire* ideas in the nineteenth century) did not actually serve to clarify the meaning of its theoretical arguments. As Brittan noted, the public debate soon became:

> hopelessly confused between (a) issues on which every citizen has a right to be informed, (b) questions of general economic theory, and (c) highly technical questions best left to a few banking specialists. The confusions among the experts played into the hands of those who used the term 'monetarism' as a generalised term of abuse for the policies associated with Margaret Thatcher when she ousted Edward Heath as Leader of the Conservative Party.[45]

In the end, argument was replaced by a sense of just waiting for it all to go wrong. As J. K. Galbraith commented in the *Observer* after the election of Mrs Thatcher:

> Britain has, in effect, volunteered to be the Friedmanite guinea pig. There could be no better choice. Britain's political and social institutions are solid . . . British phlegm is a good antidote for anger; but so is an adequate system of unemployment insurance.[46]

However, by the time of the famous letter of the 364 university economists in March 1981, asserting that there was no basis in economic theory for the government's policies, it was too late for what the *Guardian* termed refurbishment of old ideas and the promotion new ones.[47]

Monetarist and supply-side economics and anti-big-government ideas as they were taken up in the media were manifestations of a search for a new legitimating discourse at a time when the economic system and political order was under severe pressure resulting from the prevailing international economic situation and the demise of the old economic nostrums and trade-offs. Inevitably, in practice the ideas failed to work out in the manner hoped for by their proponents. Milton Friedman was quick to distance himself from the early errors of the Thatcher government. In evidence before the Commons Treasury Select Committee in 1980 and given full coverage by the *Observer*'s economics (anti-monetarist) editor, William Keegan, Professor Friedman berated the government's preoccupation with the Public Sector Borrowing Requirement, and urged more cuts in government spending and incentives for free enterprise.[48] The changing attitude towards Mrs Thatcher's monetarism was marked most graphically in *The Times* – the paper which had done so much to straighten the paths and prepare the way in the 1970s. When Harold Evans succeeded Rees-Mogg as editor in 1981 he was soon out of favour with the paper's new proprietor, Mr Rupert Murdoch, for his anti-monetarist opinions. Mrs Thatcher herself was none too pleased either. As far as Evans was concerned, the Prime Minister was just 'Wrong, Wrong, Wrong'. Mrs Thatcher, apparently, was worried by the fact that the paper which had, under the ownership of Thompson and the editorship of Rees-Mogg, been so much for her, was now, under Murdoch and Evans, so outspoken a critic of her economic policy.[49]

Evans who, unlike Rees-Mogg, was actually an economics graduate, had clear ideas about the human consequences of 'sado-monetarism'. Whilst editor of the *Sunday Times* he had frequently commented on the need for the fundamental structural and regional defects of the British economy to be tackled by government. As we noted earlier, he was instrumental, for example, in promoting the theories of Bacon and Eltis – although in his memoirs he is curiously quiet about this particular contribution to the development of Thatcherite economics! The conflict between himself and Murdoch over economic policy came to a head after Evans had given James Tobin, who had just received his Nobel prize for economics (October 1981), a chance to assess (and damn) the monetarist experiment. Murdoch was furious. Evans recounts the exchange in *Good Times, Bad Times*:

'Why d'ya run that stuff?'
'Well, it's timely.'
'And it's wrong! Wrong! What does he know anyway?' We spilled out on to the pavement,
'Come on,' I retorted. 'He won the Nobel Prize.'
'Intellectual bullshit!'[50]

Tobin and Evans had indeed trod on sacred ground and to Mr Murdoch's – and no doubt, to Mrs Thatcher's – great relief, Harry Evans resigned in 1982, complaining of editorial interference and expressing the view that for Murdoch the 'business of the press is more business for Murdoch. It is the subjugation of journalism to marketing and personal power-broking'.[51]

The government's commitment to a strict monetary regime was, however, only a little longer lived than Mr Evans's tenure of *The Times*'s editorial chair. By March 1982 the Thatcher government had accepted the need to broaden its monetary targets and came to adopt a far more pragmatic strategy based on the Medium Term Financial Strategy (MTFS): an approach which had been advocated by Samuel Brittan, Terry Burns at the London Business School, Tim Congdon (in *The Times*) and Gordon Pepper. Under Mr Lawson the old monetarism was finally dispatched in favour of a less narrow interpretation of monetary and fiscal targets. The government's response to the October 1985 sterling crisis served to confirm that M3, the touchstone of the government's early monetarism was abandoned. As the *Financial Times* reported, monetarism was 'dead – official'.[52] Cutting expenditure gave way to holding the line, if not (with an election in view) to boasting of how much the government was spending – as did Mr Lawson in November 1986. Some, like Gordon Pepper and Tim Congdon, kept the faith; others, like the former editor of *The Times*, Rees-Mogg, finally confessed that in the light of experience he had doubts about whether controlling the money supply was as easy a matter as he had once maintained.[53] Although, as John Pardoe (a former Liberal Party economics spokesman) commented, it was ironic that such a confession was forthcoming from 'one of that select band of Pied Pipers who misled a whole generation of British political children into believing the monetarist rubbish of the 1970s'[54] Another correspondent noted with unashamed glee that Sir William (he had been knighted in 1981) now seemed to admit that the money supply defied definition, controlling it was thereby very difficult, and the old monetarist hosepipe had not a few weaknesses which allowed liquidity traps to develop:

Ten years ago, Sir William was stating that 'the money supply . . . is like water flowing from a tap attached to a hosepipe which is about two years in length. Once you have turned the tap nothing will stop the water coming out of the other end of the hosepipe in the form of price increases.' Now with the wisdom of hindsight, and the embarrassment of the evidence, he has rediscovered the points his opponents were making all along . . . The confident inevitabilities of earlier predictions, complete with Friedman's imprimatur, have dissolved into an attempt to explain away the facts.[55]

The story of the supply-side revolution and monetarism was that of the defeat of ideas and, as Stockman put it, 'the triumph of politics'. As far as Friedman was concerned, the Reagan revolution had been deadlocked by the 'tyranny of the status quo': high spending, politicians and bureaucrats.[56] In practice, economic policy was, in both countries, shaped by what Lindblom once termed 'muddling through', or flying by the seat of the pants, rather than by the influence of the gurus and theories of the 1970s. It was ironic that Mrs Thatcher chose to announce the official end of 'Friedmanism' in an interview with someone who had, more than most, done so much to spread the word: Peter Jay. In 1984 she confessed that, although she had looked at Professor Friedman's theory, it was not one to which she had actually subscribed!

What the experience of monetarism and supply-side economics confirms is that the making of economic policy owes in reality far more to the dynamics and contingencies of the political process and to market forces than ever it does to the influence of 'scribblers'. As the British economic journalist David Smith has observed: 'In certain circumstances, fixed ideas will take hold of policy, pushing pragmatism temporarily out of the way. This is perhaps the best way in which to view the monetarist experiments of the 1970s and 1980s.'[57] And as the *Economist* reported in the week of the stock market crash of October 1987, the biggest thing that Thatcherism and Reaganomics had in common was that:

> judged by their early claims made for them both went badly wrong. America's tax cuts of 1981 led – regardless of the Laffer curve – to a ballooning budget deficit and thence to high interest rates, an over-valued dollar and an unsustainably large current-account deficit. Britain, in contrast, added fiscal austerity to its own high interest rates, produced a sharp recession and – regardless of the MTFS – the highest unemployment rate of any large OECD economy.[58]

The actuality of US supply-side economics and British monetarism greatly strengthens the thesis that economic policy all too often is the product of what Henderson has described as DIYE – Do It Yourself Economics[59] – rather than what we might term GIFE – Getting It From Experts.

In the closing decades of the twentieth century ideas and experts count for much less than they did in the age of economic controversy. In the public mind economists have proved a quarrelsome and unreliable bunch, even if in academic terms the margin of disagreement between opposing camps has narrowed in the last decade. Public uncertainty about economic knowledge and the fact that (especially for the younger generation of more technically orientated economists) the big questions are out of favour, the social and political impact of economic ideas is not what it was in the days when economists would talk of tuning, brakes and accelerators, and argue the toss over 'Keynesianism' and 'monetarism', and when the Laffer curve was but a gleam in a journalist's eye. Indeed, with the benefit of hindsight we can now say that the 1970s was one of those periods when *ideas* actually mattered. Gurus, the men with *new* ideas for old, or *vice versa*, were in demand: politicians and voters were hungry for fresh economic recipes. Clearly, however, what has happened since these ideas were first taken up by Mr Reagan and Mrs Thatcher is that more pragmatic political and academic attitudes towards economic policy have evolved.[60] The demand for scholarly commentary and explanation has declined since the great debates of the 1970s: gurus are not what they used to be. Editors in search of economic or financial comment are more likely to turn to insider expertise from Wall Street or the City than, as in the past, to college professors or journalists with ideas. Nowadays, in times of economic turmoil television news producers usually turn to a young man sitting on a desk amidst flickering dealing screens and discarded coffee cups.

Economics for Everyman is changing. In the first place, the reference points of economic opinions are no longer purely Anglo-American or theoretical. This book has itself, for example, been concerned with the flow of ideas in and between Britain and America. Such a focus well reflects the intellectual and cultural dominance which Anglo-American economics has so long enjoyed in our societies. Opinion has, for the most part, been entirely framed with reference to the ideas of British, American and, to a lesser extent, European economists. However, as J. K. Galbraith has forecast in his *History of Economic Ideas*, in the next few decades:

> Japan, hitherto a prime consumer of American ideas, will become the source of economic thought for yet newer countries on the industrial scene, and in reverse flow, for the United States and Europe . . . The industrial world, and not least the United States, has already become deeply concerned with the economic ideas and more especially their practice in Japan, making that country and its economic life an important field of study.[61]

Another aspect of the changing context of economic opinion is that the scale and pace of economic communications is larger and faster than ever before. The nature of economic communications has, over the last decade, undergone a revolution as significant as that which occurred as a result of the introduction of the printing press. As Anthony Smith has noted:

> The reader of the economic pages of a newspaper is less likely to be satisfied today than in the past with the level of information he is reading, even though the daily provision of financial information is far greater now than a decade ago.[62]

The selling of supply-side economics and monetarism in the financial press was a great testament to both the influence of Anglo-American economic controversy and to the power of the printed word to formulate and disseminate an economic discourse. Bagehot characterized the nineteenth century as being an 'economic age' – a time when economic ideas and concepts actively informed public opinion. The 1970s was in many ways a period which witnessed the close of Bagehot's economic age and the dawn of another era: the electronic age. This may be characterized as a period when economic opinion is being influenced by the *information* process itself as well as by ideas and interests. The expansion of information which has occurred in the 1980s has meant that there has emerged another *electronic* agenda which imposes a different context on the pace of business life and on the national and international economic agenda than that which has long been provided by the printed word. Economic and financial information and ideas, which once upon a time were mediated largely through the press and professors, have now outgrown the capacity of any aggregative process. Business, financial and economic news have consequently become altogether more *granulated* products geared to meeting the needs of various specialized market segments. In turn, the changing market for economic information means that the role of the printed page in the making of the economic agenda has, in a very short time indeed, altered from what it was ten years or so ago. Then, as the impact of journalists like Wanniski, Jay and Brittan *et al.* attest, the crisis which the UK and America faced was ideological as well as material. The discourse of free-market economics was quickly incorporated by policy makers, whilst the original disseminators fell out of favour equally as fast. Mrs Thatcher denied Friedman, the Lafferites were discredited and, as the *Investors Chronicle* noted with regard to Gordon Pepper, once elected and the fashion for monetarism established, Conservatives 'no longer needed him'.[63]

Ironically, despite the story of 'monetarism' and 'supply-side' economics coming to a rather different end to that which would have been preferred by their advocates, one of the most interesting features of politics in the 1980s has been what the *Economist* succinctly described as 'Politics without Economics'.[64] In comparison with the controversial 1970s, we now inhabit a post-economic world. Free markets and sound money policies are, so the paper argued in 1988, the aim of governments of every label, from the Soviet Union to Mitterand's France. Political 'isms' based on economic ideas are on the way out.

As the 1980s come to a close, the capitalist and non-capitalist world is now driven along by structures of global communications and information which are more powerful than any government and more influential than any man of ideas. The globalization of world markets, satellites and computers have meant that information, news and events travel at a speed which makes economic commentary and analysis an essentially different activity from the days when national frontiers and geographical distance imposed a more limited context on the economic environment and national political agendas. In this brave new world ideas count for much less than knowing what is going on at the moment. As the final chapter discusses, in saying goodbye to Gutenburg we may also be bidding farewell to gurus and worldly philosophers.

NOTES

1. See Peter Jenkins, *Mrs Thatcher's Revolution: the ending of the socialist era* (Jonathan Cape, London, 1972) p. 42. *The Economist* was also responsible for the introduction of another key term in British political discourse, 'Butskellism'. See 'Mr Butskell's Dilemma', *The Economist*, 13 February 1954.
2. See, for example, Keith Smith, *The British Economic Crisis: its past and future* (Penguin, Harmondsworth, 1984) pp. 135–6; and William Keegan, *Mrs Thatcher's Economic Experiment* (Penguin, Harmondsworth, 1984) p. 60.
3. Milton Friedman, *Free to Choose* (Penguin, Harmondsworth, 1980) p. 12.
4. Samuel Brittan, *The Economic Contradictions of Democracy* (Temple Smith, London, 1977) p. xii.
5. Samuel Brittan, *Participation Without Politics*, Hobart Paper (Institute of Economic Affairs, London, 1975) p. 43.
6. See, for example, Smith, op.cit., pp. 135–6, when he describes Brittan (and Jay) as taking an 'utterly uncritical acceptance of free-market positions'.
7. Introduction to Nick Bosanquet, *After the New Right* (Heinemann, London, 1983) p. vii.
8. Samuel Brittan, *Second Thoughts on Full Employment Policy* (Institute of Economic Affairs, London, 1975) p. 129.
9. Samuel Brittan, *Two Cheers for Self Interest, 17th Wincott Memorial Lecture* (Institute of Economic Affairs, London, 1985) p. 34.
10. In an article first published in the *Spectator* and later in R. Skidelsky (ed.) *The End of the Keynesian Era* (Macmillan, London, 1977) p. 49.
11. The paper was given originally to Section F of the British Association at its 1974 Annual Meeting. A revised version was published in the *British Journal of Political Science* (April 1975).
12. Norman Barry, *The New Right* (Croom Helm, London, 1987) p. 116.
13. *Sunday Times*, 11 November 1984.
14. Peter Jay, *The Crisis for Western Political Economy* (Andre Deutsch, London, 1984). Mr Jay went on to become Chief of Staff [sic] to Mr Robert Maxwell. In an interview with Carol Sarler Mr Jay confessed to feeling that, 'I don't know what I've done apart from being the first person to tell Mrs Thatcher about monetarism . . .'. See 'Captain's Mate: Whatever Happened to Peter Jay?' *Sunday Times Magazine*, 5 February 1989.
15. Peter Jay and Michael Stewart, *Apocalypse 2000: economic breakdown and the suicide of democracy, 1989–2000* (Sidgwick and Jackson, London, 1987). The book predicted (amongst other things) the collapse of the economic system and democracy, the election of a Democratic American President in 1988, and the emergence of a right-wing European movement. Interested readers may also seek out their 'Still on Course for Apocalypse 2000', *New European Quarterly Review*, vol. 1, no. 2 (1988).
16. See *The Times*, 16 May 1968.
17. Ibid., 31 May 1986.
18. Ibid., 15 October 1968.
19. Ibid., 1 July 1974.
20. Ibid.
21. Jay and Brittan have been frequent contributors to IEA seminars; see, for example, *Inflation: causes, consequences, cures*, IEA Readings, no. 14 (1974). The Institute also brought many other prominent journalists into its discussions; see for example, *Is Monetarism Enough?* IEA Readings, no. 24, 1980, which included Colin Jones, editor of the *Banker*, William Keegan of the

Observer, Rodney Lord of the *Daily Telegraph*, Russell Lewis of the *Daily Mail*, Hamish McRae of the *Guardian* and William Rees-Mogg of *The Times*.

22. Jay, *The Crisis for Western Political Economy*, op.cit., p. 33.
23. *The Listener*, August 1972, pp. 239–41.
24. William Keegan and Rupert Pennant-Rea, *Who Runs the Economy: control and influence in British economic policy* (Maurice Temple Smith, London, 1979) p. 140.
25. *Investors Chronicle*, 15 April 1988, p. 21.
26. *Sunday Times*, 10 November 1974.
27. Ibid., 2 November 1974.
28. Ibid., 9 November 1975.
29. Ibid., 16 November 1975.
30. Ibid., 23 November 1975.
31. Ibid., 30 November 1975.
32. Ibid.
33. Ibid., 14 December 1975.
34. In Peter Jackson (ed.), *Implementing Government Policy Initiatives: the Thatcher Administration, 1979–1983* (Royal Institute of Public Administration, London, 1985) p. 28.
35. M. Friedman, *The Counter-Revolution in Monetary Theory: the first Wincott Memorial Lecture* (Institute of Economic Affairs, London, 1970) p. 21.
36. *Daily Telegraph*, 15 and 16 October 1974.
37. *The Times*, 6 September 1974.
38. Ibid., 8 September 1974.
39. Ibid., 10 September 1974.
40. Ibid., 15 September 1974.
41. Ibid., 20 September 1974.
42. *The Economist*, 21 September 1974.
43. *The Times*, 7 October 1974.
44. *The Economist*, 7 February 1987.
45. S. Brittan, *How to End the Monetarist Controversy: a journalist's reflections on output, jobs, prices and money* Hobart Paper (Insitute of Economic Affairs, London, 1982) p. 16.
46. *The Observer*, 31 August 1980.
47. *The Guardian*, 30 March 1981.
48. *The Observer*, 6 July 1980.
49. Harold Evans, *Good Times, Bad Times* (Weidenfeld and Nicolson, London, 1983) p. 3.
50. Ibid., p. 288.
51. Ibid., p. 6.
52. *Financial Times*, 18 October 1985. As we noted earlier, Sam Brittan himself took the line of supporting British membership of the EMS and stabilizing inflation around 5 per cent. Some commentators have seen Mr Brittan's advocacy of these policies as being a crucial factor in explaining the development of economic policy under Mr Nigel Lawson. The less influential case for controlling inflation and a balanced budget was taken up by *The Times* – under the editorship of Charles Douglas-Home. See, for example, leaders on 8 February 1983; 14 March 1983; 3 October 1983; 13 October 1983; and 20 January 1984. Tim Congdon's signed *Times* articles, which were aimed at bringing the government around to 'sound money' policies, should also be consulted. See, for example, 'Nil Norm for Prices', 9 February 1983; 'What Keynes Can Teach the Chancellor about Inflation', 15 April 1984; 'Lawson's Surprise in Annex 4', 21 March 1984; and 'The Brave New World of Zero

Inflation', 13 June 1984. Mr Brittan's position is summed up in his postscript to the 1988 edition of *Capitalism and the Permissive Society*, published as *A Restatement Of Economic Liberalism*, (Macmillan, London, 1988) pp. 210–315.

53. *Independent*, 13 January 1987.
54, Ibid., 19 January 1987.
55. Ibid., 16 January 1987.
56. See Milton and Rose Friedman, *The Tyranny of the Status Quo* (Penguin, Harmondsworth, 1985).
57. David Smith, *The Rise and Fall of Monetarism: the theory and politics of an economic experiment* (Penguin, Harmondsworth, 1987) p. 147.
58. *The Economist*, 24 October 1987.
59. David Henderson, *Innocence and Design: the influence of economic ideas on Policy* (Basil Blackwell, Oxford, 1986).
60. As David Lipsey commented in the *Sunday Times*, 12 January 1985:

    Keynesians and monetarists now share sufficient of a theoretical framework to talk the same sort of language. Freed from the dead hand of narrow, technical monetarism, economics as a political science is again freed to live.

61. J. K. Galbraith, *A History of Economics: the past as the present* (Hamish Hamilton, London, 1987) p. 292.
62. Anthony Smith, *Goodbye Gutenburg: the newspaper revolution of the 1980s* (Oxford University Press, London, 1980) p. 18.
63. *Investors Chronicle*, op.cit.
64. *The Economist*, 6 August 1988.

7.   Governing without gurus?

The decade which has passed since the 'monetarist' and 'supply-side' controversies, contained in the pages of the London *Times* and the *Wall Street Journal*, has witnessed many changes in the world of economic journalism, in the general standing of economics and economists as well as in the role of the printed word itself. In retrospect, the mid-1970s was something of a golden age, both for economic ideas and scholarly campaigning journalism. It was a period when an international crisis, inflation and unemployment prompted the revival of political economy and the renewal of economic liberalism. Underlying these changes was, however, a remarkable continuity in the financial system which had been set up in the late nineteenth and early twentieth centuries. As Stephen Fidler has noted:

> An extraordinary aspect of the last century in the world's financial markets has been not so much the speed of their transformation in the last 10 years but that there had been so little change in the preceeding 90.[1]

In great part, the uncertainty which characterizes the 1980s stems from the fact that the old structures of the financial markets and the rapid innovations in financial institutions and communications are still in the process of being comprehended. No one knows quite where it will all end. The role of the press in the 1970s in confidently articulating and disseminating a 'new' political economy was indicative of the belief that there were indeed alternatives to the economic consensus which had held sway since the 1940s. It was a time for exchanging new gurus for old; and the part played by the press in transmitting this change in opinion was also a sign of the fact that there was actually an intellectual spirit of the times capable of being distilled into popular economic opinion. As in the nineteenth century, the press had a mediative and synthetic function. The same can not be said of the press in the bullish 1980s, even after the crash of '87. If there has been a *geist* abroad it is more one of there being a sense of the old gods having failed.

Inevitably, as the practice of economic policy-making has discredited the more simplistic rhetoric of an earlier decade, policy-
making and politics in the 1980s are noticeable for being less
theoretically informed than in the recent past and more susceptible
to being influenced by *international* developments and competition
than by intellectual 'academic scribblers'. The gurus of the 1970s –
Friedman, Laffer, *et al.* – have thus given way to a more old-
fashioned pragmatism. In power Mrs Thatcher proved to be a
short-lived monetarist, and Mr Reagan a long-lived Keynesian (of
sorts). Alongside this *policy pragmatism* there has evolved, as a
result of the great expansion of the financial media and information networks, an *informational pluralism* which, as we discuss in
this concluding chapter, mirrors and informs the absence of an
ideological fixity which pertains in the world of politics. Indeed, it
is the contention of this chapter that the two phenomena – political
pragmatism and informational pluralism – are not entirely un-
related aspects of the contemporary state of the economic agenda.

During the 1970s there occurred not only the break-up of the old
economic consensus but also a build-up of new information
systems which increased the flow of information and the capacity
of markets to function internationally. It was a period when the
market for information as well as for ideas was changing rapidly. It
was the former, however, which grabbed the headlines. In the first
half of the 1970s there was, therefore, the genesis of an intellectual
change – as we have discussed in Chapters 5 and 6 – but also the
beginning of a much wider revolution in the nature of the
economic communications network. Due to the break-up of the
Bretton Woods system of fixed exchange rates in 1971 and the
subsequent deregulation of the financial markets, Reuters and
Telerate, the two biggest players, together with Quotron in the US
and Extel and Datastream in Europe, developed systems which
not only displayed prices but allowed users to exchange information. Within a decade (by 1984) Telerate could claim 24 000 VDUs
in 41 countries and Reuters, 40 000 in 100. As Lawrenson and
Barber note with regard to Reuters' Monitor service which evolved
out of earlier Stockmaster (1964) and Videomaster (1969) services:

> By the end of 1981, subscribers from New York, Moscow and across
> Peking were able to reach and deal in money with their opposite
> number in just four seconds, a critical eleven seconds faster than by

telephone. The concept of a global electronic market place over a ten-year period had multiplied Reuters' revenue by nearly thirteen times.[2]

As in the nineteenth century, Reuters have been in the advance of the informational revolution and in transforming the nature of economic communications. And, as in the 1880s, during the 1980s it has been the informational (market) role of the financial media which has been in the ascendant, as opposed to the kind of ideological or opinion-forming role which preceded it. Indeed, the parallel between the 1980s and the 1880s is an interesting one: both were periods which witnessed, on the one hand, the internationalization of economic information through the development of telegraphy, electronics and satellite communications, and on the other, a transformation of the cultural context of capitalism *qua* stock market game. Developments in computers and communications, the deregulation of financial markets, floating exchange rates and the freer flow of capital, combined with the election of Mrs Thatcher and Mr Reagan, meant that playing the stock market was back in fashion in the 1980s, as in the 1880s and 1920s. As Mihir Bose comments: 'In the 1960s and 1970s nobody talked about stock markets. They were considered 'square', along with Brylcream on the hair and turned-up-trousers. Now, in the mid 1980s, everybody was talking stock markets.'[3]

In retrospect, the 'selling of the supply side' and monetarism bear witness to the power of the printed word to shape and disseminate the policy agenda and its accompanying rhetoric at a time when economic *ideas* were in demand. Historians in the future may perhaps characterize the 1980s as a decade which experienced an information revolution in the wake of a change in the tide of economic opinion. The main difference between these two phases is that, whereas the economic revolution which took place in the 1970s was a phenomenon of 'the printed word', the information revolution of the 1980s has been essentially a process which involved the addition, if not the replacement, of printed communications by electronic media. But perhaps this is merely symptomatic of a larger change which has occurred in the role of the 'intellectual' and 'ideas' in public life. As John Berger has observed:

The intellectual and the journalist were born at about the same time, to work in the same field. Their roles could overlap, but they were different. The intellectual offered opinions; the journalist offered events.[4]

As we have seen, the relationship between economic journalism and economic ideas in the early nineteenth century, during the 1930s, and in the 1960s and 1970s were instances of such an overlap when journalists used events to illustrate ideas and were a manifestation of the existence of a specifically intellectual context informing and fashioning political and economic opinion. Ideas and their mode of distribution are, by nature, inextricably interwoven aspects of the fabric of knowledge. It will, therefore, be fascinating to discern what the effects of a new mode of electronically disseminated economic and financial information will ultimately have on the development of the future economic agenda as on other aspects of post-industrial culture. As a report to the British government noted in 1983:

> new technology is eroding many of the distinctions that have previously distinguished one form of information medium from another: publications, film, and news services are now all becoming aspects of an expanding 'tradeable information' sector.[5]

The structure of financial communications clearly lies at the centre of this process. New technologies are increasingly facilitating the *commoditization* of information. And, as Herbert Schiller argues:

> Electronic Communication provides a common denominator for an ever growing share of the production of *all* goods and services. And information, which has become an important part of the production process, as well as being a good in its own rights, is governed too by market criteria.[6]

Advances in the technology of business and financial communications and instantaneity of the economic information network has now evolved beyond the point where any single medium of the printed word such as a newspaper can aggregate it into some form of coherent body of news so much as it can list and report all those activities and events which interest its various readership segments. In a world where all information has a price and is 'tradeable', the role of the printed word has undergone considerable change over the last decade and a half. As the *Economist* pointed out in 1988:

A market that did not exist 15 years ago is today worth $3 billion a year worldwide, has been growing at roughly 35% a year throughout the 1980s and will probably grow as fast in the 1990s. Electronic financial information is booming, thanks to the (continuing) deregulation of the world's financial markets, and the ability of new computers to process billions of bits of information quickly and cheaply. Hungry for up-to-the-second prices are traders in all securities from cadmium to convertibles, butter to bonds.[7]

The financial news industry is increasingly more involved in retailing information via data bases and (expensive) specialized reports than in simply selling newspapers; and in responding to the market for financial information publishers have increasingly sought to cater for ever more specialized segments of the market for economic news. Allied to this is the fact that modern transnational companies are far less dependent on outside sources of information and mass national communications than they were in the past. Telematics, the combined use of computer and telecommunications technologies, is more autonomous a process than the paper-based communications systems of the past. Such developments in transnational data flows have to be considered as massively reinforcing the segmentation or disaggregation of news and information networks and signifying a revolution in the way in which economic news-gathering and dissemination has worked for over a century.

The contemporary information network has expanded both in terms of the printed word and in terms of financial journalism and advertising, and in the availability of electronic information and communications. Ironically, as our reliance on this greatly expanded information industry has grown so our faith in economic knowledge seems to have declined from its heyday in the 1960s and 1970s when leading economic gurus were in demand to write newspaper columns, present television series and advise governments. The academic community no longer has such a tight monopoly on economic wisdom. One of the most interesting aspects of the changing state of economics is the way in which the profession has widened. Newspapers today are more likely to call upon economists employed by stockbrokers and merchant banks for 'economic expertise' than they are to turn to economists drawing college salaries. Other kinds of economic expertise – tipsters and economists employed by private companies and firms

– have, in many cases, taken over from university professors and it is they who now enjoy the public celebrity and limelight. Indeed, as Anne Ashworth has commented, the rise of the 'teenage scribblers' has been one of the more notable developments in the media in the 1980s. It has become, as she says:

> Impossible to turn on television news . . . without having a young economic guru from stockbrokers Phillips and Drew or the apparently double Dutch Barclays de Zoete Wedd expounding knowledgeably. But like it or not . . . these pundits have become an important feature in the running of the British economy. Whatever the Chancellor does, there is the man from one of the stockbroking firms or another – invariably filmed before a bank of computer terminals – to pronounce judgement.[8]

The new generation of media gurus are economically well-educated, articulate and representative of the kind of person who now sits in front of the VDU screens. They are far more informed than was the case in the 1950s, and as a group are more narrowly preoccupied than journalists in the 1960s, since as the *Economist* has pointed out:

> In the past twenty years or so, financial journalists have increasingly had to compete not only with each other, but with in-house economists and analysts employed by City firms. They have also had to survive the specialisation of their own profession: where once only a financial editor wrote, there are now industry correspondents and banking reporters and energy editors and Euromarket reporters.[9]

This in itself is only another illustration of the fact that, thanks to the expansion of higher education in the 1960s, there are inevitably far more economists earning a living in Wall Street, the City and in industry and commerce than in university faculties. They also get paid (far) more than their old professors.

Not only has the scale of the economics community been transformed: the audience for, and context of, economic news has, especially during the great bull market of the 1980s, also experienced a number of changes. In the 1980s we have seen, for instance, a widening in the audience for business and financial news on television which in Britain was boosted with the launching of 'popular capitalism' in 1984 with the privatization of British Telecom. The Telecom sell-off itself marked a new phase in the coverage of the stock market by the British media as the highly effective and extensive press campaign proved to be a key element in the sale. As Karin Newmann concludes, it was the financial journalists' editorial coverage 'which was absolutely vital in converting interest in British Telecom to purchasers':

> Journalists vied with each other to explain the attraction to small shareholders and advise purchasers of the share sale as a 'once in a lifetime' chance for small investors to make money. [10]

For the first time, a share issue received – as the government had intended – big coverage in general news and spread on to 'non-City' pages. This growth of business coverage on British television in the wake of Mrs Thatcher's 'privatization' programme is, as Hird has noted, something which is not just a response to advertising revenues but also a measure of significant cultural change in attitudes towards money and profits, as well as reflecting the perceived 'usefulness' of economics. [11] The development of programmes originally aimed at a fairly narrow professional market reflects a steady development of popular financial journalism which dates from growth in the middle 1960s of personal finance columns in newspapers. Ever in pursuit of the affluent reader to boost advertising income, newspapers geared to high income groups have eagerly given over features to pull in the appropriate sponsors. Such developments have proved a subtle form of distorting economic news values and the economic agenda itself. As James Curran has argued, such advertising encouraging participation in the stock market or unit trusts, insurance, pensions, investment schemes, and the rest, influences what topics are covered and how they are covered:

> Sponsorship helps to set the editorial agenda of sponsorship features and, perhaps more important, to define their intended audiences. In this discreet and indirect way, rather than in the more obvious sense of overt pressure, advertising sponsorship has come to colour the portrayals of reality in the press. [12]

Curran's study of such advertising shows that, with a few exceptions, economic comment is overwhelmingly given to tipping, investment advice, company news and gossip, rather than to critical analysis. The actual national economy comes a poor third. [13]

Alongside this expansion of 'business' and personal financial coverage is the contraction of economic commentary and explanation to all but the serious 'up-market' press. The coverage of economic and financial news in the mass circulation dailies, which for obvious advertising reasons has never been great, has – with the demise of the *Daily Herald* (1964), *News Chronicle* (1960) and *Sunday Citizen* (1967) – sunk to an all time low.[14] No more graphic an illustration of the polarization of the press between 'quality' and tabloid may be seen than in the fact that the 'qualities' have greatly expanded their business coverage, dating from the great boom in unit trusts in the mid-1960s, whilst the popular tabloids continue to offer a poor service to their readership in explaining economic affairs. This has not stopped (even) the *Sun* from launching a financial section (*sic*) to attract advertising revenues. Sadly, though it is possible for television to make science attractive, British and American broadcasters have failed to do for the economic world what Carl Sagan did for the Cosmos and what David Bellamy has done for the aspidistra. As Louis Rukeyser, the presenter of *Wall Street Week*, has noted:

> Too often, network T.V. still tends to cover the subject of business and the economic system, if at all, in one of two ways: either totally superficially, as when it throws out a raw statistic and leaves it lying there . . . or else in an occasional mood of crusading exposé . . . And even when bias or intellectual laziness are not operative handicaps, television coverage of economics is inhibited by the search for exciting pictures . . . Nor, I believe, are most newspapers doing the job they should be doing in helping the average citizen better to understand the way in which the economic system really works.[15]

Although business journalism on television has improved in more recent years with, for example, the introduction of the *Financial News Network* and, in Britain the growth of programmes like *Money Week*, *The City Programme*, and *Business Daily*, it has not begun to equal the quality of political reporting. Little had changed, certainly in Britain in 1987, when, as Mihir Bose reported, television was completely caught out by how to deal with the stock market crash:

> T.V. news programmes simply do not have the expertise to deal with the complex business subjects, nor have they devised a format to cope with unusual events. . . They could have done more than report the fall; they should have explained why it happened.[16]

Even those programmes geared to meeting the demands of popular capitalism were shown, as Bose noted, to lack authority. Of course, this may well change in time as television programmes acquire the *gravitas* that comes with age. Until such time when television business journalism attracts a larger audience and more advertising revenues, there will be a growing tendency for an increasing polarization of information available to different sections of the market. With the education and information that is now available to the average citizen a two-tier effect is emerging: on the one hand, a morass of ill-informed and largely ignorant opinion, and on the other, a more élite sector catered for better than ever before with bulging financial pages and electronic information. It is a gap which the *mass media* seem unable or reluctant to fill. One explanation for this is the fact that the more élite papers derive large revenues from financial and business advertising, revenues which are obviously not available to those papers geared to lower social classes. It will be interesting to see if 'popular capitalism' will change all this. We may yet see 'Sid' – the eponymous hero of an advertising campaign to sell off British Gas – preferring to keep his eye on his British Gas shares rather than on a page three girl.

The signs are that Sid has been turning to the increasing number of tip sheets which thrived on the bull markets of the 1970s and 1980s. Newsletters are, of course, nothing new. Indeed, as Peter Brimelow has noted:

> There is . . . a definite parallel between today's investors' letters and the newspapers appearing in the eighteenth century. In those days, newspapers were basically small format digests of information, often compiled and commented upon by one hardworking hand, deriving most of their revenues from high subscription prices rather than from the sale of space to advertisers . . . With the newsletter phenomenon, the newspaper business has come full circle. Benjamin Franklin lives.[17]

So present newsletters are, by adopting modern technology, to meet the demands of the contemporary speculative culture, simply carrying on a long tradition in publishing. The expansion of the financial and business pages and tip sheets has followed on from the bull markets of the early 1970s and that of 1982–7. Tip sheets in particular have been one of the most significant outcomes of the combination of an information revolution (desk top publishing) and a long bull market. The newsletter industry has come to play an important part in the information-gathering of private investors which supplements the existing sources contained in newspapers and magazines. Tip sheets have traditionally had a more important place in the US investment scene. However, newsletters in the City of London have recently flourished as the participation in stock market investment has widened (to some 9 million by the time of the 1987 general election). Tip sheets cater to the speculative small investor as sports papers cater to the punter. They provide advice and tips for a price which is modest in comparison with the profits which they claim can be made by following their tips – at the time of writing their annual rates vary from £48 to £144 in Britain and from $40 to $540 in the USA. Perhaps their growth most significantly reflects the fact that economic expertise is no longer seen to be the monopoly of the established financial press. Again, as Brimelow points out: 'The failings of Wall Street and of the established economic authority have been crucial to the rise of the investment letter industry.'[18] The years of economic stagflation and the impact of economic recession, together with the crash of 1987, have done nothing to enhance the street credibility of either economic or financial experts or Wall Street gurus, academic or otherwise.[19] As David Chase, a Wall Street broker, has commented:

> The closer you look at economists and their recent bad calls, the more they seem like an endangered species running out of survival techniques. Those who listen to them do so at increasing risk.[20]

Even so, as Chase concedes:

> The economist-as-celebrity is here to stay. Economists like John Kenneth Galbraith, Henry Kaufman, Edward Yardeni, David Stockman and Milton Friedman have become personalities in financial news and our TV screens because, whether we like it or not, they affect our lives, and so do their theories.[21]

Inevitably, then, it has been the case that, *parri-passu* with the expansion of financial, business and economic information, there has been a decline in big theory (personality) economics itself. In the last decade or so it is not only the Keynesian era which has come to an end. A number of theoretical experiments have also come unstuck. Ironically, the Thatcher-Reagan years have not seen the triumph of the 'supply-side' or 'monetarist' revolutions so much as, on the one hand, what David Stockman described as the 'triumph of politics', and on the other, the development of an information economy. Inevitably, economic commentary and reporting on both sides of the Atlantic is reflecting this retreat from mouthing the rhetoric of the past in favour of listening more attentively, if not exclusively, to the beat of the market drums. Even though the intellectual initiative has, as Will Hutton has observed, passed to free-marketeers there remains a good deal of unease amongst the non-partisans:

> They are suspicious of planning and economic blueprints . . . but they are concerned about trends in the economy. If it *is* true that Keynesian economics no longer has anything to offer, and if the claims and policies of the free market theorists *are* at the very least contestable, then what next?[22]

What next, indeed. Well, if the experience of the 1980s is anything to go by, the trend has been for the tipsters to outnumber and replace the scholars (teachers): selling stocks and shares, rather than ideas and explanation. In other words, catering to the needs of their readers *qua* investors and public relations men rather than to a market interested in general (outsider) opinions and theoretical context. The teachers – like Shonfield, Brittan and Jay – were close to the world of ideas, whereas the tipsters have become close, some would say too close, to the very areas of business and finance that they are supposed to be reporting and analysing in an objective manner. As the CBI pointed out in October 1987:

> Speculation about possible takeovers in financial columns, often without any foundation other than City rumours, can actually distort share prices . . . The extent to which share prices can be manipulated by such press comment and the scope for profit by those initiating the rumours requires more detailed . . . investigation.[23]

The danger is that, as in the past, the financial press may become more participants and 'puffers' than observers and more extensions of PR companies than independent commentators and reporters. For example; one publication which gives advice on

How to Get a Highly Paid Job in the City, by Richard Roberts and Luke Johnson, makes the point that:

> One of the main criticisms now being levelled at the business is that increasingly the news side of financial journalism is being controlled by the news producers rather than journalists. Press conferences are far more common than they used to be and these are in many cases designed to set the agenda rather than disseminate information. By calling a press conference you can determine what the press should be given and restrict your information to just that . . . So although there is a huge investigative role to be played in financial journalism it is becoming less and less evident . . . PR firms are increasingly dominating the business and they like reporters to play their game.[24]

That the financial press is increasingly seen to be too closely involved with the financial and business worlds gives some credence to the argument that the press have over the years consistently failed to be as rigorous in its investigation of 'white-collar', corporate crime than it should have been. The financial press will continue to make healthy profits, as Lawrenson and Barber conclude in their study of Reuters, so long as 'it successfully sells useful information that enables businessmen to trade profitably'.[25] And that it has been able so to do has made the whole business of selling business information one of the most sought-after areas of the contemporary communications and publishing field. In the new conditions of global capitalism, information is everything.

The reality of the information revolution became all too evident with the stock market crash of October 1987. It is tempting to over-extend the parallel between 1929 and 1987. 1987 was technically much worse than 1929 since the technology (by all accounts) facilitated a speed of response which could not have been contemplated in 1929, although it could have been foreseen in September 1987. Clearly, the existence of a global financial village cannot be said to have caused the crash of 1987. Yet it was the case that the existence of a system of computerized market trading, with little regulation or monitoring, undoubtedly made everything happen so much faster than could have been the case a few years earlier. Even so, as J. K. Galbraith (whose comments were much in demand after the 1987 crash) observed: 'Modern technology spreads disaster a little more rapidly but it is not terribly important.'[26] In the end, as always, the system of financial communications cannot be held responsible for the kind of speculative mania that preceded Black Monday: garbage in, garbage out. However, the existence of newspapers eager to make (a lot of) money from advertisements urging their readers to come and play, cannot be lightly dismissed as having played an unimportant role in contributing to the cultivation of a speculative mentality and sustaining what Galbraith termed the 'mythology of the market'. One magazine, *Family Wealth*, for example, (not untypically) launched itself in March 1987 as a 'new kind of money magazine' to help its readers make money; after all: 'Making money isn't the exclusive preserve of the bulls and stags of the stock market. Anyone can do it . . . Everybody deserves the chance to be rich.' Whilst another, *Investors Digest* promised: 'Now you can get the best ideas, tips, and advice from the financial press . . . in less than an hour a month . . . for just pennies a day.'

In this respect, the cultivation of playing the stock market game by the advertising carried in newspapers and magazines does present a valid comparison between the way in which the press in both crashes, as in other periods of speculation since the South Seas Bubble, uncritically fed the stock market booms which preceded the fall. By 1987 the economy had become a speculative game on the stock market which could, as Jesse Livermore put it in the 1920s, be 'played for the price of an evening paper'. Unlike the 1920s, however, the corruption of financial journalism has, as far as we know, been a rarer phenomenon in the 1980s, with financial journalists having to live up to very tough ethical standards of behaviour. The most notorious exception to this was that of R. Foster Winans, a journalist on the *Wall Street Journal*, who was found guilty of insider trading. Winans, whose column 'Heard on the Street' reached an audience of 2½ million, fell prey to Peter Brands, a broker. Overworked and underpaid, leastways by the standards of Wall Street Wizz Kids, Winans agreed to forward information to Brands in advance of his column being published: 'No one will ever know. Its just between us. You write the columns and I'll make the trades. No one gets hurt, no one knows.'[27] Needless to say, they did.

Explanation has been far thinner on the ground than tipping and advertising space devoted to encouraging readers to play the 'market game'. Finance and the workings of markets which affect everybody are presented in a manner which, as Philip Coggan argues, is designed to perpetuate the myth of the infallibility of

'the man in the pinstripe suit' and which obscures information
rather than informs the outsider even though:

> Although the details of individual financial deals can be very complex,
> there are basic principles which everybody can understand and which
> apply as much to the finances of Mr Smith, the grocer, as to Barclays
> Bank.[28]

Yet, as he points out: 'The more fully people understand these
principles, the more they will be able to criticise, and perhaps even
participate in the workings of the financial system. Like all areas of
public life, it needs criticism to ensure its efficiency.'[29] Perhaps
from the point of view of the man in the pinstripe suit that's one
good reason why poor press coverage is no bad thing. However, in
a world in which – like Livermore's 1920s – it is now possible, as
Business Week notes, for 'even the average citizen or company to
take a financial position almost instantaneously in just about
anything, anywhere'[30] the need for critical commentary is a *sine
qua non* of good business and an informed democracy.

We may no longer have grand theories but we do have the
technology for investment information to be right there on the
home micro, and for the whole family to feel, as an advertisement
for the Dow-Jones News/Retrieval service expressed it, 'at home
with the stockmarket'.

> Dow Jones News/Retrieval is the surprisingly affordable, online finan-
> cial news resource with exclusive electronic access to the *Wall Street
> Journal*. The combination of New/Retrieval and Dow Jones Software
> makes personal investment decisions easier by giving you a clear,
> organized picture of the facts.
>   Use News/Retrieval to check on your stocks or read up on com-
> panies and industries that interest *you*. Get tomorrow's business news
> today – 90 seconds after it appears on the Dow Jones News Service . . .
> See what impact government or world news is having on the
> marketplace.[31]

Increasing the level of speculative participation is, however, not
the same as making it more comprehensible to those millions of
people who nowadays through their pensions, savings and insurance have a very big investment stake in the money game. To
quote Louis Rukeyser again on this point, most newspapers
peddle clichés, politicians' press releases and investment advice

rather than give its readers the kind of 'solid economic analysis and commentary, which the public needs'.[32] Rukeyser suggests that the problem is due to the lack of journalists trained to operate in the economic arena who can go beyond the clichés and get at the real issues which are covered up and obscured. However, does the problem of the poor coverage of economics involve more than just training? Or, does it have more to do with the demand and supply of economic information and tipping exceeding that for more scholarly political economy?

As we saw in Chapter 1, in the beginning the press and political economy evolved in the context of a debate in which the educated classes were participatory observers. However, by the 1870s economics began to develop in an altogether more closed academic environment. This tendency towards the privatization of its discourse has continued apace in our own times. With the growing technical and mathematical content of economics the profession itself has inevitably become less accessible to the outsider. To some extent this has been a function of the mode of discourse employed by professional economists: mathematical metaphors have long been in the ascendant. And, as McCloskey comments:

> Books on technical economics are no longer even superficially accessible to lay people; and young economists overvalue a narrow, and occasionally silly, ingenuity of technique.[33]

There have been costs. As Leonard Silk of the *New York Times* has pointed out, there has been a growing gap between the internal agenda of economics and the policy agenda of the real world. If economists are to make more of a contribution to the political agenda than they have in recent years Silk suggests that they 'need to escape from the straightjacket imposed upon economic thought by an uncritical use of mathematical symbol'.[34] It is essential for the vitality of our modern democracies that, as in earlier times, political economy should come to the fore to inform public choices. This requires that economists should endeavour to communicate their ideas to as wide a public as possible so as to explain, educate and inform. Significantly, this wider audience has been found for natural sciences: there is no reason why economics cannot find a public voice. As Adam Smith and all the great political economists since have demonstrated, the metaphors of economic theory are the instances and language of the everyday. This is a task for economists themselves rather than, as has happened in the recent past, journalists and politicians. Yet much stands to prevent this improvement in the presentation of economics actually happening.

The academic gains prestige and advancement from developing expertise in a narrow field. This begins with the PhD and carries through the rest of his or her professional life. There are no faculty points for journalism and television appearances. From the career point of view, narrowness, technical ability and 'normal science' pays. At the same time, there are similar pressures making for specialization in journalism. The boom in financial and business journalism over the last decade or so has been in the market for specialists rather than generalists: the casino society has not brought forth *macro* commentators so much as ever more *micro*-orientated journalists and publications. As Colin Chapman notes, nowadays:

> most media organisations . . . have an army of financial journalists . . . There are people who specialise in company news and comment, and there are specialists on everything from energy and chemicals to banking and telecommunications. There are economic writers, and personal finance writers, who spend most of their working lives writing to fill the spaces left after the salesmen have filled their sections up with advertisements . . .[35]

This *disaggregation* of economic news which has taken place alongside the increasing specialization of economics has a number of causes. First of all, as Chapman suggests, the breaking-up of economic news into more specialist bits is something which is very much the result of advertising and commercial pressures. Had it not been for the money to be derived from advertisements, it is very doubtful if a great explosion of finance and business news would have happened in the first place! At another level, it is also a reflection of the fact that the powerful macro frameworks of the past are no longer adequate as contexts of reporting modern transnational capitalism. The continued privatization of economic discourse has not helped to provide any new popular paradigm. But another reason for this splintering process is the sheer expansion in the availability of greater quantities of information itself.

Since markets began, information has been at the heart of the economic order. Today, more than at any time in history, it is the linchpin of the new world economic system. Indeed, as Walter Wriston, former Chairman of Citibank, has argued in his Op Ed pieces in the *New York Times*, in many senses, the 'information standard'[36] has effectively replaced the old gold standard as the basis of world finance. The existence of this new common currency means that news and information, rumour, gossip and anxieties can be spread around the globe in a matter of seconds. From Wriston's point of view, this revolution in world communications has greatly improved the efficiency of markets: information is now available to anyone who has the technology. The VDU represents the most recent stage in a communications revolution which has informed the evolution of capitalism since its genesis. In the nineteenth century markets grew as information became more widely disseminated. The printed word had a key role in creating a new climate of business activity. The fact, for example, that the news of other countries – both of a political and of an economic nature – could be read at the morning breakfast table gave Victorian investors a confidence to invest abroad to an extent unparalleled before. Britain, or rather the City, stood at the hub of an Empire but also, more significantly in the long run, at the centre of a world economic information system. Today's technologies, therefore, have transformed the way in which that information system functions more radically than at any time since the introduction of the electric telegraph and transatlantic cables in the nineteenth century. The impact of new technology on the structure of the communications underpinning the capitalist system will be as dramatic, if not more so, than that of the telegraph. As David Ayling notes:

> The amount, nature and speed of information available to marketeers and market users is an important aspect of and a driving force behind the internationalisation of stockmarkets . . . The more information is available, the more able is the market to arrive at fair prices so that prices reflect current values of the securities for sale and purchase.[37]

The improvement in the internal and external efficiency of markets is clearly a function of increasing the speed and quality of information. However, more information requires ever more specialized knowledge. And for this reason, if not for many others, the financial communications network has grown in terms of instant information exchange and analysis.

In the circumstances which now pertain in the world of economic communications, what role is there for the printed word? The financial press has adapted to meet the challenges of the information revolution by expanding into the electronic information business. Indeed, economic journalism seems to have come full circle to the days when news came in the form of privately commissioned intelligence. The most significant development in financial writing has been not in 'popular', over-the-news-agent's-counter journalism so much as in the emergence of electronic news and information services for a more limited subscription audience.

New technology and transnational information flows have meant that information *qua* commodity can now be traded across the world, and the development of data bases and information networks which can be accessed by subscribers has meant that the *Wall Street Journal* and the *Financial Times* and the *Economist* now compete for large international markets in selling their information to those willing to pay. Computer link-ups provide information on stocks and shares, analysis, general news and research as well as facilitating fast communications. Dow Jones is now a leading provider of this type of service and is being joined by others: E. F. Hutton, Merrill Lynch, Chase Manhattan, Charles Schwab, Fidelity and Dean Witter. In Britain, too, the range of services now available is very extensive and growing. The *Financial Times* runs FINSTAT, Reuters, Extel, Citibank, and Bridge Data, as well as Dow Jones all provide computer-to-computer information exchange at a relatively low cost. In addition to this, Teletext carries detailed financial and business pages and Prestel has a Citiservice. And, as in America, there is a range of telephone services for the price of a phone call.[38] In Japan *Nihon Keizai Shimbun* (Nikkei) now offers a 'total economic information system' which makes available to subscribers the reports of over 100 journalists. The system feeds four newspapers, seven magazines, and over 300 other publications, as well as television and radio. The Nikkei electronic data bank services (NEEDS) and the Total Research System for Enterprise Data (TREND) provide an analytical service for the *Nikkei Industrial Daily* and the *Nikkei Marketing Journal*. Costs are falling and the competition to provide information services and the data to firms and individuals is becoming ever more competitive and ever more interactive. And, as these various levels and kinds of information evolve, the 'efficiency' of markets themselves will increase and, by definition, will greatly assist in the internationalization of markets and of the attitudes and expectations of those who play what 'Adam Smith' called the 'money game'.[39]

As in the past, the development of economic communications has many implications for the future of the economic agenda. In the first place, the existence of an electronic tier of information and exchange will mean that, as the response to the crash of 1987 demonstrated, there is an inherent gap between the national economic policy and news agenda and that generated by international 'electronic' agenda. The new technology has created another dimension to an information network long dominated by relatively local gossip and the printed page, and powerfully influenced by national politics, economic circumstances and expectations. It is inevitable that the ability of the financial media and communications to mediate economic opinion is greatly enhanced by the existence of an information and data network which functions at a different level and at a much faster pace than was possible only a few years ago. This became apparent to Mrs Thatcher when she protested in February 1985 that: 'Those whose eyes are glued to the screens and ears to the telephones of the world's exchanges have missed the point.' The point being, of course, that the news being flashed around the green screens and the pronouncements and forecasts of (young) economic gurus is less subject to being constructed around government press releases. Again, it is ironic that a former financial journalist, Nigel Lawson, who was also young once, should have become so openly critical in the summer of 1988 of the 'teenage scribblers' in the City of London. The attempt by Mrs Thatcher and Mr Reagan to assure the international markets of the sound basis of the 'real' economy in the wake of the 1987 crash is another graphic illustration of the fact that national economic news has become ever more something which is shaped by an evolving global (and western dominated) information network.

In addition to this, the existence of freely floating international currencies and international markets has meant that the markets themselves are, more than ever before, susceptible to news stories and leaks which are instantly interpreted into price and currency movements. The power of the economic news agencies and information services to structure the agenda has become a major influence on the climate of political opinion and business sentiment. The development of a global financial information industry has, therefore, implications which extend far beyond how the economic system functions, and ultimately challenges the capacity of national governments to manage their economic agendas as in the past. That the financial information industry is one which involves but a few major players (and is in many instances too closely involved with PR companies) cannot then be healthy, either for the information business or for the authority of elected governments or for consumers. Clearly, the existence of a global financial village facilitates, as the 1987 crash bore out, a pace of information exchange which is inherently less susceptible to the influence of the printed word and what Keynes described as the 'ideas of economists' as well as purely national political and economic news. Given this new pace and scale of the information network, the role of both the press and politicians and economic gurus is undergoing a fundamental change.

Alongside this emerging 'electronic agenda' is the break-up of the old context of economic news and the vastly increased range of business and financial journalism. The coherence of economic news of the 1950s and 1960s, when there was comparatively little economic news in newspapers, must be contrasted with the sheer quantity now available in today's press. Compared with the past, it is now more difficult – if not impossible – to pull all these various aspects of economic commentary, personal finance, company news, money market news, commodity news, and so on into one framework. (It is as if the *meta-economy* has outgrown the capacity of anyone to comprehend it, rather as the *meso-economy* has outgrown the capacity of any one nation state or government to control it.) The sheer increased quantity of information places new stresses on the information environment which sustains markets, as well as on the theoretical or intellectual community which endeavours to make sense of it all. Hence, the most important development in the information business is the development of data bases which offer the business community and the financial journalist the ability to access market intelligence from a multiplicity of sources at a speed which would have been impossible ten years ago. As Jean-Claude Nicole, publisher of *La*

Suisse, noted when reviewing the IFRA data bank symposium in 1987:

> Analysis shows computer-based communications has entered a phase of intensive development. Today, we are on the verge of what may be a veritable revolution . . . The computerisation of newspaper companies opens up a range of opportunities for the storage of information, for transferring it and selling it . . .[40]

The *New York Times* was the first newspaper (1971) to put its articles and editorials on a data base: by 1987 over 30 had done so. In Britain the main data base was started in 1984 by Datasolve, a subsidiary of Thorn EMI. *World Reporter* provided the text of stories from a number of major newspapers, including the *Guardian* and the *Washington Post*. Later on, services geared to the business community were added – *World Exporter* and *Magic*. In 1987 Datasolve sold its services to the *Financial Times*. In 1988 the FT's *Profile* was expanded to include coverage of stories in *The Times* and *Sunday Times*. It is planned to introduce more titles. As Sarah Pebody, manager of the *FT* Business Information Service, observed at the IFRA conference:

> with the huge expansion of externally-hosted on-line services, the newspaper is probably available to substantially more readers on-line than it is in hard copy. A sobering thought for those of us in the publishing industry.[41]

The financial newspaper is therefore becoming increasingly a source of data for the economic communications network rather than just a product on a printed page. As new information services emerge so the need for filing away press clippings will, for both journalists and businessmen, become a rather antiquated activity. Cards and other printed media will become redundant in the face of ever more display-based modes of communication and analysis.[42]

The rate of information growth today, as oftentimes in the past, exceeds that of the development of ideas which can serve to organize new information into concepts and discourse. The present position is one in which the global information economy has outpaced the growth of theoretical frameworks. In such conditions the fragmentation of knowledge is almost inevitable. And as the world of finance moves increasingly away from the printed page to electronic information, so the problem of actually organizing economic life into a *news* context, much less an intellectual context, becomes more and more difficult, if not downright impossible: we may have to face the prospect of being information rich and knowledge poor! It may well be that this is what distinguishes Bagehot's 'Economic Age' from our own 'information society'. In the past, for example, British economic commentators, in the tradition of Bagehot, could endeavour to provide their readers with an intellectual context that offered a general perspective on the relationship between economic theories and events. Keynes, as we saw in Chapter 2, and Brittan and Jay were very much part of that style of addressing essentially intellectual questions and issues: ideas journalism. Nowadays, they appear very much as an extinct literary tradition – echos of a time when economics had a literary mode and economists celebrity. The problem today, however, is that the very complexity and global structure of economic news and information makes 'the economy' less and less capable of being aggregated into the kind of political economy which Bagehot provided for his readers in the nineteenth century and which Shonfield, Brittan, Jay, *et al.*, attempted in the 1960s and 1970s. Furthermore, as we mentioned earlier, Galbraith has suggested that the source of new ideas will come not from within the western tradition of economic theory but from the East: the Japanese economic 'miracle'.[43]

Perhaps, however, this turning to the East is but a symptom of a more fundamental condition of cultural decline: the demise of the kind of intellectual controversy which has characterized earlier times. As William Rees-Mogg has suggested, one of the most remarkable changes in British and American political life has been the virtual disappearance of the 'political intellectual'.[44] What is absent from contemporary economic debate is that which characterized the great age of the literary review in the nineteenth century, and the weeklies in the interwar period: *intellectual collision*, as John Gross terms it in his book, *The Rise and Fall of the Man of Letters*.[45]

The specialization of knowledge which accelerated rapidly in the 1960s with the expansion of institutional research and learning, together with the changing demand for publications which cater for a narrower, more segmented market, has meant that the reference points for the kind of economic debate which we have discussed in the preceding chapters have largely disappeared. The arena of influential opinion is not as narrow as in the past, when Keynes could shift the terms of the debate amongst 'inside opinion' through a letter to *The Times*. Since the late 1970s we have seen the phenomenon of an expansion of economic communications – more and faster information and more financial publications – at the same time as we have witnessed a contraction of economic controversy predicated on theoretical or intellectual disagreement. Having abandoned one illusion – the pursuit of big economic theories – we are in danger of embracing another which may prove to be even more transitory: a faith in the wonders of micro-information technology.

The critical question remains, therefore, what will be the role of the printed word in a world economic order girded by what Cable and Wireless describe as a 'Global Digital Highway'? Decision-taking in the financial markets of the world, driven along by the pace of information exchange and data retrieval and analysis, will take place at a speed which will both subvert the old notions of national economic policy and alter the behaviour and responses of market traders. Nonetheless, as Boris Sedacca has noted:

> technology does not make the trader omnipresent. There is no way that all possible information about every trade can be made available every time at the push of a button. . . . Even if such information is made available, a trader could not afford to dwell on it too long. The problem is not necessarily a shortage of information, but the reverse – often of making sense of masses of data.[46]

The modern trading room is a world away from the leisurely style of business in the past when *The Wall Street Journal* or the *FT* provided a gentleman with all the basic information for the day's business. Contemporary traders are now on the receiving end of a multiplicity of sources of information, surrounded by numerous terminals flashing the latest up-to-the-second news. And, as Jane Bird notes: 'The trouble is that often they are drowning in data rather than turning it into useful information.'[47] The problem, however, tends to be seen as less of a (human) intellectual issue so much as one of improving the software so that computers can process the information overload and filter relevant information. As David Ure, managing director of Reuters Europe claimed in

1988: 'We are now in a position to provide a whole spectrum of services at one workstation, from anonymous prices, to generally-held news and quotes to filtered news, backing into historical databases.'[48]

The increased availability of more specialized and filtered information and its speed of dissemination and access only makes the problem of general intelligibility – making sense of it all – ever more urgent. Our need for 'scholars' in the financial media may therefore be greater today than in the past.[49]

Throughout history man's capacity to get information has always gone in advance of his capacity to understand and organize it: knowledge. The electronic agenda is the most recent example of the lag between information and knowledge. The function of the printed word in general, and of good financial journalism in particular, will, it seems to the present author, be to provide another, less rapid rhythm and pace of appraisal to balance that flickering across the VDU screen. The growth of the financial press in the last decade has, after all, been alongside that of the growth of electronic information. The communications revolution will not make the printed page redundant: its ease of use will take some beating. But it will alter the way in which printed information is used. Using data bases and desk-top computers, the reader of the future will be able to construct a newspaper or newsheet to suit their personal or company interests, rather than print out material which is of no immediate use or relevance. The new technology may consequently narrow and constrain horizons rather than widen them. The economic news agenda may be more of a series of individualized, bespoke products, as opposed to all-purpose off-the-peg jobs as at present. As Sarah Pebody has forecast, this means that 'where we are really heading is bundling added value information for specialist vertical markets . . . tailoring specialist information for particular market niches'.[50] There is no reason, therefore, to doubt that the newspaper will continue to have a role in propagating economic ideas and opinions and in mediating the flow of opinion between business, industry and the state, but the big question is whether that role will be anything like that of the past hundred years. My guess is that it will not, since the changeover from the printed word to electronic technology also expresses, as Anthony Smith has argued, a challenge to the 'philosophical underpinning of reporting and collecting information'.

'Victorian objectivity' is giving way to the relativism of the electronic age. Words have lost their hard edges in the age of the audio-visual. A world of facts is dissolving into a factless world overloaded with information, dominated by images.[51]

The electronic revolution is also a challenge to the previous patterns of access to, and ownership of, information. The gap between the 'haves' and the 'have-nots', in terms of access to expensive data and information systems, means that it is no longer the case that what information is to be had is available to all who can afford the price of a newspaper. Paradoxically, the internationalization of information by the use of electronic technology makes the market more exclusive and less accessible than in the past when printed information held sway. And, the fact that the provision of economic information is likely to be dominated by relatively few producers (and owners) has many serious consequences for both price and accessibility, as well as the political and economic power of the information market. Keynes optimistically believed that in the end it was ideas and not interests which determined policies. What, however, would he have made of the situation where policy-making is shaped less by the 'ideas of economists' than by informatics: the application of computers, data bases and transnational information flows to economic, social and political problems?

Technology cannot solve the basic problem of turning all this vast array of financial and business information into something called economic knowledge. Ever more information does not necessarily lead to an increased understanding. The Wriston thesis, that the global financial village makes crashes and panics less likely than in the past where information was less available, looks somewhat dented after the crash of '87. As a *Wall Street Journal* journalist exclaims in a Robert Erdman novel:

'Oh, yeah Walter... Well, I'm plugged in and, true, I've got information coming out of my ears. But what that information *means* I haven't got a clue about.'[52]

The intellectual function of the printed word remains what it has always been: to place events in the framework of ideas and concepts and *vice versa*. As Theodore Roszak reminds us:

news, which is the daily pulse of politics, is never simply information; it is not raw factual material that simply drops out of the world into a data base. It is focused enquiry and interpretation based on a solid set of ideas about the world: what matters, where is the history of our time heading, what's at stake, what are the hidden agendas, what is the big picture? The answers to these questions are the ideas that determine the value of information. Often what a good journalist must do is cast out tons of obfuscating data glut in order to get down to the living truth . . . At most the computer makes a limited and marginal contribution to that goal.[53]

With the relationship between business, industry and the state changing so rapidly, and not just in Western capitalist economies, the need for critical journalism capable of handling the 'information glut' is just as important as (if not *more* important than) improving the 'flow of data'. And, given the scale and complexity of business and finance in the modern world, the existence of a press equipped to analyse and hold it to public accountability is a necessary component of democracy in a market society.

The existence of global financial and informational networks and databases offers the prospect of a more complex and inter-dependent international economic agenda which challenges both the position of national news reporting and commentary and the context of governmental and business decision-making. In the future the international market for the economic communications media may prove to have far more influence on the formation of national economic agendas and the possibilities of political control of the economy than any new theoretical message.

NOTES

1. *Financial Times*, 15 February 1988, p. 54.
2. J. Lawrenson and L. Barber, *The Price of Truth: the story of Reuters Millions*, (Sphere Books, London, 1986) p. 119. See also Alex Murray, 'Reuter–Fleet Street our Success Story', *Sunday Telegraph*, 19 September 1982.
3. Mihir Bose, *The Crash: the fundamental flaws which caused the 1987–8 world market slump and what they mean for future financial stability* (Bloomsbury, London, 1988) p. 7.
4. *New Statesman*, 11 March 1988.
5. Cabinet Office, Information Technology Panel, 'Making A Business of Information' (HMSO, London, 1983) p. 11.
6. Herbert I. Schiller, *Information and the Crisis Economy* (Oxford University Press, New York, 1986) p. 81.
7. *The Economist*, 23 July 1988. Paul Norkett also makes the same point with regard to the spectacular growth of the information sector:

    The provision of business related information and the means of communicating it are high growth industrial sectors. A decade ago a large part of business information was published . . . This traditional hard copy form of storing and communicating information is still a mainstream activity. But the real growth industry sector is the database where information is stored in digital form. There are now thousands of databases and that number is growing daily. Even the most traditional of hard copy publishers are moving into what is generally called electronic publishing. (P. Norkett, *Guide to Company Information in Great Britain* (Longmans, London, 1986) p. 24.

8. *Mail On Sunday*, 21 August 1988. She lists amongst the new gurus: Steven Bell, Morgan Grenfell; Michael Hughes, Barclays de Zoete Wedd; John Shepperd, Warburg Securities; Richard Jeffrey, Hoare Govett; and the guru's guru, Gavin Davies, Goldman Sachs. In connection with Mr Lawson's attack on the 'teenage scribblers' see Tim Congdon, 'Scribblers in the Stocks', *The Times*, 27 September 1988.

9. *The Economist*, 26 December 1987.

10. Karin Newmann, *The Selling of British Telecom* (Holt, Rinehart and Winston, London, 1986) pp. 142–4.

11. Christopher Hird, 'Decoding the Message of the Money Programmes', *The Listener*, 28 January 1988.

12. James Curran, 'Advertising and the Press', in J. Curran (ed.), *The British Press: a manifesto* (Mackmillan, London, 1978), p. 240.

13. Ibid., p. 141.

14. See J. Curran, A. Douglas and G. Whannel, 'The political-economy of the human interest story', in A. Smith (ed.), *Newspapers and Democracy* (MIT Press, Cambridge, Mass., 1981) p. 295; and P. Mosely, *The British Economy as Represented by the Popular Press* (University of Strathclyde, Centre for the Study of Public Policy, Glasgow, 1982).

15. Louis Rukeyser, *What's Ahead for the Economy?* (Simon and Schuster, New York, 1983) pp. 34–5.

16. *Sunday Times* 25 October 1987.

17. Peter Brimelow, *The Wall Street Gurus: how you can profit from investment newsletters* (Random House, New York, 1986).

18. Ibid.

19. See Peter Brimelow, 'The Gurus Gored', *The Times*, 21 October 1987.

20. C. David Chase, *Mugged On Wall Street: an insider shows you how to protect yourself and your money from the financial pros* (Simon and Schuster, New York, 1987) p. 141.

21. Ibid., p. 139.

22. Will Hutton, *The Revolution that Never was: an assessment of Keynesian economics* (Longman, London, 1986).

23. *Business*, March 1988.

24. R. Roberts and L. Johnson, *How to Get a Highly Paid Job in the City* (Kogan Page, London, 1987) p. 79. On the use of the press by business see R. B. Irvine, *When You Are the Headline: managing a major news story* (Dow-Jones Irwin, New York, 1987).

25. Lawrenson and Barber, op.cit.

26. *Sunday Times*, 25 October 1987.

27. R. Foster Winans, *Trading Secrets: seduction and scandal at the Wall Street Journal* (Macmillan, London, 1986) p. 120.

28. P. Coggan, *The Money Machine: how the City Works: a report from the inside* (Penguin Books, Harmondsworth, 1986) p. 11.

29. Ibid.

30. 'Playing with fire', *Business Week*, 16 September 1985, p. 78.

31. September 1985. Ad shows Mom and Dad feeling at home with the stock market while son looks on eagerly.
32. Rukeyser, op.cit,
33. Donald McCloskey *The Rhetoric of Economics* (Wheatsheaf Books, Brighton, 1986), p. 4.
34. Leonard Silk, *The Economists* (Avon Books, New York, 1978) p. 236.
35. C. Chapman, *How the New Stock Exchange Works: buying and selling stocks and shares in the new stock-market* (Hutchinson, London, 1986) p. 127.
36. Cited in Adrian Hamilton, *The Financial Revolution*, (Penguin, Harmondsworth, 1986) p. 30.
37. D. E. Ayling, *The Internationalisation of the Stockmarkets: the trend towards greater foreign borrowing and investment* (Gower, Aldershot, 1986) p. 181.
38. *Independent*, 18 July 1988. In the summer of 1988 the new *Independent* added to the list by the introduction of a telephone service, 'Independent Index'. it argued that, in the light of the 1987 crash, the customer needed, 'if ever proof were needed', *more* information than could be provided on the printed page! See 18 July 1988.
39. Alias George Goodman, *The Money Game* (Dell Publishing, New York, 1969).
40. *Newspaper Techniques* (the monthly publication of the INCA–FIES research association) April 1987, p. 1.
41. Ibid., p. 9.
42. For example, a report on *Analysis News*, a company planning to take on EXTEL claims that its service will guarantee 'total accuracy of company information with the immediacy of company news'. A key point is that it will aim to be a 'comprehensive financial news service which does away with the need to store press clippings', *Independent*, 9 June 1988.
43. J. K. Galbraith, *A History of Economics: the past as the present* (Hamish Hamilton, London, 1987) p. 292.
44. *Independent*, 1 December 1987.
45. John Gross, *The Rise and Fall of the Man of Letters: English literary life since 1800* (Penguin Books, Harmondsworth, 1969) p. 311.
46. *Financial Times*, 3 December 1987.
47. *Sunday Times* 6 March 1988.
48. *The Economist*, 23 July 1988.
49. See Mihir Bose, 'Fallen Stars of the City Pages', (*Business*, March 1988) which suggests that the scholars are indeed making a comeback.
50. *Newspaper Techniques*, April 1987.
51. Anthony Smith, *Goodbye Gutenburg: the newspaper revolution of the 1980s* (Oxford University Press, London, 1980) p. 325.
52. Paul Erdman, *The Crash of '89* (Sphere Books, London, 1987) p. 197.
53. Theodore Roszak, *The Cult of Information: the folklore of computers and the art of true thinking* (Paladin Books, London, 1988) pp. 191–2.

Bibliography

This bibliography lists those books and academic journal articles cited in the text as well as other relevant material which may be of interest to the reader.

BOOKS (including contributions to multi-author works)

Abrams, A. E., *Journalist Biographies and Master Index* (Gale Research Company, Detroit, 1979).

Allen, G. C., *Economic Fact and Fantasy: a rejoinder to Galbraith's Reith Lectures* (Institute of Economic Affairs, London, 1967).

Anderson, M. (ed.), *The Unfinished Agenda: Essays on the political economy of government in honour of Arthur Seldon* (Institute of Economic Affairs, London, 1986).

Andrews, A., *History of British Journalism*, 2 vols (Richard Bentley, London, 1859).

Armstrong, F. E., *The Book of the Stock Exchange* (Pitman, London, 1949).

Attaroni, Yair, *The Foreign Investment Decision Process* (Harvard University Press, Boston, 1966).

Attwood, Thomas, *Selected Writings* ed. Frank Whitson Fetter (London School of Economics and Political Science, London, 1964).

Ayerst, D., *Guardian: biography of a newspaper* (Collins, London, 1971).

Ayling, D. E., *The Internationalisation of Stockmarkets: the trend towards greater foreign borrowing and investment* (Gower, Aldershot, 1986).

Bacon, R. and W. Eltis, *Britain's Economic Problem: too few producers* (Macmillan, London, 1976/1978)

Bagehot, Walter, *The Collected Works*, ed. Norman St John Stevas (*The Economist*, London 1965) vols 9, 10, 11, (the economic writings).

Bagehot, Walter, *Economic Studies*, ed. Richard Holt Hutton (Longman, London, 1880).

Bagehot, Walter, *Literary Studies*, vol. 1 (Dent, London, 1916).

Baistow, T., *Fourth Rate Estate: an anatomy of Fleet Street* (Comedia, London, 1985).

Barry, N., *The New Right* (Croom Helm, London, 1987).

Bartlett, Bruce., *Reaganomics: supply side economics in action* (Arlington House, Westport, Conn., 1981).

Bartlett, Bruce and Timothy P. Roth, *The Supply-Side Solution* (Macmillan, London, 1984).

Beer, Samuel, *Modern British Politics* (Faber and Faber, London, 1965).

Bell, Daniel, 'Models and Reality in Economic Discourse' in Bell and Kristol (eds).

Bell, Daniel and Irving Kristol (eds), *The Crisis in Economic Theory* (Basic Books, New York, 1981).

Bender, Thomas, *New York Intellect* (Knopf, New York, 1987).

Benson, J., *The Penny Capitalists* (Gill and Macmillan, Dublin, 1983).

Berger, P., *The Capitalist Revolution: fifty propositions about prosperity, equality and liberty* (Wildwood House, Aldershot, 1987).

Birnie, A., *Single Tax George* (Nelson, London, 1939).

Black, J., *The English Press in the Eighteenth Century* (Croom Helm, London, 1987).

Black, R. D. Collison (ed.), *Ideas in Economics* (Macmillan, London, 1986).

Black, R. D. Collison, A. W. Coats and Crauford D. W. Goodwin, *The Marginal Revolution in Economics* (Duke University Press, Durham, North Carolina, 1973).

Blaug, Mark, *Economic Theory in Retrospect* (Cambridge University Press, Cambridge, 1979).

Bond, D. H. and W. Reynolds Mcloed (eds), *Newsletters to Newspapers: eighteenth century journalism* (papers presented at a bicentennial symposium at Morgantown, West Virginia, 31 March–2 April 1976) (School of Journalism, West Virginia University, 1977).

Bond, R. P. (ed.), *Studies in the Early English Periodical* (University of North Carolina Press, Chapel Hill, 1957).

Bosanquet, Nick, *After the New Right* (Heinemann, London, 1983)

Bose, Mihir, *The Crash: the fundamental flaws which caused the*

1987–8 world stock market slump – and what they mean for future financial stability (Bloomsbury, London, 1988).

Boston, R. (ed.), *The Press We Deserve* (Routledge and Kegan Paul, London, 1970).

Boyd-Barrett, Oliver, *The International News Agencies* (Constable/Sage, London and Beverly Hills, 1980).

Boyd-Barrett, Oliver, C. Seymour-Ure and J. Tunstall, *Studies on the Press*, Royal Commission on the Press, Working Paper 3 (HMSO, London, 1977).

Boyle, A., *Poor, Dear Brendan: the quest for Brendan Bracken* (Hutchinson, London, 1974).

Breit, W. and Roger L. Ransom, *Academic Scribblers* (Dryden Press, Chicago, 1982).

Breit, W. and R. Spencer (eds), *The Lives of the Laureates* (MIT Press, Cambridge, Mass., 1986).

Brett, Michael, *How to Read the Financial Pages* (Business Books, London, 1987).

Brewer, J., 'Commercialisation and Politics' in N. McKendrick *et al.*, *The Birth of a Consumer Society: the commercialisation of 18th century England* (Hutchinson, London, 1983).

Brigham, C. S., *History and Bibliography of American newspapers, 1690–1820*, 2 vols (American Antiquarian Society, Worcester, Mass., 1947).

Brimelow, Peter, *The Wall Street Gurus: how you can profit from investment newsletters* (Random House, New York, 1986).

Brittan, Samuel, *The Economic Consequences of Democracy* (Temple Smith, London, 1977).

Brittan, Samuel, *How to End the 'Monetarist' Controversy: a journalist's reflections on output, jobs, prices and money*, Hobart Paper (Institute of Economic Affairs, London, 1982).

Brittan, Samuel, *Is There an Economic Consensus? An attitude survey* (Macmillan, London, 1971).

Brittan, Samuel, *Participation Without Politics*, Hobart Paper (Institute of Economic Affairs, London, 1975).

Brittan, Samuel, *A Restatement of Economic Liberalism* (Macmillan, London, 1988).

Brittan, Samuel, *The Role and Limits of Government: essays in political economy* (Temple Smith, London, 1983).

Brittan, Samuel, *Steering the Economy; the role of the Treasury* (Penguin, Harmondsworth, 1971).

Brittan, Samuel, *Two Cheers for Self Interest*, seventeenth Wincott Memorial Lecture, (Institute of Economic Affairs, London, 1985).

Bronfenbrenner, Martin, 'On the Superlative in Samuelson', in Feiwell (ed.).

Bronson, B. H., *Printing as an Index of Taste in Eighteenth Century England* (New York Public Library, 1963).

Brookes, Warren T., *The Economy in Mind*, (Universe Books, New York, 1982).

Brown, Lucy, *Victorian News and Newspapers*, (Oxford University Press, Oxford, 1985).

Browning, Peter, *The Treasury and Economic Policy, 1964–1985* (Longman, London and New York, 1986).

Burton, John (ed.), *Keynes's General Theory Fifty Years On: its relevance to modern times* (Institute of Economic Affairs, London, 1986).

Byland, Terry, *Understanding Finance with the Financial Times* (Harrap, London, 1988).

Cairncross, Alec, 'Academics and Policy Makers', in F. Cairncross (ed.).

Cairncross, Francis (ed.), *Changing Perceptions of Economic Policy: essays in honour of the 70th birthday of Sir Alec Cairncross* (Methuen, London, 1981).

Cameron, A. and R. Farndon, *Scenes from Sea and City: Lloyds List, 1734–1984* (Lloyds of London, 1984).

Camrose, Viscount, *British Newspapers and their Controllers* (Cassell, London, 1947).

Canterbury, E. Ray, *The Making of Economics* (Wadsworth, Belmont, California, 1987).

Carswell, John, *The South Sea Bubble* (Crescent Press, London, 1960).

Chandler, A. D., *The Visible Hand: the managerial revolution in American Business* (Harvard University Press, Cambridge, Mass., 1977).

Chapman, Colin, *How the New Stock Exchange Works* (Hutchinson, London, 1986).

Chase, C. David, *Mugged on Wall Street* (Simon and Schuster, New York, 1987).

Cipolla, C. M., *The Industrial Revolution* (Fontana/Collins, London, 1973).

Clarke, W. M., *How the City of London Works* (Waterlow Publishers, London, 1986).

Clive, J., *Scotch Reviewers: the Edinburgh Review, 1802–1815* (Faber and Faber, London, 1957).

Coats, A. W. (ed.), *The Classical Economists and Economic Policy* (Methuen, London, 1971).

Coggan, Philip, *The Money Machine: how the City works* (Penguin, Harmondsworth, 1986).

Corry, B. A. 'Torrens', in *The International Encyclopaedia of the Social Sciences* (Macmillan and Free Press, London, 1968).

Cranfield, G. A., *The Development of the Provincial Newspaper, 1700–1760* (Clarendon Press, Oxford, 1962).

Cranfield, G. A., *The Press and Society from Caxton to Northcliffe* (Longman, London, 1976).

Crawford, Alan, *Thunder on the Right* (Pantheon Books, New York, 1980).

Crowther, Geoffrey, *Economics for Democrats* (Thomas Nelson, London, 1939).

Cruise-O'Brien, Rita (ed.), *Information, Economics and Power: the north–south dimension* (Hodder & Stoughton, London, 1983).

Curran, J., 'Advertising and the press', in Curran (ed.).

Curran, J., 'Capitalism and Control of the Press 1800–1975', in Curran *et al.* (eds).

Curran, J. and Jean Seaton, *Power without Responsibility: the press and broadcasting in Britain* (Routledge and Kegan Paul, London, 1985).

Curran, J. (ed.), *The British Press: a manifesto* (Macmillan, London, 1978).

Curran, J., M. Gurevitch and J. Woollacott (eds), *Mass Communications and Society* (Edward Arnold/Open University, London, 1977).

Darby, M. R. and J. R. Lothian, 'Economic Events and Keynesian Ideas: the 1930s and the 1940s', in Burton (ed.).

Davenport, Nicholas, *Memoirs of a City Radical* (Weidenfeld and Nicolson, London, 1974).

Davenport, Nicholas, *The Split Society* (Gollancz, London, 1964).

Davenport-Hines, R. P. T. (ed.), *Speculators and Patriots: essays in business biography* (Frank Cass, London, 1986).

Davis, H. and P. Walton (eds), *Language, Image, Media* (Blackwell, Oxford, 1983).

Dean, James W., 'The Dissolution of the Keynesian Consensus', in Bell and Kristol (eds).

Desmond, R. W., *The Information Process: world news reporting in the twentieth century* (University of Iowa Press, Iowa City, 1978).

Donavan, Hedley, *Roosevelt to Reagan: a Reporter's Encounters with Nine Presidents* (Harper and Row, New York, 1987).

Drucker, Peter R., 'Toward the Next Economics', in Bell and Kristol (eds).

Duguid, C., *How to Read the Money Article* (Effingham Wilson, London, 1908) and 1905 6th edn, rev. F. W. H. Caudwell, 1931. 7th edn (W. Colin Brooks, London, 1936).

Eagly, R. V. (ed.), *Events, Ideology and Economic Theory* (Wayne State University Press, Detroit, 1968).

Economist, *The Economist 1843–1943* (Economist Newspaper, London, 1943).

Einzig, Paul, *In the Centre of Things: the autobiography of Paul Einzig* (Hutchinson, London, 1960).

Ellis, A., *The Penny Universities: a history of the coffee houses* (Secker and Warburg, London, 1957).

Emery, E. and H. L. Smith, *The Press and America* (Prentice Hall, New York, 1954).

Emmison, Mike, 'The Economy': its emergence in media discourse', in Davis and Walton (eds).

Erdman, Paul, *Money Guide* (Sphere Books, London, 1985).

Erdman, Paul, *The Panic of '89* (Sphere Books, London, 1987).

Ermann, M. David and Richard J. Lundman (eds), *Corporate and Governmental Deviance* (Oxford University Press, New York, 1987).

Evans, Harold, *Good Times, Bad Times* (Weidenfeld & Nicolson, London, 1983).

Evans, M. K., *The Truth About the Supply Side Economics* (Basic Books, New York, 1983).

Evans, Sandra S. and Richard J. Lundmann, 'Newspaper Coverage of Corporate Crime', in Ermann and Lundmann (eds).

Feather, J. *The Provincial Book Trade in Eighteenth Century England* (Cambridge University Press, Cambridge, 1985).

Feiwell G. R. (ed.), *Samuelson and Neo-classical Economics* (Kluwer Nijhoff, Boston, 1982).

Fels, R. (ed.) *The Second Crisis of Economic Theory* (General Learning Press, New Jersey, 1972).

Ferguson, M. (ed.), *New Communication Technologies and the Public Interest: comparative perspectives on policy and research*, (Sage, London, 1986).

Fink, R. H. (ed.), *Supply-side Economics: a critical appraisal* (Aleheia, University Publications of America, Maryland, 1982).

Fishman, W. J., *East End 1888: a year in a London borough among the Labouring poor* (Duckworth, London, 1988).

Fleet, K. G., *The Influence of the Financial Press* (Annual Livery Lecture, The Worshipful Company of Stationers and Newspaper Makers, London, 1983).

Fontana, Biancamaria, *Rethinking the Politics of Commercial Society; The 'Edinburgh Review', 1802–1832* (Cambridge University Press, Cambridge, 1985).

Foster Winans, R., *Trading Secrets: seduction and scandal at the Wall Street Journal* (Macmillan, London, 1986).

Frank, J., *The Beginnings of the English Newspaper, 1620–1660*, (Harvard University Press, Cambridge, Mass., 1961).

Franklin, Benjamin, *Benjamin Franklin's letters to the Press, 1758–1775*, ed. V. W. Crane (University of North Carolina Press, Chapel Hill, 1950).

Fraser, W. H., *The Coming of the Mass Market: 1850–1914* (Macmillan, London, 1981).

Friedman, Milton, *Bright Promises, Dismal Performance: an economist's protest* (Harcourt Brace Jovanovich, New York, 1983).

Friedman, Milton, *Capitalism and Freedom* (Chicago University Press, Chicago, 1962).

Friedman, Milton, *The Counter-revolution in Monetary Theory:* the first Wincott Memorial Lecture (Institute of Economic Affairs, London, 1970).

Friedman, Milton, *An Economist's Protest: columns in political economy* (Thomas Horton, New Jersey, 1972).

Friedman, Milton, *From Galbraith to Economic Freedom* (Institute of Economic Affairs, London, 1977).

Friedman, Milton, 'Has Liberalism failed?' in Anderson (ed.).

Friedman, Milton, *There's No Such Thing as a Free Lunch* (Open Court, La Salle, Ill., 1975).

Friedman, Milton and Rose Friedman, *Free to Choose* (Penguin, Harmondsworth, 1980).

Friedman, Milton, and Rose Friedman, *The Tyranny of the Status Quo* (Penguin, Harmondsworth, 1985).

Galbraith, J. K., *The Affluent Society* (Houghton Mifflin, Boston, 1958).

Galbraith, J. K., *The Age of Uncertainty* (BBC/Andre Deutsch, London, 1977).

Galbraith, J. K., *Economics, Peace and Laughter* (Penguin, Harmondsworth, 1971).

Galbraith, J. K., *The Great Crash, 1929* (Houghton Mifflin, Boston, 1955).

Galbraith, J. K., *A History of Economics: the past as the present* (Hamish Hamilton, London, 1987).

Galbraith, J. K. *A Life in Our Times* (Houghton Mifflin, Boston, 1981).

Galbraith, J. K., *A View from the Stands: of people, politics, military powers and the arts* (Hamish Hamilton, London, 1987).

Gambs, John S., *John Kenneth Galbraith* (St Martin's Press, New York, 1975).

George, Henry, *Progress and Poverty* (Dent, London, 1977).

Gilder, George, *Wealth and Poverty* (Bantam Books, New York, 1981).

Ginswick, J. (ed.), *Labour and the Poor in England and Wales, 1849–1851: letters to the* Morning Chronicle *from the correspondents in the manufacturing and mining districts, the towns of Liverpool and Birmingham and the rural districts*, 3 vols (Frank Cass, London, 1983).

Gleeson, A., *People and their Money: 50 years of private investment* (Hobsons Press for M & G Group, London, 1981).

Goodman, George, *The Money Game* (Dell Publishing, New York, 1969).

Gordon, Barry, *Political Economy in Parliament, 1819–1823* (Macmillan, London, 1976).

Graham, David and Peter Clarke, *The New Enlightenment: the re-birth of liberalism* (Macmillan/Channel 4 Books, London, 1986).

Grant, J., *The Newspaper Press: its origin, progress and present position*, 3 vols (Tinsley, London, 1871).

Gramp, W. D., *The Manchester School of Economics* (Stanford University Press, Stanford, 1960).

Greenstein, Fred I. (ed.), *The Reagan Presidency: an early assessment* (Johns Hopkins University Press, Baltimore, 1983).

Gross, J., *The Rise and Fall of the Man of Letters: English literary life since 1800* (Penguin, Harmondsworth, 1973).

Halbertstam, D., *The Powers that Be* (Knopf, New York, 1979).

Hamilton, Adrian, *The Financial Revolution* (Penguin, Harmondsworth, 1986).

Hannah, Leslie, *The Rise of the Corporate Economy* (Methuen, London and New York, 1983).

Harris, M. and A. Lee (eds), *The Press and English Society from the Seventeenth to Nineteenth Centuries* (Associated University Press, London, 1986).

Harris, R. and A. Seldon, *Not from Benevolence: twenty years of economic dissent* (Institute of Economic Affairs, London, 1977).

Harrod, R. F., *The Life of John Maynard Keynes* (Macmillan, London, 1951).

Hayek, F. A., *Studies in Philosophy, Politics and Economics* (Routledge and Kegan Paul, London, 1978).

Hazlitt, H., *The Failure of the New Economics: an analysis of Keynesian fallacies* (Van Nostrand, New York, 1959).

Hazlitt, H. (ed.), *The Critics of Keynesian Economics* (Van Nostrand, New York, 1960).

Heinzelman, Kurt, *The Economics of the Imagination* (University of Massachusetts Press, Amherst, 1980).

Heilbronner, Robert L., *Business Civilisation in Decline* (Penguin, Harmondsworth, 1977).

Heilbroner, Robert L., *The Worldly Philosophers: the lives, times and ideas of the great economic thinkers* (Penguin, Harmondsworth, 1983).

Henderson, D., *Innocence and Design: the influence of economic ideas on policy* (Basil Blackwell, Oxford, 1986).

Henderson, H. D., *The Inter-war Years and Other Papers: a selection from the writings of Hubert Douglas Henderson* ed. H. Clay (Clarendon Press, Oxford, 1955).

Hennesey, Peter, *What the Papers Never Said* (Portcullis Press, Politics Association, London, 1985).

Hession, Charles H., *John Kenneth Galbraith and His Critics* (New American Library, New York, 1972).

Hetherington, A., *Guardian Years* (Chatto and Windus, London, 1981).

Hindle, W., *The* Morning Post, *1772–1937: portrait of a newspaper* (Greenwood Press, Westport, Conn., 1974).

Hirsch, Fred *The Social Limits to Growth* (Routledge and Kegan Paul, London, 1977).

Hirsch, Fred and David Gordon, *Newspaper Money: Fleet Street and the search for the affluent reader* (Hutchinson, London, 1975).

Hirst, F. W., *The Stock Exchange: a short study of investment and speculation* (Holt, Rinehart and Winston, New York and Butterworth, London, 1911, 1927).

Hobson, Oscar, *How the City Works* (News Chronicle, London, 1938).

Horner, Francis, *The Economic Writings*, ed. Frank Whitson Fetter (London School of Economics and Political Science, London, 1957).

Horner, Francis, *Memoirs and Correspondence of Francis Horner M.P.*, ed. L. Horner (London, 1853).

Horowitz, I. L., *Communicating Ideas: the crisis of publishing in a post-industrial society* (Oxford University Press, New York, 1986).

Houghton, W. E. (ed.)., *The Wellesley Index to Victorian Periodicals, 1824–1900* (University of Toronto Press, and Routledge and Kegan Paul, London, 1966).

Hubback, D., *No Ordinary Press Baron: a life of Walter Layton* (Weidenfeld and Nicolson, London, 1985).

Hudson, F., *Journalism in the United States, 1690–1872* (Harper and Row, New York, 1973).

Hutchison, T. W., *Economics and Economic Policy in Britain, 1946–1966: some aspects of their interrelations* (Allen and Unwin, London, 1968).

Hutchison, T. W., *The Politics and Philosophy of Economics* (Blackwell, Oxford, 1981).

Hutchison, T. W., *A Review of Economic Doctrines, 1870–1929* (Clarendon Press, Oxford, 1966).

Hutchison, T. W., *On Revolutions and Progress in Economic Knowledge* (Cambridge University Press, Cambridge, 1978).

Hutton, Will, *The Revolution that Never Was: an assessment of Keynesian economics*, (Longman, London and New York, 1986).

Hyams, Edward, *The* New Statesman: *the history of the first fifty years, 1913–1963* (Longman, London, 1963).

Illich, Ivan, *The Right to Useful Unemployment and Its Professional Enemies* (Marion Boyars, London, 1978).

Innis, H. A., *Political Economy in the Modern State* (University of Toronto Press, Toronto, 1946).

Innis, H. A., *The Press: a neglected factor in the economic history of the twentieth century* (Oxford University Press, London 1949). Stamp Memorial Lecture.

Irvine, R. B., *When You are the Headlines: managing a major news story* (Dow Jones, New York, 1987).

Jackson, Peter (ed.), *Implementing Government Policy Initiatives: the Thatcher Administration, 1979–1983* (Royal Institute of Public Administration, London, 1985).

Jay, Douglas, *Change and Fortune: a political record* (Hutchinson, London, 1980).

Jay, Peter, *The Crisis for Western Political Economy, and other essays* (Andre Deutsch, London, 1984).

Jay, Peter and Michael Stewart, *Apocalypse 2000* (Sidgwick and Jackson, London, 1987).

Jenkins, Peter, *Mrs Thatcher's Revolution: the ending of the socialist era* (Jonathan Cape, London, 1972).

Johnson, E. A. J., *Predecessors of Adam Smith: the growth of British economic thought* (Kelley, New York, 1965).

Johnson, E. S., 'Keynes as a Literary Craftsman', in Johnson and Johnson.

Johnson, E. S. and H. Johnson, *The Shadow of Keynes: understanding Keynes, Cambridge and Keynesian economics* (Basil Blackwell, Oxford, 1978).

Kadish, A., *The Oxford Economists in the Late Nineteenth Century* (Clarendon Press, Oxford, 1982).

Keegan, W. and Rupert Pennant-Rea, *Who runs the Economy: control and influence in British Economic Policy*, (Maurice Temple Smith, London, 1979).

Keegan, W., *Mrs Thatcher's Economic Experiment* (Penguin, Harmondsworth, 1984).

Keleher, R. E. and W. P. Orezchowski, 'Supply-Side Economics: an historical analysis of a rejuvenated idea', in Fink (ed.).

Kemps, J., *An American Renaissance* (Basic Books, New York, 1979).

Keynes, J. M., *The Collected Writings* (Macmillan, London, 1971–).

Keynes, J. M., *The General Theory of Employment Interest and Money* (Macmillan, London, 1936).

Keynes, Milo, (ed.), *Essays on John Maynard Keynes* (Cambridge University Press, London, 1975).

Kindelberger, C. P., *Manias, Panics and Crashes: a history of financial crises* (Macmillan, London, 1978).

King, Desmond S., *The New Right: politics, markets and citizenship* (Macmillan, London, 1987).

Kobler, John, *Luce, His Time, Life and Fortune* (MacDonald, London, 1968).

Kramer, Kenneth, *Economic commentary: reflections and critiques from the pages of* Business Week (Business Week, New York, 1966).

Krieger, Joel, *Reagan, Thatcher and the Politics of Decline* (Polity Press, Cambridge, 1986).

Kristol, I., *Two Cheers for Capitalism* (Basic Books, New York, 1978).

Kuhn, T. S., *The Structure of Scientific Revolutions* (University of Chicago Press, Chicago, 1970).

Kynaston, David, The Financial Times: *a centenary history* (Viking Press, London, 1988).

Laffer, A. B. and Jan Seymour, *The Economics of Tax Revolt* (Harcourt Brace Jovanovitch, New York, 1979).

Larenson, J. and Lionel Barber, *The Price of Truth: the story of Reuters millions* (Sphere Books, London, 1986).

Lee, Alan J., *The Origins of the Popular Press, 1855–1914* (Croom Helm, London, 1976).

Lee, F., *The City Page* (Nelson, London, 1939).

Lekachman, Robert, *The Age of Keynes* (Allen Lane, London, 1967).

Lekachman, Robert, *Greed is Not Enough: Reaganomics* (Pantheon Books, New York, 1982).

Lysaght, Charles E., *Brendan Bracken* (Allen Lane, London, 1979).

McCloskey, D., *The Rhetoric of Economics* (Wheatsheaf Books, Brighton, 1986).

McFadzean, J., *The Economics of John Kenneth Galbraith: a study in fantasy* (Centre for Policy Studies, London, 1977).

McGrane, R. C., *The Panic of 1837: some financial problems of the Jacksonian era* (University of Chicago Press, Chicago, 1924).

McKendrick, Neil, John Brewer and J. H. Plumb, *The Birth of a Consumer Society* (Hutchinson, London, 1983).

McLachlan, D., *In the Chair: Barrington Ward of* The Times (Weidenfeld and Nicolson, London, 1971).

Madden, L. and D. Dixon, *The Nineteenth Century Periodical Press in Britain: a bibliography of modern studies, 1901–1971* (Garland, New York and London, 1976).

Malabre, Alfred J. Jr, *Investing for Profit in the Eighties: the business cycle system* (Doubleday, New York, 1982).

Malabre, Alfred J. Jr, *Understanding the Economy: for people who can't stand economics* (Mentor, New York, 1976).

Marriner, S. (ed.) *Business and Businessmen: studies in business, economic and accounting history* (Liverpool University Press, Liverpool, 1978).

Marshall, A., *Essays in Biography* (Norton, New York. 1951).

Martin, F., *The History of Lloyds Marine Insurance in Great Britain* (Lloyds, London, 1976).

Martin, Kingsley, *Editor: a volume of autobiography, 1931–1945* (Hutchinson, London, 1968).

Harriet, Martineau, *Autobiography*, 3 vols (Smith Elder, London, 1877).

Matatko, J. and D. Stafford, *Key Developments in Personal Finance* (Blackwell, Oxford, 1985).

Mathias, P., 'Dr Johnson and the Business World' in Marriner, S. (ed.) *Business and Businessmen: studies in business, economic and accounting history* (Liverpool University Press, Liverpool, 1978).

Meiselman, D. and A. B. Laffer, *The Phenomenon of World-wide Inflation* (American Enterprise Institute, Washington, 1975).

Middleton, K. R., 'Commercial Speech in the Eighteenth Century', in Bond and Mcloed (eds).

Milne, J. M., *The Politics of Blackwood's, 1817–1846: a study of the political, economic and social articles in* Blackwoods Edinburgh Magazine *and selected contributors* (University of Newcastle, PhD thesis, 1984).

Minchinton, W., 'Patterns of Demand, 1750–1914' in Cipolla (ed.).

Morgan, E. Victor and W. A. Thomas, *The Stock Exchange: its history and functions* (Elek Books, London, 1962).

Morison, S., *The English Newspaper: some account of the physical development of journals printed in London between 1622 and the present day* (Cambridge University Press, Cambridge, 1932).

Mosley P., *The British Economy as Represented by the Popular*

Press (University of Strathclyde, Centre for the study of Public Policy, Glasgow, 1982).

Nevett, T. R., *Advertising in Britain: a history* (Heineman, London, 1982).

Newman, Karin, *The Selling of British Telecom* (Holt, Rinehart and Winston, London, 1986).

Norkett, Paul, *Guide to Company Information in Great Britain* (Longman, London, 1986).

Noyes, Alexander Dana, 'Economic Problems during the War and Afterward', in E. M. Friedman (ed.), *American Problems of Reconstruction* (Dutton, New York, 1918).

Noyes, Alexander Dana, *The Market Place: reminiscences of American finance* (Little Brown, Boston, 1938).

Noyes, Alexander Dana, 'Present Value of Past Economic History', in *Addresses and Discussion at a Conference of Universities under the auspicies of New York University and the Waldorf-Astoria in New York November 15th–17th, 1932* (New York University Press, New York, 1933).

O'Brien, D. P., *The Classical Economists*, (Clarendon Press, Oxford, 1975).

O'Brien, D. P., *J. R. McCulloch: a study in classical economics* (Allen and Unwin, London, 1970).

O'Brien, D. P. and J. R. Presley (eds), *Pioneers of Modern Economics in Britain* (Macmillan, London, 1981).

O'Connor, Richard, *The Scandalous Mr Bennett* (Doubleday, New York, 1962).

Palmer, John, 'The Harlot's Perogative' in R. Boston (ed.) *The Press we Deserve* (Routledge & Kegan Paul, London, 1970).

Parsons, D. W., *The Political Economy of British Regional Policy* (Routledge & Kegan Paul, London, 1988).

Patinkin, D., *Anticipations of the General Theory? and other essays on Keynes* (University of Chicago Press, Chicago, 1982).

Pennant-Rea, Robert and Clive Crook, *The Economist Economics* (Penguin, Harmondsworth, 1986).

Phillips, A., *Glasgow's* Herald: *two hundred years of a newspaper, 1783–1983* (Richard Drew, Glasgow, 1983).

Pigou, A. C., *The Theory of Unemployment* (Macmillan, London, 1933).

Plumb, J. H., *England in the Eighteenth Century* (Penguin, Harmondsworth, 1963).

Polanyi, Karl, *The Great Transformation* (Beacon Press, Boston, 1957).

Political and Economic Planning, *Report on the British Press* (PEP, London, 1938).

Porter, Dilwyn, 'A Trusted Guide of the Investing Public, Harry Marks and the *Financial News*, 1884–1916', in Davenport-Hines (ed.).

Rees-Mogg, William, *Democracy and the Value of Money: the theory of money from Locke to Keynes* (Institute of Economic Affairs, London, 1977).

Rees-Mogg, William, *The Reigning Illusion* (Hamish Hamilton, London, 1974).

Reisman, David, *Galbraith and Market Capitalism* (Macmillan, London, 1980).

Rhea, Robert, *The Dow Theory* (Barron's, New York, 1932).

David, Ricardo, *The Works and Correspondence of David Ricardo* (Royal Economic Society, London, 1951–5).

Rima, I. H., *Development of Economic Analysis* (Richard D. Irwin, Homewood, Ill., 1978).

Robbins, Lord [Lionel], *Autobiography of an Economist* (Macmillan, London, 1971).

Robbins, L., *The Nature and Significance of Economic Science* (Macmillan, London, 1935).

Robbins, Lionel, *Robert Torrens and the Evolution of Classical Economics* (Macmillan, London, 1958).

Roberts, R. and L. Johnson *How to get a Highly Paid Job in the City* (Kogan Page, London, 1987).

Roberts, P. C., *The Supply Side Revolution: an insider's account of policymaking in Washington* (Harvard University Press, Cambridge, Mass., 1984).

Roll, Eric, *A History of Economic Thought* (Faber, London, 1973).

Rolph, C. H., (ed.), *Kingsley: the life, letters and diaries of Kingsley Martin* (Gollancz, London, 1973).

Rosenberg, J. M., *Inside the* Wall Street Journal (Macmillan, New York, 1982).

Roszak, Theodore, *The Cult of Information* (Paladin Books, London, 1988).

Rubner, Alex, *The Price of a Free Lunch: the perverse relationship between economists and politicians* (Wildwood House, London, 1979).

Rukeyser, Louis, *What's Ahead for the Economy* (Simon & Schuster, New York, 1983).

Rutland, R. A., *The Newsmongers: journalism in the life of the nation, 1690–1972*, Dial Press, New York, 1973).

Samuelson, P. A., *The Collected Scientific Papers*, vols 1–4 (MIT Press, Cambridge, Mass., 1972).

Samuelson, P. A. (ed.), *Readings in Economics*, 7th edn (McGraw Hill, New York, 1973).

Sayers, R. S., 'Bagehot as an Economist', in Bagehot, vol. 9, pp. 27–43.

Schiller, Herbert I., *Information and the Crisis Economy*, (Oxford University Press, New York, 1986).

Schlesinger, A. M., *The Coming of the New Deal*, (Houghton Mifflin, Boston, 1965).

Schlesinger, A. M., *Prelude to Independence: the newspaper war on Britain, 1764–1776* (Alfred A Knopf, New York, 1957).

Schumpeter, Joseph A., *Capitalism, Socialism and Democracy*, (Allen & Unwin, London, 1974).

Schumpeter, Joseph A., *History of Economic Analysis* (Allen & Unwin, London, 1965).

Schumpeter, Joseph A., *Ten Great Economists – from Marx to Keynes* (Oxford University Press, New York, 1951).

Schwartz, G. L., *Bread and Circuses, 1945–1958* (Sunday Times, London, 1958).

Scottish Central Library, *Scottish Newspapers held in Scottish Libraries* (Scottish Central Library, Edinburgh, 1956).

Seitz, D. C., *The James Gordon Bennetts: father and son* (Bobs-Merrill, Indianapolis, 1928).

Seldon, A. (ed.), *The Emerging Consensus: essays on the interplay between ideas, interests and circumstances in the first 25 years of the IEA* (Institute of Economic Affairs, London, 1981).

Sergeant, Patrick, 'Tip for Tap in the City', in *100 Years of Fleet Street* (Press Club, London, 1982).

Seymour-Ure, C., *The Political Impact of the Mass Media*, (Constable, London, 1974).

Seymour-Ure, C., *The Press, Politics and the Public* (Methuen, London, 1968).

Shaddock, J. and M. Wolff (eds), *The Victorian Press: samplings and soundings* (Leicester University Press, Leicester, and Toronto University Press, Toronto, 1982).

Shanks, M., *Planning and Politics: the British Experience 1960–78* (Political and Economic Planning and Allen and Unwin, London, 1977).

Shanks, Michael, *The Stagnant Society* (Penguin, Harmondsworth, 1961).

Sharpe, M. E., *John Kenneth Galbraith and the Lower Economics* (Macmillan, London, 1973).

Shell, Marc, *The Economy of Literature*, (Johns Hopkins University Press, Baltimore, 1978).

Shonfield, Andrew, *British Economic Policy Since the War* (Penguin, Harmondsworth, 1958).

Shonfield, Andrew, *Europe: journey to an unknown destination* (Penguin, Harmondsworth, 1973).

Shonfield, Andrew, *Modern Capitalism* (Oxford University Press, London and New York, 1965).

Silk, Leonard, *Economic Commentary: reflections and critiques from the pages of* Business Week. (Business Week, New York, 1966).

Silk, Leonard, *Economics in the Real World* (Simon & Schuster, New York, 1984).

Silk, Leonard, *The Economists* (Avon Books, New York, 1978).

Skidelsky, R., *John Maynard Keynes: hopes betrayed, 1883–1920* (Macmillan, London, 1983).

Skidelsky, R. (ed.), *The End of the Keynesian Era* (Macmillan, London, 1977).

Smith, Adam (pseud. of George Goodman), *The Money Game* (Dell Publishing, New York, 1969).

Smith, Anthony, *The Newspaper: an international history* (Thames & Hudson, London, 1979).

Smith, Anthony, *Goodbye Gutenburg: the newspaper revolution of the 1980s* (Oxford University Press, London, 1980).

Smith, Anthony (ed.), *Newspapers and Democracy: international essays on a changing medium* (MIT Press, Cambridge, Mass., 1980).

Smith, David, *The Rise and Fall of Monetarism: the theory and politics of an economic experiment* (Penguin Books, Harmondsworth, 1987).

Smith, Keith, *The British Economic Crisis: its past and future*, Penguin, Harmondsworth, 1984).

Smith, Trevor, *Anti Politics: consensus, reform and protest in Britain*, (Chas. Knight, London, 1972).

Smith, Trevor, *The Politics of the Corporate Economy* (Martin Robertson, Oxford, 1979).

Snyder, H. L., 'Newsletters in England, 1687–1715, with special reference to John Dyer – a byway in the history of England', in Bond and Mcloed (eds).

Sobel, Robert, *The Great Bull Market: Wall Street in the 1920s* (W. W. Norton, New York, 1968).

Sobel, Robert, *Inside Wall Street: continuity and change in the financial district* (W. W. Norton, New York, 1977).

Sobel, Robert, *Panic on Wall Street: a history of America's financial disasters* (Macmillan, London, 1970).

Sobel, Robert, *The Worldly Economists* (Free Press, New York, 1980).

Sola Pool, Ithiel de, *The Prestige Press: a comprehensive study of political symbols* (MIT Press, Cambridge, Mass., 1970).

Spengler, J. J., 'Exogenous and Endogenous Influences in the formation of Post–1870 Economic Thought: a sociology of knowledge approach'., in Eagly (ed.).

Steel, R., *Walter Lippmann and the American Century* (The Bodley Head, London, 1980).

Stein, Herbert, *The Fiscal Revolution in America* (Chicago University Press, Chicago, 1969).

Steinfels, Peter, *The Neo-Conservatives: the men who are changing American Politics* (Touchstone Books, New York, 1979).

Stigler, G. J., *The Economist as Preacher* (Basil Blackwell, Oxford, 1982).

Stigler, G. J., *Essays in the History of Economics* (Chicago University Press, Chicago, 1965).

Stockman, David A., *The Triumph of Politics* (The Bodley Head, London, 1986).

Storey, G., *Reuters' Century, 1851–1951* (Max Parrish, London, 1951).

Sullivan, A. (ed.), *British Literary Magazines*, 4 vols (Greenwood Press, Westport Conn., 1983–6).

Sunday Times, *A Pictorial History of one of the World's Greatest Newspapers* (Sunday Times, London, 1961).

Sutherland, E. H., *White Collar Crime* (Holt, Rinehart and Winston, New York, 1949).

Temin, P., *Did Monetary Forces Cause the Great Depression?* (W. W. Norton, New York, 1976).

Thomas, G., and M. Morgan-Witts, *The Day the Bubble Burst: a social history of the Wall Street Crash* (Hamish Hamilton, London, 1979).

Thurow, L. C., *Dangerous Currents: the state of economics* (Oxford University Press, Oxford, 1983).

The Times, *The History of* The Times, *1785–1966*, 5 vols (Times Books, London, 1935–84).

Tobin, J., *The New Economics One Decade Older* (Princeton University Press, Princeton, New Jersey, 1974).

Tomita, Tetsuro, 'The New Electronic Media and Their Place in the Information Market of the Future', in Smith (ed.).

Torrens, R., *Letters on Commercial Policy* (London School of Economics and Political Science, London, 1958).

Tribe, K., *Land, Labour and Economic Discourse* (Routledge and Kegan Paul, London, 1978).

Tullock, G., 'Wanted: New Public Choice Theories', in Anderson (ed.).

Tunstall, J., *Journalists at Work* (Constable, London, 1971).

Tydeman, John and Elen Jakes Kelm, *New Media in Europe: satellites, cable, VCRs and videotex* (McGraw-Hill, London, 1986).

Tydeman, John *et al.*, *Teletext and Videotex in the United States: market potential, technology and public policy issues* (McGraw Hill, London, 1982).

Ulrich's International Periodicals Directory, 1986–1987 ('25th ed., vol. 1 (Bowker, New York, 1986).

Walker, M., *Powers of the Press: the world's great newspapers* (Quartet Books, London and New York, 1982).

Walters, M., *How to Make a Killing in the Share Jungle* (Sidgwick and Jackson, London, 1986).

Wanniski, Jude, *The Way the World Works* (Simon & Schuster, New York, 1983).

Ward, W. S., *British Periodicals and Newspapers, 1789–1832: a bibliography of secondary sources* (University of Kentucky Press, Lexington, 1972).

Webb, R. K., *The British Working Class Reader* (Allen & Unwin, London, 1955).

Weisberger, B. A., *The American Newspaperman* (Chicago University Press, Chicago, 1961).

Wendt, Lloyd, *The* Wall Street Journal (Rand McNally, New York, 1982).

Whale, J., *Journalism and Government* (Macmillan, London, 1972).

Wiles, P. J. D., *Economic Institutions Compared* (Basil Blackwell, Oxford, 1977).

Wiles, R. M., *Freshest Advices: early provincial newspapers in England* (Ohio State University Press, Columbus, 1965).

Williams, Francis, *Dangerous Estate* (Arrow, London, 1959).

Williams, Francis, *Nothing So Strange: an autobiography* (Cassell, London, 1970).

Williams, Francis, The Times *on the Economy* (Collins, London, 1984).

Wilson, C., *First with the News: the history of W. H. Smith, 1792–1972* (Cape, London, 1985).

Wilson, R., 'Newspapers and Industry: the export of wool controversy in the 1780s', in Harris and Lee (eds).

Winch, D. N., *Economics and Policy* (Hodder and Stoughton, London, 1982).

Winch, D. N., 'The Emergence of Economics as a Science, 1750–1870', in Cipolla (ed.).

Wincott, H., *The Business of Capitalism* (Institute of Economic Affairs, London, 1968).

Wintour, C., *Pressures on the Press* (Andre Deutsch, London, 1972); see pp. 35–6 on influence of advertisers.

Wright, C. and C. E. Fayle, *A History of Lloyds from the Founding of Lloyds Coffee House to the Present Day* (London, Macmillan, 1928).

ARTICLES

Aspinall, A., 'The Circulation of Newspapers in the Early Nineteenth Century', *Review of English Studies*, (Jan. 1946).

Black, J., 'Flying a Kite: the political impact of the 18th century British press', *Journal of Newspaper and Periodical History*, vol. 1, no. 2 (1985).

Bose, Mihir, 'Fallen Stars of the City Pages', *Business* (March 1988).

Bruttini, A., 'Advertising and Socio-Economic Transformations in England, 1720–1760', *Journal of Advertising History*, no. 5 (1982).

Canterbery, E. Ray (ed.), 'Galbraith Symposium', *Journal of Post Keynesian Economics*, vol. 7 (Fall 1984).

Checkland, S. G. 'The propagation of Ricardian Economics in England', *Economica*, vol. 16 (1949).

Dershowitz, A., 'Newspaper Publicity and the Electrical Conspiracy', *Yale Law Journal*, vol. 71 (1961).

Dordick, H. S., 'The Emerging World Information Industry', *Economic Impact*, no. 46, (1984).

Fetter, F. W., 'The Economic Articles in *Blackwood's Edinburgh Magazine* and Their Authors' 1817–53', *Scottish Journal of Political Economy*, vol. 71 (1960).

Fetter, F. W., 'Economic Articles in the *Westminster Review* and Their Authors, 1824–1851', *Scottish Journal of Political Economy*, vol. 70 (1962).

Fetter, F. W., 'The Economic Articles in the *Quarterly Review* and Their Authors', *Journal of Political Economy*, vol. 64 (1958).

Fetter, F. W., 'Economic Controversy in the British Reviews, 1802–1850', *Economica*, n.s, vol. 32 (1965).

Fouraker, L. E. 'The Cambridge Didactic Style', *Journal of Political Economy*, vol. 66 (1958).

Giffen, R., 'Bagehot as an Economist', *Fortnightly Review*, vol. 27 (1880).

Gilbert, G., 'The *Morning Chronicle*: poor laws and political economy', *History of Political Economy*, vol. 117, no. 4 (1985).

Gordon, B. J., 'Criticism of Ricardian Views on Value and Distribution in the British periodicals, 1820–1850', *History of Political Economy*, vol. 1 (1969).

Gordon, B. J., 'Say's Law, Effective Demand, and the Contemporary British Periodicals, 1820–1850', *Economica*, vol. 32 (1965).

Gossop, M., 'News as a Drug: it relieves anxiety', *Journalism Studies Review*, (July 1982).

Hird, Christopher, 'Decoding the Message of the Money Programmes, *The Listener* (28 January 1988).

Innis, H. A., 'The Newspaper in Economic Development', *Journal of Economic History*, vol. 2 (1942).

Johnson, E. S. and H. G. Johnson, 'The Social and Intellectual Origins of the General Theory', *History of Political Economy* vol. 6 (1974).

Keynes, J. M., 'The Works of Walter Bagehot', *Economic Journal* vol. 25 (Sept. 1915).

Laffer, A., 'Government Exactions and Revenue Deficiencies', *Cato Journal*, vol. 1 (Spring 1981).

Levermore, C. H., 'The Rise of Metropolitan Journalism, 1800–1840', *American Historical Review*, vol. 7 (1931).

Marshall, A., 'The Old Generation of Economists and the New', *Quarterly Journal of Economics*, (January, 1987).

Marwick, Arthur, 'Middle Opinion in the Thirties: planning, progress and political 'agreement', *English Historical Review*, vol. 79 (1964).

McCloskey, D., 'The Rhetoric of Economics', *Journal of Economic Literature*, vol. 31 (1983).

McCombs, M. E., and D. L. Shaw, 'The Agenda Setting Function of the Press', *Public Opinion Quarterly* vol. 36 (1972).

McCusker, J. J., 'The Business Press in England before 1775', *Library*, vol. 8 (1986).

Mcloed, J. M., L. B. Baker and J. E. Byrnes, 'Another Look at the Agenda Setting Role of the Press', *Communications Review*, vol. 1 (1974).

Mill, J. S., 'The Claims of Labour', *Edinburgh Review* (1845).

Newmann, E. K., 'The Origin and Development of Company Meeting Reports', *Journal of Advertising History*, no. 6 (1983).

Parsons, D. W., 'Keynes and the Politics of Economic Ideas', *History of Political Thought*, vol. 4 (1983).

Parsons, D. W., 'Politics Without Promises: the crisis of overload and governability', *Parliamentary Affairs*, vol. 35 (1982).

Parsons, D. W., 'Was Keynes Kuhnian?: Keynes and the idea of theoretical revolutions', *British Journal of Political Science*, vol. 15 (1985).

Samuelson, P., 'Economists and the History of Ideas', *American Economic Review*, vol. 52 (1962).

Scott, G., 'The London *Economist* and the High Tide of *Laissez Faire*', *Journal of Political Economy*, vol. 63 (Dec. 1955).

Seymour-Ure, C. 'Editorial Policymaking in the Press', *Government and Opposition*, vol. 4 (1969).

Smith, T. A., 'Politics, Economics, and Political Economy', *Government and Opposition*, vol. 8 (1973).

Solow, R., 'Does Economics Make Progress?' *Bulletin of the*

American Academy of Arts and Sciences, vol. 36 (December 1981).

Spengler, J. J., 'Notes on the International Transmission of Economic Ideas', *History of Political Economy*, vol. 2 (1970).

Stafford, D. C., 'Bank Advertising: from the shade to the limelight', *Journal of Advertising History*, No. 6, (1983).

Stigler, G. J., 'The Economics of Information', *Journal of Political Economy*, vol. 69, no. 3 (1961).

Stigler, G. J., 'Nobel Lecture: The Process and Progress of Economics', *Journal of Political Economy*, vol. 91, no. 4 (1981).

Tomlinson, J., 'Where Do Economic Objectives Come From? The case of full employment', *Economy and Society*, vol. 12, no. 1 (1983).

Walker, R. B., 'Advertising in London Newspapers, 1650–1750', *Business History*, vol. 15, no. 2 (1973).

Wanniski, J., 'Taxes, Revenues and the Laffer Curve', *Public Interest* (Winter 1978).

Watson, W. L., 'The Press and Finance', *Blackwood's Magazine* (Nov. 1898).

Name index

Subject index